The LAST DAYS of Letterman

The

LAST DAYS

of

Letterman

THE FINAL 6 WEEKS

by **Scott Ryan**

foreword by **Bill Scheft**

The Last Days of Letterman
© 2018 Scott Ryan Productions

Book designed by Mark Karis
Edited by David Bushman

Published in the USA by Fayetteville Mafia Press
in association with Scott Ryan Productions
Columbus, Ohio

Contact Information
Email: fayettevillemafiapress@gmail.com
Website: fayettevillemafiapress.com

ISBN: 978-1-949024-00-5
eBook ISBN: 978-1-949024-01-2

This book is dedicated to that poor monkey on a rock.

The desk of David Letterman. Photo courtesy of Jill Goodwin.

The *Late Show* loot of writer Jim Mulholland. Photo courtesy of Jim Mulholland.

Contents

Fans wait in line to see a taping of *Late Show With David Letterman*. Photo by Scott Ryan.

Foreword

BY BILL SCHEFT

(Spontaneous exchange just before reading "Top Ten Memorable Moments in Comic Strip History," July 15, 2014. The list had been inspired by an item that the beloved Archie Comics series would end in the next issue with the accidental murder of Archie.)

DAVE: So, that's it. Archie's dead. Gone. Adios. What's going to happen to Betty, Veronica, Jughead, Reggie? They're all unemployed.

PAUL: Archie made specific instructions that his staff would continue to be paid after he was killed.

IN TEN YEARS OF ALL-BOYS BOARDING SCHOOLS, I had two headmasters. Both had catchphrases they were fond of. One, David Pynchon of Deerfield Academy, would constantly use a line he copped from his predecessor, Frank Boyden: "Finish up strong." The other, Robert P.T. Coffin, Jr., of the Fessenden School, frequently trotted out one that was all his: "Twenty minutes to pack and leave."

(If I find a pack of cigarettes in a boy's desk, I'll give him twenty minutes to pack and leave. . . . If I hear a boy talk back to one of the kitchen staff, twenty minutes to pack and leave. . . . If I see a boy wearing underpants on his head without a note from the school nurse, twenty minutes to pack and leave. . . .)

Both turns of phrase lovingly apply to whatever it was that transpired in the last six weeks of the late-night life of David Letterman. Not the underwear on the head, but the rest of it.

We really did finish up strong. Ask anyone. Ask all the not-yet-fake media people who called the last show "perfect" and all those viewers who met Dave for the first time on his way out and all the prodigal devotees who flocked back to the dock where they might not have trod since half-past NBC to see him off.

But don't ask any of us. We were in the middle of it. Carried by a momentum that built on itself, rather than the lurching adrenaline-based urgency of getting a strip (nightly) show on the air and in the ether five times a week.

"I am living these shows," executive producer Barbara Gaines said to me on more than a few occasions. We all were. We all knew it, and we didn't. We knew it because we knew it was unavoidable and finite. We didn't because when it was over, we got twenty minutes to pack and leave. Like it never happened.

So, I don't know about the rest of you, but I would love to know what happened. If only there was a book. . . .

The irony that it takes an outsider to aptly chronicle the last twenty-eight installments of the *Late Show* is not lost on me, or any of us who alternately skipped and trudged that surreal road of destiny. I say "surreal" because I remember almost none of it now, just what I am without. Which was the all-oars-pulling pursuit of a glorious finish, but not thinking about the, you know, end.

You don't see this scene on TV anymore, but you used to all the time. It's the scene where the guy has finally left his wife and moved in with the girlfriend. And they're all set up in the new apartment and it's about a month in and one night after dinner the girlfriend walks into the kitchen and finds the guy sobbing over the sink. She thinks he's broken a glass and says, "Hey, don't worry about it." But there's no broken glass. He just looks at her, blubbering, and says, "I miss my family."

You don't see this scene anymore because television has decided it's not realistic or relevant. And it's not, unless instead of a month, it's three years later and it's you blubbering over the sink. And there's no broken glass. And no girlfriend. And no wife to go back to anymore. But you still miss your family.

You are going to see a lot of names here. Names you may have known. Names you didn't know, and frankly, should have. Names who humbly give credit to other names. Names worth fifty points in Scrabble (Mike Buczkiewicz). Pay attention, I am begging you.

BILL SCHEFT (*LATE NIGHT* 1991–1993, *LATE SHOW* 1993–2015)
MANHATTAN, MARCH 2018

Barbara Gaines and Bill Scheft. Photo courtesy of Bill Scheft.

Desperados Under the Eaves

THE PARTICIPANTS

Listed here are the people who were interviewed for this book, their job title at the end of the series, and the day they were interviewed.

BARBARA GAINES   Executive Producer
(August 4 & December 5, 2017)

SHEILA ROGERS   Supervising Producer/Talent Executive
(August 10, 2017)

RANDI GROSSACK   Associate Director
(August 17, 2017)

KATHY MAVRIKAKIS   Supervising Producer
(August 22, 2017)

RICK SCHECKMAN   Associate Producer
(August 25, 2017)

BRIAN TETA   Supervising Producer/Segment Producer
(August 31, 2017)

SHERYL ZELIKSON   Music Producer
(September 7, 2017)

JAY JOHNSON   Creative Director, Digital Media
(September 18, 2017)

JERRY FOLEY   Director
(September 19, 2017)

MICHAEL BARRIE   Writer
(September 21, 2017)

LEE ELLENBERG	Writer (September 25, 2017)	
JIM MULHOLLAND	Writer (September 26, 2017)	
JOE GROSSMAN	Writer (September 27, 2017)	
JEREMY WEINER	Writer (September 28, 2017)	
STEVE YOUNG	Writer (October 3, 2017)	
VINCENT FAVALE	East Coast Executive, Late Night Programing, CBS (October 11, 2017)	
EDDIE VALK	Stage Manager (October 26, 2017)	
BILL SCHEFT	Writer (November 14, 2017, & quotes from his blog)	
JANICE PENINO	Vice President, Human Resources Worldwide Pants (November 16, 2017)	
JILL GOODWIN	Writer (November 17, 2017)	
MIKE BUCZKIEWICZ	Senior Producer/Segment Producer (March 5, 2018)	
RUPERT JEE	Hello Deli Owner (March 30, 2018)	

Since the majority of these interviews were conducted conversationally, the author has occasionally shaped some of the sentences. Memories come back in spurts, not complete sentences. Every attempt has been made to make as few changes as possible. Email exchanges were also used for follow-up questions.

1

Mutineer

MY MONOLOGUE

"I'M REGRETTING THIS ALREADY." Not quite what you hope to hear at the beginning of an interview for your next book. I also heard, "I can't imagine what this book will actually be" and "Is anyone really going to be interested in this?" Heck, I gave up trying to figure out what people were interested in years ago. That's probably what made me a devoted *Late Show With David Letterman* fan to begin with. Dave fans tended to be on the outside, didn't we? Dave never tried to please the home viewing audience at large. Why would I? I had been raised on David Letterman. As his long-time writer Bill Scheft put it: For a generation of people, Dave came with the television set. I was part of that generation.

I caught the Dave bug in the summer of 1987, between my junior and senior years of high school. I had regularly stayed up and watched Johnny Carson with my father on Friday nights, but he always turned the TV off when Johnny said goodnight and before Dave's *Late Night* came on. When my father laughed at Johnny Carson, I laughed. Although I rarely got the references. (Who was Red Skelton, anyway?) That summer, I stayed up every night on my own, but I left the TV on when Johnny finished. Dave wasn't Johnny at all. Dave was something completely different. He was something I got. When Dave said something, I laughed all on my own.

By the time Dave moved to CBS in 1993, I was a full-on fan. He had guided me through high school and college and had already shaped the way I spoke, the way I told a story, and the music I listened to. I am pretty sure I watched every installment of the *Late Show* on CBS from 1993-2015. I don't have the paperwork on that, but I don't ever remember missing a show. Watching Dave was part of my daily routine. Dave got me through my first marriage. He was there when I was a stay-at-home dad of twins. That was when I started taping the show and watching it the following morning. When I started traveling on a weekly basis, I would listen to the VHS tapes in the minivan's VCR. I watched through marriage and divorce, in my parents' house, my own house, back to my parents' house, and on to another marriage. When I got my corporate job, I streamed Dave every morning through the internet, pretending to be answering emails but really listening to Top Tens and great interviews and dancing in my swivel chair to music by Paul Shaffer and the CBS Orchestra.

In 2015, I recorded Dave on my DVR, because it was free with my job at a cable company. It was on that DVR that I decided to keep the final six weeks of the *Late Show*. "Decided" is a strong word. I just couldn't bring myself to actually hit that delete button. The final weeks of the *Late Show* stayed there for two years, taking up valuable family hard-drive space. ("Dad, can I delete these *Late Show* episodes to tape *Teen Wolf?*" NO.) That is when my job was downsized.

"Downsized" is a word that corporate stooges made up. The kind of stooges that Dave would try to deliver a fruit basket to and then be thrown out. I wasn't downsized; I was fired. When your place of employment asks you to not come back, you're fired. I didn't care. I was ready to go off into the world and become a writer anyway. There was only one part of being let go that hurt—I had to turn my DVR back in. That meant giving up Dave for good. I looked at the calendar. I had just about twenty-eight workdays left. Dave had been there for me through all my changes in life, why not through this one as well? I would rewatch one episode a day. Dave was losing his job; I was losing mine. We would get fired/retired together.

I hadn't watched late-night television since Dave said "Thank you and goodnight" to all of us on May 20, 2015. After twenty-eight years of watching him, I didn't see much point in trying someone new. I also hadn't watched a moment of Letterman since he left the air. No, I had kicked the late-night habit cold *canned ham* . . . I mean cold turkey. But it was now or never. The equipment was going back whether I watched the episodes or not. I started my rewatch of the *Late Show* almost two years after it ended. I went right back down the rabbit hole. I watched these magnificent hours with a fresh perspective. The country was completely different now. The world had been turned upside down. Every part of pop culture had been radically changed by the events of 2016. Everything, that is, but the six weeks of the *Late Show* episodes that had been frozen in time on my DVR.

Conversation, dignity, class, and even comedy had all drastically changed. The world had become less civil; face-to-face conversation was almost nonexistent. Dave and his guests actually talked to each other. Very few of the guests were appearing on the show to promote their latest movies. They were coming on the show to *talk* to their friend. The few guests who actually did appear only to promote a movie stuck out like a sore thumb. Somehow the producers and staff of the *Late Show* had broken the late-night mold again. This time they brought it back to the days of Jack Paar and Johnny Carson. For six weeks of time, conversation was the true king of late night. Sitting there, watching these mesmerizing television moments again, I got an idea. As Dave always said, "There is no 'off' position on the genius switch."

I would document the last six weeks of David Letterman's time as the longest-running late-night talk show host, 1982-2015. My plan was to skip the first thirty-two years and forty-six weeks (what could possibly have happened during that time anyway?) and look only at the end. I would conduct interviews with the people who had crafted what may very well be the end of television as I knew it. Television wasn't even televised any more, it was streamed. Any star who came after Dave would be an internet or YouTube sensation. David Letterman was a broadcaster, and the last of his kind. I set out to capture the moments of those episodes and color them with comments from writers, directors, producers, and crew. If things had changed that much in the world in less than two years, how much would things change ten or twenty years from now? How much would be totally forgotten? Now was the time.

As I started interviewing the *Late Show* staff, I discovered that just about everyone thought this idea was a little nuts. They were skeptical that the show still mattered. They doubted anyone would care, or even remember what they had done. Every time someone on the staff said that, it only inspired me more. Not because I wanted to prove them wrong, but because their reaction was so Dave. They had his sensibility and predilection for self-deprecation. How could they not? They had spent years trying to write and create a world where Letterman was the centerpiece. Dave never understood why he mattered so much to us. Every time a guest tried to explain how much he meant to them, he dodged and ducked. I imagine he would think it was crazy that I watched him faithfully for well over half my life. From job to job, from state to state, in the car, at work, on vacation, through an antenna, a cable wire, a computer screen, and, inconceivably, on a telephone. There was no way I was the only one.

This book will cover those final twenty-eight shows, from Sarah Jessica Parker on April 3, 2015, Dave's 6,000th show, all the way to the Foo Fighters on May 20, 2015, Dave's 6,028th installment. That is correct, I am ignoring the first 6,000 hours. So Joaquin Phoenix, Drew Barrymore, Madonna, and late-night wars are not rehashed in this book (not counting my coverage of the special that CBS aired during those final weeks about Dave's career). The hope is that by focusing the lens tightly on twenty-eight specific episodes, this book will reflect the artistry of past episodes as well.

I was fortunate to get the enthusiastic (and sometimes reluctant) participation of over twenty people who worked at the *Late Show*, which allowed this book to become a detailed look at what they had accomplished. Everyone was extremely generous with their memories, time, and photos. But, I would be remiss if I didn't single out executive producer Barbara Gaines. She was my first interview and a true champion of the book. She said she wanted to help because those six weeks were the highlight of her professional career. I strongly agree. I think it was the highlight of all involved. The staff's dedication in supporting Dave's farewell is something that television history needs to be mindful of.

What you will learn from reading their combined interviews, which are dispersed among recapitulations of the twenty-eight episodes, is that the *Late Show* staff was a family. They were loyal, not just to Dave but to each other. Some of them worked there for a decade or two, or, in

Barbara's case, three and a half decades. That is loyalty. That is family. That is also unheard of in the television industry. And while I never did get an interview with Dave for this book, I know that if I had, he would have had just one thing to say: "I'm regretting this already."

2

I'll Sleep When I'm Dead

THE ANNOUNCEMENT

LATE SHOW WITH DAVID LETTERMAN had a big Wednesday night show on April 2, 2014. The guests were Bill Murray and Lady Gaga. The audience walked up 53rd Street in the middle of the show to watch Lady Gaga perform live from the famed Roseland Ballroom. Dave, Bill Murray, and Lady Gaga were seen in the commercial bumpers walking up the street along with the audience. Lady Gaga performed two songs live on that stage. Bill Murray took selfies. The staff was more than pleased with how this show came out. There were surprises, the show was full of energy, and Dave seemed to be having a great time. The next day, April 3, David Letterman called a meeting with his senior staff.

Photo courtesy of @Letterman.

6

BARBARA GAINES (Executive Producer): That day he called a bunch of us into his dressing room. We were in rehearsal and Dave wants to see us in his dressing room? What could this be? It's the middle of the afternoon and Jude Brennan [executive producer] and I have got a lot to do. We went up to his room and Mary Barclay [Dave's executive assistant] said, "Wait here. Other people are coming."

BILL SCHEFT (Writer): The day before we had done this great show with Lady Gaga and Bill Murray. It was really a kind of spectacular show. Dave was buoyed by that show. I was pretty sure that he was gathering the senior staff together to say, "Hey, that was great" and "Let's do more of that."

BARBARA GAINES: We had done the Lady Gaga show, and it had been such a big, crazy show. It felt like we were rocking.

SHEILA ROGERS (Supervising Producer/Talent Booker): I was among those that were called into the dressing room. It would be unusual of him to hold a meeting of ten or twelve of us in his dressing room at that time of day. Normally he would meet with a couple of his top producers in his dressing room closer to showtime. I remember thinking, "Maybe he is calling us in to tell us what a great job we did the night before." [Laughs] He would never hold a meeting to do that.

BILL SCHEFT: It happened once, at the beginning of the CBS show. We had been on for about ten weeks. He called us together. I thought we were gonna get yelled at, but he said, "This is great. I have never been number one. I know you are tired; I am tired. Keep doing it." That was the only time we were called into a meeting with everybody. When you do 200 shows a year, you finish the show, you pat yourself on the back or you don't. Then you do tomorrow's show. It is like putting out a newspaper.

KATHY MAVRIKAKIS (Supervising Producer): A call came in from Dave's assistant, Mary Barclay. She said, "Dave would like you to come up to the dressing room." I realized Jerry Foley [director] got the same call. So we both head upstairs and then other producers were there.

STEVE YOUNG (Writer): I got a call from Mary asking if I could run up to the dressing room. It was too early in the afternoon for Dave to be in the dressing room according to the usual schedule. So something seemed odd. I said, "I will get up there as soon as I can." I was running around, not only with the monologue, but with the usual monologue videotaped pieces in the editing room. I didn't get up to the dressing room.

SHEILA ROGERS: I think people had a sinking feeling. I was the eternal optimist. I really loved working there. I was very happy with my job and loved the people there. I never wanted it to end.

BILL SCHEFT: I came in and there were people there already, maybe twenty. Jude Brennan, Barbara Gaines, Nancy Agostini [executive producer], Jerry Foley, Kathy Mavrikakis, and a few others. It was the senior staff.

BARBARA GAINES: We are like, "This is an odd group of people to be congregating at 1:00 in the afternoon." We all come in and Dave was having his lunch.

SHEILA ROGERS: Dave was sitting there and he made a couple of jokes.

KATHY MAVRIKAKIS: Freakishly enough, he had cut himself shaving. He had a big bandage on his top lip. We were all like, "What happened to you?" He said, "I cut myself." He was making jokes about it and being very funny.

BARBARA GAINES: He said, "I want you know that in an hour I am calling Les Moonves [president of CBS Corporation] to tell him I am going to retire. I wanted you to all know first. I am going to announce it on the air tonight." We were like, "What? What do you mean?" I didn't know he was going to retire. I didn't find out till right then.

KATHY MAVRIKAKIS: Then somebody asked, "Is this something that you want?" He said, "This is my decision and I want to do this." Someone said, "What is the time frame?" He said, "In about a year we will probably be finishing up here."

BARBARA GAINES: Why now? Then he told us the story about spending the day asking about the bird—the story he told that night on the air—that clearly he wasn't involved like he used to be and it was time to go.

SHEILA ROGERS: He told us that he had decided that it was time to end, to quit, to retire, as it were. I just felt like I got punched in the gut, because I didn't want to accept it. I was very sad, really sad. . . . It was just sad, honestly. And fear: What's gonna be next for me, personally?

JERRY FOLEY (Director): It was not something that was particularly pleasant. I was deeply affected by it. My coworkers and these people that I saw every day were very warm, supportive, and funny. I was concerned about my future and appreciative of my association with them and our friendships.

KATHY MAVRIKAKIS: I just remember standing there, and the stereo was playing Pharrell's song "Happy" in the background. And he was basically saying that in a year we are all getting divorced. So now every time I hear that song, it brings me right back to that moment.

BILL SCHEFT: Dave didn't talk for very long. He wasn't very specific about the timeline. Then Kathy had the presence of mind to start applauding.

KATHY MAVRIKAKIS: After he said that we all started clapping to give him a "Well done, you've chosen what you wanna do. We will support whatever you want." Then we kind of stumbled back to the control room, but couldn't tell other people because he was gonna do that during the taping. We got back with our coworkers and kind of did our jobs and pretended we didn't know anything.

STEVE YOUNG: It was a nice gesture on Dave's part. He wanted to personally inform some of the senior staff. It was nice that I was on that list of people that he thought he would tell ahead of other people. Such was the pace of work that I couldn't take advantage of that.

BILL SCHEFT: I only had two thoughts. My first thought was, "We are all gonna make it to the end of the show." There were a lot of us who had been there a long time. The second thought was, "This is so great, because unlike anybody else he is gonna get to end it on his own terms. Unlike Johnny Carson or anybody, he gets to decide." I was very happy for him that *he* had made the decision. It wasn't made for him.

JAY JOHNSON (Media Content): I was in the studio to rehearse a comedy bit that I had been cast in. When I finished my rehearsal, Jude asked to speak with me. She pulled me behind the set. I thought, "Something is up, because she is pulling me off stage." That is how I found out. It was stunning. I think the comedy bit I was in got cut after rehearsal. We always knew the day was coming. Everybody talked about it. It was a favorite topic of conversation among the staff: "How much longer will Dave keep doing the show?"

LEE ELLENBERG (Writer): It was always a parlor game of guessing when Dave was gonna retire. I was a page in August '94 and a staffer in '95. Since that day in '95, staffers would try to guess when he would hang it up. That is twenty years.

JOE GROSSMAN (Writer): You were always wondering how much longer this was going to last. We knew it would not go on forever. I always felt like Dave could show up one day and say, "By the way, tonight is my last show." And we would never see him again, or he could go on for another fifteen years. You never knew.

JAY JOHNSON: I always thought that "when the day comes, it will arrive as a surprise. We know that it is coming, but we will never know when. It's not gonna be something obvious, like the result of a contract negotiation." I just knew when we would find out it would be unexpected. It turned out I was right. It was a strange day. Everyone was walking around in a bit of a daze. We all knew it was coming, but the reality of it really kind of hit hard.

EDDIE VALK (Stage Manager): At some point before the show we always met in the control room for a debrief. Jerry Foley would have his camera meeting for the crew. In that meeting, Jerry relayed to us that Dave would be making an announcement on the show, but he wanted us to know before we found out on the air.

RANDI GROSSACK (Associate Director): I was not happy. I was hoping Dave was gonna go for another five years. The show had changed drastically since it first started, but I liked it. Once he announced, he kind of relaxed and became more like himself again. I was happily plugging along. I liked the people I worked with. I liked the show he put on. I was content. I was like, "Holy shit, now what?"

JANICE PENINO (Human Resources): Kathy called me and told me that he was going to announce that night. I was working from home that day. I just remember there was a "before" and an "after." I was like the mom of that family in a lot of ways. For many years all we talked about is, "When is Dave going to retire?" We lived with this knowledge that it would happen. That year he had only signed to go one more year. So it seemed real. I had worked there for twenty-two years.

EDDIE VALK: Initially I was kind of shocked. I knew the day would come at some point, but it was definitely a blow to finally hear that it was going to happen. Although we still didn't know exactly when.

LEE ELLENBERG: We were in our offices and the writers were told to meet in the conference room. Matt Roberts [head writer] wanted to meet with us in the middle of the day. Now, we don't have meetings in the middle of the day. I think everyone was wondering what it was about.

JILL GOODWIN (Writer): Immediately everyone knew something was up. We wondered, "Oh, God, is someone ill?"

LEE ELLENBERG: I was sitting across the table from Matt and he looked a little stressed. He had a serious expression on his face. He just seemed like he had something of weight that was about to be told. We waited till the final writer came in, and Matt said, "In five minutes, Dave is going to call Les Moonves and tell him he is retiring." There is that great line in *The West Wing*, "Is it possible to be astonished and, at the same time, not surprised?" That is how it felt.

STEVE YOUNG: I was in the room where Matt said, "This evening on the show, Dave is going to announce his retirement." There was a silence of surprise.

JILL GOODWIN: I remember there being a calm in the room. I think the head writer thought there was gonna be a "WHAT?" It was not that surprising, but also so huge to take in at the same time.

JEREMY WEINER (Writer): We were all like, "Wow, this is really going to be it." It was weird to have that lead time. You normally don't get that in TV. You are usually told you are canceled and you are done. You don't usually get to prep for it. I think everyone took it in stride.

JOE GROSSMAN: We were surprised, but not shocked. It is tough, because your job is going away.

STEVE YOUNG: A silence took place for twenty seconds. I broke the silence by saying, "But Paul's not leaving, is he?"

MIKE BARRIE (Writer): Well, it's not like it was Pearl Harbor. I don't remember where I was at that exact moment. [Laughs]

VINCENT FAVALE (Executive of Late Night Programing, CBS): My office at the time was at CBS Black Rock, so I was a block away. I would be there every morning for the production meeting. I would be there every evening for the taping. Jude called me and said, "Whatever you do, don't be late tonight." The network was told above me, but I didn't know. I was surprised. It was a yearly thing where it was Dave's call if he wanted to go for another year. I had had conversations with Les Moonves that maybe this year might be it. When it was announced, I remember thinking it was like when Johnny Carson announced. It drops like a bombshell, but it was still a year away. As we got closer, it was so weird because it is like a death. But we know it well in advance.

STEVE YOUNG: I remember feeling that "this seems about right." We knew the show had to end someday. It was probably time to head to the finish line.

BILL SCHEFT: Dave had cut himself shaving. The cut opened up when the band came in, so it looked like he had been in a fight. He is bleeding while telling the band. Then he sent the band out. Now we are a little behind on the day. I haven't even gone in to do the monologue with him yet. He went into the dressing room and then he opened the door. He said to me, and I probably shouldn't tell you this, but I am gonna tell you because it meant a lot to me. He poked his head out and said, "Hey, what if I start drinking again?" I stopped drinking a long time ago and he had stopped drinking after the morning show. He knew I didn't drink. It was his way of saying, "What if I made a huge mistake?" I said, "That is what I am here for." He said, "That's what my shrink said to me." And we laughed. That was the only time we mentioned it. It has been two and a half years and I haven't thought about that until this moment. It meant a lot to me because it was a connection that we had.

Photo courtesy of @Letterman, CBS publicity photo.

That evening on the show, David Letterman addressed the studio audience: "Earlier today, the man who owns this network, Leslie Moonves—he and I have had a relationship for years and years and years—and we have had this conversation in the past, and we agreed that we would work together on this circumstance and the timing of this circumstance. And I phoned him just before the program, and I said, 'Leslie, it's been great, you've been great, the network has been great, but I'm retiring.'" The audience is silent for a moment and then there is a bit of nervous laughter. Paul says, "Do I have a moment to call my accountant?"

JERRY FOLEY: I had the opportunity to attend my own funeral when that happened. So I got to read my own obituary. It was something that in hindsight I was privileged to be a part of because I know it has a happy ending. I looked at everybody differently after that.

SHEILA ROGERS: It was hard. Then Johnny Depp [one of that night's guests] was dealing with sad people. He probably didn't know what was going on. "Why is everybody acting so morose?" We all watched him on TV announce it. Again, it was just sad. He said it was gonna end, but we had no sense of when it was happening. So I think the uncertainty was very difficult. It was a real camaraderie and great group of people and great working for Dave. I really respected him so much, and his talent.

RANDI GROSSACK: Then it became, "Crap, we've got to prepare for what is coming with the show." We have to do a nightly show. I have to figure out what happens to all the tapes. How do we close things down after all these years? How do I shut off all these same jokes that I tell people at work over and over? Because they know the punch lines.

JILL GOODWIN: We couldn't really comprehend it right away. We didn't have any answers either. "Is next week going to be the last show?" There was a lot up in the air. "Wait, is he sure? Has he really thought this over?" [Laughs]

LEE ELLENBERG: That whole week, I thought, "Wow, this is over." It was the first time in my two-plus decades of working there that I knew it was ending. It had become real.

KATHY MAVRIKAKIS: It was a gradual thing, because we had a year. We still didn't have a final day. It was still being discussed between Dave and CBS. I feel like we didn't have a final day until maybe December. It didn't seem real until we finally had the date of May 20.

VINCENT FAVALE: These final shows were going to be emotional, and it was going to get more intense. I was with the network, so I still had a job. I was very mindful of that fact, because a lot of people weren't going to have a job after that date. I was a rookie at twenty years. Can you imagine the weight that Dave must have felt thinking, "I am responsible for all of these people as an employer"? It was an emotional time.

KATHY MAVRIKAKIS: For me, I was working on an archive program to digitize all the episodes and all the paperwork that went with the episodes. It just meant I had to start immediately in making sure that was all done because it took a year to digitize all the video and all the paperwork that came with those episodes.

JANICE PENINO: I had no trouble getting interns for that spring semester. It was the most coveted time to be an intern, to see how it was gonna end and what was going to happen. There were a few people who got offered work who had to go, but not very many people did. Most people stayed till the very end.

VINCENT FAVALE: I didn't envy what Barbara and Jude had to do. They had to look forward and behind at the same time. Me, thinking as a network person, I thought we should be planning a prime-time special in conjunction with the 11:30 farewell tour. That is where we had some friction at the end.

STEVE YOUNG: I do remember that as 2014 wore on, we weren't entirely sure when the final show was going to be. I think the bulk of the year after Dave made the announcement that there was very little in the show reflecting the impending retirement. I think it was only in the last six weeks.

SHERYL ZELIKSON (Music Booker): It was sad that the show was ending, but it was the most creative time for music. So, the work itself was enjoyable for me because it almost used a different part of my brain. It really allowed me to go back in the history of the show and look at artists and think about not just putting on a song from an artist's new album. Dave wanted to hear particular songs, and trying to find those artists that would work, artists that have a history with the show that would make something special. This was really a very creative part of the end of working at the show. I wanted to do it for Dave. I wanted to do it for the viewing audience.

JERRY FOLEY: They were some of the easiest shows we have ever done because there was an outpouring of affection and good will. There was unparalleled cooperation from everyone involved. Performers, publicists, musicians, producers—it was riding that wave. The key factor in that was that Dave was super-focused on the show in ways he hadn't been in a long time. There is a routine from grinding out that many shows. You become a slave to routine, and that is what gets you through. But those last twenty-eight shows, Dave knew that was all evaporating. So Dave was really exercising his talents as a producer and writer. After we all get through patting ourselves on the back and you get through deconstructing why the shows were what they were, I can assure you that the single biggest factor was that Dave was in complete control of the creative aspect of those shows, and that is why they are as memorable as they are.

BARBARA GAINES: The last six weeks of the show were no doubt a highlight of my career there. I started on the morning show. I was there thirty-five years. The last six weeks? I love the last six weeks.

The following chapters document the final six weeks of *Late Show with David Letterman*.

3

Six Weeks Left

EPISODES 6,001-6,005

ON APRIL 13, 2015, the *Late Show* came back from a week of reruns to air its final six weeks. This began the farewell to favorite guests and friends of the show. The talent bookers worked hard to be sure the guest list would reflect the long-term relationships the show had built over the years. It was Dave's way of thanking the guests for years of great appearances. What Dave didn't expect was the guests' reactions to being given the chance to say goodbye to him.

The producers couldn't have found a better lead guest than Sarah Jessica Parker to kick off the goodbye parade. Long-time fans of the show will remember Parker appearing many times—singing *Annie's* "Tomorrow," coming into the studio surrounded by sailors during Fleet Week, participating in Alan Kalter's celebrity interviews, hitting golf balls into the audience, and even hosting a backstage show when Dave was out with heart surgery. Thanks to *Sex and the City*, Parker became a huge television star during her tenure of guesting with Dave, but never lost her fan-girl attitude. She always loved Dave. She unwittingly set the tone for the next six weeks of episodes, changing the plan from the *Late Show* saying goodbye to its guests to America saying goodbye to David Letterman.

"FROM THE MOON'S COPERNICUS CRATER..."
IT IS EPISODE 6,001
APRIL 13, 2015

After the *Late Show*'s opening credits, the first shot is always the empty stage, quickly followed by David Letterman running as fast as lightning across the stage from left to right. Then he walks out to cheers from the right side, as if he had been on that side the entire time. Dave sprinting across the stage was one thing viewers could count on to start the show. It was impressive the way director Jerry Foley timed the shot every night just as Dave ran.

> **EDDIE VALK** (Stage Manager): Biff Henderson [stage manager] would be on the headset with the control room, and he would let Jerry Foley know when Dave was about to run across.

The opening credits end and the lens blurs to the stage, Alan Kalter says, "And now, born to rock the boat . . . David Letterman." The camera pans to the stage, but Dave doesn't run across. The screen stays empty for a beat and then pans left as Dave enters through the cityscape behind the desk. He navigates around the comfy chairs and makes his way to center stage. The camera cuts to an audience member in the last row who waves to Dave with glee. Dave has altered the normal routine of the show to make an audience member happy. What else should we expect from the final series of shows other than the unexpected?

> **RANDI GROSSACK** (Associate Director): It is always a little frantic. You are trying to be on the same wavelength as Dave, thinking, "How he is thinking?" Whether he is sending a camera outside or if suddenly someone from the audience wants to drop something off the roof, you always have to be in that ready position for anything that might happen, because it was never scripted.

JERRY FOLEY (Director): You were required to be on Dave's wavelength and be inside his head. There was no other way to do it. Randi is correct. There were plenty of days when I wasn't able to decode what he was thinking, and that would make for a difficult time. All of us were required to be in the conversation with Dave, to be aware of the things he liked and didn't like and where his mind would go for a certain joke or callback. It is an interesting point that there is Randi, an AD, and she had the burden of being in sync with Dave. That burden fell on everyone—the graphics department, audio, stage manager, writers, Paul, the musicians, everybody was required to be thinking the way he was thinking. That sometimes would be an impossible task, because his mind is so fast and it goes in so many directions that you never really truly arrive at the same place. You only hope to come close.

Dave receives extended applause and does his best to hurry it along. Still, it is early April, the crowd and media are not yet focused on the end. Once the audience settles, Dave begins his monologue. The topics include income taxes, the Masters Tournament, Dave's birthday (which was the prior day), and Hillary Clinton's presidential aspirations.

The Clinton campaign had just released a video of "regular" people revealing what they will be doing in 2015, and then Hillary says, "I am running for president." The clip plays, but writer Joe Grossman is inserted into the mix of "regular people." Joe, who always plays the sad sack, says, "I'm gonna be out of a job in a month thanks to this jackass." He holds up a picture of David Letterman.

JOE GROSSMAN: Someone pitched that videotaped piece that morning. I never pitched myself for the show. Those were usually written the morning of and then assembled during the day. We had done a few of those of me in my office with some boring thing for me to talk about. It was another variation of that. A few of those had me putting my head on my desk in despair. That's my catchphrase: "guy in despair." It was just an opportunity to put the awkward guy on camera, and Dave always enjoyed that.

The Act 2 desk piece begins but is interrupted when Paul and the band start playing uptempo music, which Dave calls to a halt to say, "As that unmistakable music tells me, once again it is time for Pea Boy." Cut to the back of the studio; the doors open and a man in a green suit with a yellow "P" on his chest runs through the studio throwing peas at everyone. Pea Boy runs on stage and then out the back of the theater. This skit appears to have been planned, but in fact was another unexpected moment. The staff hadn't planned the Pea Boy appearance. It all came up during the preshow question and answer between Dave and an audience member.

> **JERRY FOLEY:** We ran into a stretch in this period of time where people who were visiting the show for the final time were inclined to go down memory lane. They would throw these memories out to Dave, who would then kind of turn them around to be challenges to the staff.

> **JOE GROSSMAN:** It was an audience person who asked about Pea Boy. So at the last minute they thought, "Wouldn't it be great if we could get Pea Boy on the show tonight?"

JERRY FOLEY: One of the great private amusements Dave would have is when he would hijack the entire system, the technology, the people, the format, and say, "Oh, let's see if you can jerk this thing around to an appearance by Pea Boy, who we haven't seen in several years." This amused Dave. He wanted to see whether or not we could pull it off. It was part of his managerial genius that somehow we all were motivated by the challenge. We wanted to kind of shut him down before he could complain that we couldn't do it.

BILL SCHEFT (Writer): A woman asked, "Whatever happened to Pea Boy?" and Dave said to me, "What is the song that Paul and the band used to play for Pea Boy?" I said, "It's the 'Sabre Dance.' Do you remember what to say?" He did remember. Used no cards, he nailed it.

JERRY FOLEY: You had props people who had to come up with baskets and peas. You had wardrobe people who had to get the costume. The band had to quickly come around and remember the song they played. All of us had to dig into our collective memories and say, "How did Pea Boy work?"

BILL SCHEFT: The staff put that all together during the commercial break. They had maybe twenty minutes. Pea Boy was from 1992. Donick Cary [writer] came up with that piece at the old show. We did it at the old and new show. Mike Leach was Pea Boy in 2015.

JOE GROSSMAN: Mike was one of everyone's favorite people at the show. He was a guy who was just up for anything. He was always good at his on-camera appearances. He was not the original Pea Boy, I don't know who the original was.

BARBARA GAINES: The original Pea Boy was David Ellner.

JERRY FOLEY: That mentality, that willingness to throw yourself at a particular assignment that was motivated by someone's comment in the audience warm-up, that mindset was shared by everybody.

The Top Ten List features C-3PO and R2-D2 on stage counting down lines that have never been said in a Star Wars film. Paul plays "Cantina Band" from *Star Wars Episode IV*.

Sarah Jessica Parker is the first guest. She pretends to wipe away a tear and comically wipes her nose on her sleeve. Dave hands her a box of tissues. "Thank you," she says. "I was planning on not crying." She tucks the tissue up her sleeve. Before Dave can even finish his first sentence she stops him and says, "No, no, no, I just want to take a long hard look at you. I want to do for all Americans what they will not be able to do because I am here in their place. For all the men and women who cannot be here . . . [I will] look at you and perhaps tell you about yourself and what you have meant to us. I want you to take it like a man. I want you to sit here, because I know your instinct is that you don't want to hear it."

Right there in the first minute of the first guest in the final six weeks, Sarah Jessica Parker sets the tone for what these episodes will become. The reins of the show are flipped. This would not be Dave saying goodbye to his favorite guests. This would be the guests and, by proxy, America saying goodbye to their favorite host. Sarah isn't there to promote a new movie or series, or any product. She's there to tell Dave what he's meant to her. Dave tries to joke his way out, but Parker isn't having it.

Dave responds, "I want to hear about you." Parker immediately shoots back, "I have no interest in me. I figure I have nothing to lose, because you can't not ask me back again. I don't want to make you uncomfortable, but I feel like this is my last hope."

JERRY FOLEY: Typically the guests like Sarah Jessica Parker would interact with segment producers. They would do the pre-interviews and talk through the topics that might be good for the conversation. I would deal with the guests if we used them for any kind of pretape.

BRIAN TETA (Segment Producer/Supervising Producer): Sarah and I had our first conversation that morning. Doing a live show that turns around this quickly, you focused on the show at hand. You figured out what you were doing, you banged it out and started on the next one. I think her pre-interview happened at 11:00 that morning.

BARBARA GAINES (Executive Producer): Sarah Jessica Parker came on just as a friend. She just came on to talk to Dave.

BRIAN TETA: I don't know if Sarah was booked as the first guest in the final six weeks by design so much as it just worked out. She had a history with the show. Those spots were pretty coveted. No one was saying no to coming on at this point. We didn't want to have people there that didn't have a relationship or history.

SHEILA ROGERS (Supervising Producer/Talent Booker): Sarah and Dave always had a great rapport, and she did a guest-host spot when Dave was out with his heart surgery. She was one of the first in line to do that. She hadn't been on a lot recently, so it was great to have her back. She was someone we said we had to have in the final weeks.

BRIAN TETA: I think Sarah had sincere feelings for Dave. She had been a guest since the old days at NBC. It began to be real at that point.

Parker continues her praise for Dave: "You've made us all so happy and been thoughtful, funny, and challenging and terrifying, and despite your best efforts, probably the most distinguished man on late-night television."

Dave puts his hands over his ears, as if to deflect those words from entering his consciousness, and screams, "Oh, my God." The audience erupts with applause. Paul plays a little fanfare music. Parker brings it all home by saying, "It really is the end of an era."

This is not what Dave had in mind. He will spend a ton of time over the final weeks avoiding these moments, but the best appearances will be those that lean into this sentiment. Parker had always set a high bar for what a good talk show appearance could be. Over the years, she took part in skits and came prepared with great stories. She instinctively knew that this time it would be a heartfelt declaration of her affection for the host that would make her appearance memorable.

Sarah then recounts a dream she had about Dave years ago, flirting with him in a respectful, cute way. Their conversation covers parenting, her husband (Matthew Broderick), and how to talk to their children about the birds and the bees. Dave shares a charming story about his son, Harry, and sex education at school. A strong appearance and the perfect beginning to, as Sarah put it, the end of an era.

As the show fades to commercial, a picture of Sarah Jessica Parker from her appearance twenty-four years earlier on *Late Night*, on February 8, 1991, is shown. The picture is framed to look like a baseball card. These logos were created to highlight how many years the long-term guests have been appearing with Dave.

JAY JOHNSON (Digital Content): As part of the countdown to the end of the show, Walter Kim and I began posting images on our social platforms in the style of *Late Show* baseball cards that featured behind-the-scenes photos and staff profiles. Not long after we started doing that, Jerry Foley began using that same baseball card template to showcase select moments from old shows when going into commercial breaks.

RANDI GROSSACK: The baseball cards became a big thing as the shows ticked away. We thought the guests loved them. We were always looking for the perfect shot. It wasn't always easy finding the old shows, but it became a fun thing.

The second guest is the 2015 Masters Tournament winner, Jordan Spieth. Dave typically had the winner of the prestigious golf tournament on, since it aired on CBS.

Musical Guest

The musical guest, Asleep at the Wheel, with guest vocalist Kat Edmonson, performs "I Can't Give You Anything but Love," a western swing number. Paul and the band play along. Paul even performs the piano solo. Will Lee plays upright bass, and the horn section sits in.

SHERYL ZELIKSON (Music Booker): I think that Dave does have a great fondness for Americana music, as much as he has a great fondness for music like Foo Fighters and Pearl Jam. Asleep at the Wheel did have a longevity of being on that stage. When Letterman was at NBC, he would book David Byrne and alternative rock 'n' roll, all the things you wouldn't get to see on Johnny Carson. Well, that became true with Americana in the later years of the show. You didn't see a lot of it on other shows, so we had a space for that. I think he came to these artists without hearing them on the radio. He was listening to a lot of that type of music.

WORLDWIDE PANTS TAG:

"May pants be with you."

"FROM O'HARE AIRPORT'S ECONOMY PARKING LOT F..."
IT IS EPISODE 6,002
APRIL 14, 2015

Alan Kalter introduces Dave with, "And now . . . young wiry rider of the Pony Express . . . David Letterman." The monologue topics are tax season (taxes are due the following day), the Transportation Security Administration, and the 2016 presidential campaign. Dave asks, "Can you feel the indifference?"

JIM MULHOLLAND (Writer): We developed annual topics, like "my tax accountant." We would do them during tax season. Those were things we learned from writing for Johnny Carson. There are annual things we could do, like jokes about Dave's mother or his Uncle Earle.

Act 2 has Dave at the desk, where viewers are usually given a prepared comedy piece or, in the final six weeks, a best-of clip package, but once again the show veers from the prepared to the spontaneous.

BILL SCHEFT (Writer): This is why the Letterman show has always been like no other. I wish I could tell you it has something to do with me, but it does not. We had all the elements in place for the show and then, ten minutes before Dave goes downstairs, he sees someone's phone video of Todd Seda, the cue card boy who is known on the show as "Todd the Intern," jumping over a conference table on the fourteenth floor. Instantly, that became the Act 2 comedy piece.

JILL GOODWIN (Writer): Todd is one of the most flexible people you will ever meet. He can hop over stuff or swing around poles. To see Dave buy into that and put it on the show was really fun.

BILL SCHEFT: I'm sure, like many things, this started as someone just trying to make Dave laugh. But Dave immediately saw it as something much more compelling than anything we had been working on all day. And it was. It will always be the stuff on the fly people will remember.

JILL GOODWIN: I like when there is some peek behind the curtain. That is kind of what that is. Viewers enjoyed seeing this kid doing crazy stunts and Dave getting a chuckle out of it. I don't think that is too inside or self-serving.

As the video plays in slow motion, Paul and the band perform "Also sprach Zarathustra" (the theme to *2001: A Space Odyssey*), timing it to kick in as Todd flies over the table. Dave cheers and screams, "Come on!" in his sports broadcasting voice, which makes the event even more exciting. When Dave gets excited, we get excited. This is such a Letterman moment: exciting, different, relatable, ultimately pointless, and stupidly wonderful. He proceeds to the Top Ten "Things Overheard in Hillary Clinton's Van."

The first guest is Billy Crystal, who receives a standing ovation. He and Dave chat about Billy's grandchildren. Crystal takes a different approach from Sarah Jessica Parker. Crystal has prepared great stories and catchphrase-filled material designed to make Dave laugh. Since Billy and Dave are contemporaries, the tactic is more suited to their relationship. He imitates his next-door neighbor, who keeps coming up to his security camera to ask him pointless questions. He runs up to the cameras and puts his face as close as he can. You can hear Dave laughing and clapping along.

Billy says, "Dave, you're my best friend on television, and what I can't put into words I'd like to put into a song." He moves center stage and performs a comic song set to the tune of "Sunrise, Sunset" from *Fiddler on the Roof.* Crystal co-wrote the song with composer Marc Shaiman (*Hairspray, Sleepless in Seattle*); the two had earlier collaborated on Billy's musical monologues (Can we start calling these songologues?) during the Academy Awards telecasts. The song is filled with references to great moments in Dave's career. Billy performs the song in front of two green screens, which display clips from the show as he sings about Drew Barrymore, Richard Simmons, Madonna, and more. Paul and the band accompany Shaiman, who plays the piano. It hits the right tones, the right jokes, and is a fun tribute to Dave.

RANDI GROSSACK (Associate Director): We would get the script to know what clips we needed. Then we would have to pull them and have them cut to the right length and moment. Then, at rehearsal, you are rolling the clips and making sure they time out. I would be involved in pulling the clips and putting them together. We would see if we got the right clip and then maybe pull one that might work better. It is up to Jerry Foley to run them at the right time as the song is going on.

MIKE BUCZKIEWICZ: (Segment Producer/Senior Producer): The great thing about Billy Crystal and Marc Shaiman was they reached out to the show a full two weeks beforehand. They had a fully formed idea and were ready to go. He said, "We worked up this full song." It was amazing. Billy was open to ideas. He came in and rehearsed it a couple of times. He wanted to walk through a couple of beats. I think Marc had six other things going on at the same time, but was still willing to drop everything to come in because Billy wanted to tweak something. It was a rare treat to be able to work with both those guys and then see the final product.

The *Late Show* baseball card shows a very young Billy Crystal, from August 2, 1982.

The second guest is Julie Chen, from the CBS shows *The Talk* and *Big Brother*. She oddly doesn't mention that Dave is leaving the network. She talks about The Beatles, parenting, and *The Talk*. As they go to commercial, Paul plays The Beatles' "I Saw Her Standing There," demonstrating that he is always listening to the conversation.

Musical Guest

The musical guest is country star Chris Stapleton, making his network television debut with a performance of "Traveller." The show may be ending, but it is still debuting new artists.

SHERYL ZELIKSON (Music Booker): Chris Stapleton has a certain presence about him. If you are flipping through the channels and see him, you are curious just based on his physicality. He's talented, an outlaw, and he's a maverick in what was considered popular and the norm for country music. I thought it was a really special artist and a good representation of what Dave was throughout his career in championing artists like that.

WORLDWIDE PANTS TAG:

"Press those pants."

"FROM MAPLE SHADE, NEW JERSEY..."
IT IS EPISODE 6,003
APRIL 15, 2015

"And now the goon in the room from Saskatoon . . . David Letterman." When Dave arrives at center stage, the audience leaps to its feet. This is his first standing ovation of the final six weeks. "Thank you, that is very kind," Dave says, as he keeps motioning with his hands for the audience to sit. "Please be seated . . . OK . . . all right." They won't stop, though, so Dave has to force them to.

The monologue consists of jokes about taxes, the presidential campaign, and the California drought. The desk piece is the first best-of package of the final six weeks, a taped bit from April 8, 1997, "How Many Guys in Bunny Suits Can Get into an H&R Block?" The answer is two.

The Top Ten List, delivered by ten accountants, is "Things You Don't Want to Hear from Your Accountant." Paul plays "Taxman" by The Beatles.

The first guest is Michael J. Fox. Dave announces in his intro that Fox has raised over $450 million for his Parkinson's foundation. The audience delivers the second standing ovation of the night as Fox makes his way to the guest chair.

Photo courtesy of @Letterman, CBS publicity photo.

"You've been on this show over forty times." says Dave. Fox replies, "Forty-one times. I can't believe this will be the last time I will be on the show. I just wanted to thank you for everything you have done for me and for television." It is touching to see Fox pay tribute to Dave. "I will say you are better doing what you do than I am at what I do," says Dave, deflecting. "You're taller," quips Fox.

A picture of Fox from October 23, 1985 is shown. It's everything you want the eighties to be—big hair, big glasses, and a crazy suit jacket. They talk about parenting and *Back to the Future*. They move on to Parkinson's awareness month (April) and the research that his foundation is working on.

They discuss Fox's initial reaction to being diagnosed with Parkinson's to advances in scientific research into the disease. Dave asks how the money is distributed, and Fox gives detailed answers. One of Dave's questions is so in-depth that Fox loses his place and asks Dave to repeat it. This is where Dave really shines as an interviewer. Dave is not lobbing softballs about working with Christopher Lloyd or even perfunctory questions about Fox's charitable endeavors. Rather, they are having a serious discussion about science. To put it another way, they are most certainly not playing board games out there. Dave is honestly curious about the techniques scientists are using to cure this disease.

EDDIE VALK: Dave is so curious and so wants to know a thing. It's insatiable. He wants to know why. He has an ability to absorb everything, but keeps that low-key atmosphere.

SHERYL ZELIKSON: Letterman is an anomaly. He's a very curious, smart person that had a very distinctive viewpoint. I always think of him as quality.

"I have great admiration for you," says Dave. "Thank you, I do for you, too," answers Michael. Dave finishes, "You're the original tough guy. It was a great pleasure and an honor. I am happy to have known you."

This is an emotional, wonderful appearance. Viewers are witness to two television legends talking about substantial topics and having fun. You can feel the respect that each has for the other. For twelve minutes on network television, two respectable adults are sharing their mutual admiration.

KATHY MAVRIKAKIS: I do feel that people were coming on to take a victory lap with Dave. It wasn't about selling a project. It was about acknowledging that they had a history with somebody who is a legend. The people that we chose for those appearances, in most instances, had long-term relationships with us. They are entitled to take a victory lap with him. I am very proud of those episodes.

BRIAN TETA: Michael J. Fox is another person whom I idolized as a kid. I was always excited to work with him. What struck me about Michael and Dave is the history there. Michael is somebody who was a star in the early NBC days. *Back to the*

Future is 1985. They did the old *Late Night* film festival bit in 1986. Dave respected him a lot. He immediately made sense to me as a guest we should have in those final weeks.

Dave introduces his second guest as "one of the funniest people we know, Amy Sedaris." Full disclosure from your author: Amy Sedaris is hands down my all-time favorite *Late Show* guest. She wastes no time with her final appearance. She leaps out to the chair and says, "I have seven minutes and I didn't leave any wiggle room for you to say anything."

She is visibly nervous, grimacing and fidgeting (more than normal) as she first makes eye contact with Dave. The realization that this is her final appearance is weighing on her. Another true professional, she shakes it off and recalls how Dr. Phil once told her to make a list of the five most important men (or animals, she couldn't remember). Either way, Dave is on her list. She admits she has thought about him every single day since 2001. She bursts into a short improvisational song, then admits she doesn't know how to sing.

Amy says, "This is my thirty-fourth time on your show since 2001. You have the best audience, best crew, lighting, band, Paul, you guys are the best. When you get off set everyone is cheering you on. No one has ever said a bad thing about you." Dave replies, "You've always been very generous to come and be on the show. Sometimes we call you—" Amy explodes, "Last minute! I get that call, 'Hi it's Sheila Rogers from the *Late Show*.' And I panic. I always have a dress hanging up in case you call."

SHEILA ROGERS: Amy was always an amazing guest. She would say to me, "Tell me when and I will be there." She was a given as a final guest and not a "Hollywood" interview.

BRIAN TETA: She, Regis, and a couple of the sports guys would fill in for guests that dropped out. Amy was so funny, original, and different. Their conversations were different from Amy's appearances on other talk shows. She became one of the most quintessential *Late Show* guests. There was something special about the two of them together.

Amy starts to realize her time is almost up. She digs into her bag of compliments and comes up with maybe one of the best descriptions of Dave: "You are like scaffolding." It is perfectly Amy. Funny, crazy, and spot on. Dave is just as big a part of New York City as scaffolding.

"Is this really gonna be it? I'll never see you again . . . Well, I'll see you at home," she jokes, but starts to get emotional. "I'm in love with you. You've just been the best. Seriously, this is really hard." She kisses him on the cheek, then announces that she is wearing Spanx backward.

JERRY FOLEY: If Amy Sedaris was an older man, she'd have the same beard as Dave has now. There are willful eccentrics and then there are eccentrics. Amy is truly an eccentric in the most playful, creative, offbeat way.

BILL SCHEFT: I have often said this about Amy Sedaris: If she wasn't Amy Sedaris, she'd be in a state hospital. But she has two qualities I admire. One, she never stops moving, she never stops trying to make you look. Which, for television, is kind of important. Second, she really loves Dave. Now, a lot of guests love Dave and it makes him uncomfortable. But Amy Sedaris is so uncomfortable to begin with, he gets to settle right down. What a blessed relief.

BARBARA GAINES: Amy is almost like having a human-interest guest even though she is an actress, because she talked about her fake boyfriend, her rabbit, or a craft she is doing. But she really is doing crafts, and she really does have a rabbit.

JERRY FOLEY: When Amy talks about her bunny, she spins something exaggerated, but she has a relationship with rabbits. Her home decorating and arts and crafts and skills with a glue gun, that is all real. That is what she does.

RICK SCHECKMAN: Amy was one of those actresses that came to play. She was on our 4 a.m. show. Dave loved her and her brother, David Sedaris.

BRIAN TETA: Amy was a lot of people's favorite guest. When someone would tell you they were a fan of the show, and they would start rattling off the guests they like, when they said Amy Sedaris, you knew, "Oh yeah, you get it. You are one of us." She was fantastic. I only worked with her a couple of times. That was a name that came up immediately: "We have to make sure we have Amy in the final weeks," because she is one of the classic *Late Show* guests in the later run of Dave's history.

LEE ELLENBERG: I always got the sense as a viewer, Dave wasn't impressed by people who just act. He still wanted to be engaged by the person. I think he was a hard person to entertain. I think it became harder the more celebrities he spoke to.

JERRY FOLEY: You sit and do a couple thousand shows and your laugh nerve gets a little deactivated. You find yourself appreciating a joke more than laughing at it. But when Amy came out, you laughed out loud. She was perfectly ridiculous. She is truly thinking differently from the rest of us.

BARBARA GAINES: I think that is enormously appealing to Dave, that she is this quirky woman. He loves people who are naturally interesting, odd, and funny who talk to him, who aren't just sitting down and saying, "I want to talk to you about my movie and nothing else." Which Amy doesn't do.

JERRY FOLEY: People like Amy and Dave are truly different from the rest of us. When you get two truly different people in the same room together, they elevate each other. Amy was always very appreciative that Dave could give her a platform to be weird and entertaining. It goes beyond an act or publicity opportunity. Those two people would be acting the same way if they were riding in a car together going to Boston. There just happened to be cameras there.

Musical Guest

The musical guests are Iron & Wine and Ben Bridwell. They perform "No Way Out of Here."

SHERYL ZELIKSON: They sang a song out from their new album. I can't remember if Ben also made his debut on the show. A lot of the artists were invited back during those final weeks. It was like a trip down memory lane.

WORLDWIDE PANTS TAG:

"Mmm . . . mmm . . . mmm."

"FROM THE SUNNYSIDE RAIL YARD IN QUEENS..."
IT IS EPISODE 6,004
APRIL 16, 2015

"And now . . . it's a Webkinz . . . David Letterman." The audience is standing before he even dashes across the stage. "Thank you, that is very kind of you," Dave says, then begs everyone to take a seat. After three cuts to the standing audience, Dave says, "Knock it off or you will wake the people at home." The monologue topics are New York City construction workers, the gyrocopter that landed on the Capitol lawn, and Hillary Clinton's Twitter account.

Sue Hum, the costume designer, interrupts Dave to hand him a pantsuit made out of tortilla shells (Hillary Clinton had stopped at a Chipotle earlier that week). She tells him she and her entire family hate him. She walks off stage with the pantsuit.

BRIAN TETA: There are people who are characters and part of the regular show. I made some appearances on the show, but I was never Sue Hum.

JOE GROSSMAN (Writer): Dave always liked someone who didn't belong on camera—Larry "Bud" Melman, Rupert Jee, George Clark [building engineer], Sue Hum. It's always someone who has an awkward presence. I was basically one of those people.

BILL SCHEFT: We had this concept going that the staff had no respect for Dave during the monologue and no one was listening to him. We did that "B" storyline for years. No other show did that. I feel that the show never got the credit for what the staff was doing. It takes a lot of humility to go out there night after night and have someone on the staff just not pay attention to you. We would do the monologue interrupts where Pat Farmer [stage hand] would come out and say, "While it's quiet and I have your attention . . ."

JOE GROSSMAN: Over the years we did a lot of passive-aggressive jokes about how hard it was to work for him. Those were sometimes his favorite things to put on the show, so you have to give him a lot of credit for that.

JILL GOODWIN: Other hosts are too precious to put up with that. It was surprising Dave could take it. There would be a tinge of "It is almost too real." Even if Dave knew it, Dave loved it. He thought it was ballsy and funny. He didn't take offense at it.

At the desk Dave reads the Top Ten "Questions to Ask Yourself Before Landing a Gyrocopter on the United States Capitol Lawn." Then he plays a best-of montage in which he makes all kinds of strange noises, faces, and gestures through the years with the classic line "I'm the only thing on CBS right now."

The first guest is Kevin James, promoting *Paul Blart Mall Cop 2*. He also announces that he will be returning to CBS in the fall. He does mention Dave leaving at the end of the segment, presenting him with farewell gifts, including fitness equipment, a blueberry pie, and peanut butter. This is more of a regular talk-show appearance, not one enriched by history. An accomplished comedian, James comes prepared with bits that would be fitting during a standard talk-show appearance.

BILL SCHEFT: Kevin James is, I believe, the best physical comic on TV since Jackie Gleason. He can do big and subtle. He did a bit on the show about how he doesn't play blackjack because he doesn't like the pressure of having to add and then went into a pantomime of him trying to count up his cards.

Tom Dreesen is the second guest. Paul plays the classic Sinatra song "Come Fly with Me," which is appropriate, since Dreesen opened for Sinatra for years. Dave and Dreesen, who have known each other for forty years, discuss the old days at The Comedy Store in Los Angeles. Dreesen says he was there the first time Dave ever did stand-up. They show a picture of Dave, Dreesen, and George Miller from back in the day.

Tom tells a story about going to a L.A. Lakers game where Dave gave the best under-pressure comic response he had ever heard. They're sitting in the stands and a menacing-looking man sits down next to Dave. He pulls out a hunting knife and says to Dave, "You got any money?" Dave retorts, "No, but ask around." Dreesen also shares a Frank Sinatra story. He ends his appearance by saying to Dave, "You're the best friend a guy could have. I wish for you that you get half the joy in your retirement that you have given to the world. I love you, pal." Dave thanks him; fade to a baseball card of Dreesen on *Late Night* from April 21, 1982.

STEVE YOUNG (Writer): Tom went back to when Dave started out in the seventies. There was a group of stand-ups that all knew each other from Los Angeles. Dave was very supportive of his friends from that era, and had on the show various people, like John Witherspoon, Jimmie Walker, and George Miller. I don't know if other shows were putting them on, but Dave enjoyed the connections running through the decades.

RICK SCHECKMAN: Tom Dreesen was an incredible friend of Dave's. Dreesen was a smart man in the seventies and he befriended all those people at The Comedy Store. Those people became very big and they never forgot him. He eventually became Frank Sinatra's opening act. He was a sweetheart.

Musical Guest

Dave explains that when Harry was a child he would read him a story and sing him a song every night before bed. He would sing him one of two songs. One was "America" by Simon & Garfunkel. The other was "Stand by Me." He remembers the night when he put Harry to bed and asked him which of the two songs he would like to hear. Harry's response? "No song." So ended Dave's singing career. He introduces the artist who will perform the Ben E. King classic "Stand by Me." He says, "To hear Tracy Chapman sing it is heaven."

Alone with an electric guitar and amp, Chapman stands center stage and performs this loving tribute to Dave and his son. This is the first, but not the last, song that will highlight how important music is to David Letterman and his history with television. Stop reading this book right now, YouTube the performance, and then come back. Be sure to grab a tissue because this is an emotional performance.

JERRY FOLEY: For Tracy Chapman to sing "Stand by Me," referencing something deeply personal in Dave's life, that kind of works center stage—scaled down, darker. It is a private, personal moment.

SHEILA ROGERS: Tracy was, kind of, all Dave's idea. I had a great relationship with Tracy's manager. I think she said yes pretty quickly. If Dave asked for something, you wanted to deliver. That was always what one tried to do.

SHERYL ZELIKSON: I enjoyed the creativity of those last six weeks and working closely with Sheila and Dave. At the end, Dave had very specific songs he wanted to hear. It was sort of my job to come up with a list of people who could sing these songs.

JERRY FOLEY: There was a heightened awareness that your opportunities to fix things you screwed up or redeem yourself in Dave's eyes were shrinking as time was getting shorter, but honestly any time the cameras were on that stage there was a lot of pressure to be sure you had it right for Dave. I can't tell you it was a greater pressure because of the importance that Dave put on that song. Anytime someone was on that stage, he was so heavily invested, and that was years before there was any talk of retirement.

RICK SCHECKMAN: Dave would say, "I want to hear Tracy Chapman," and they would book her. They would call the artist and say, "Dave has asked for you." It was very personal, as opposed to someone coming on and singing their latest single.

SHERYL ZELIKSON: This is where I can't remember. I think Dave would say, "I'd like to hear this song," very matter of factly. And I can't remember exactly with Tracy Chapman how it happened. I would start to write lists. Who would do a beautiful job with the song? Of course Tracy Chapman would. Given that she had history with the show, she would be perfect. That's another thing that I kept in mind. Who has history with the show? Who is an artist we debuted on the show?

JERRY FOLEY: You also have an awareness that these are historical moments. Tracy Chapman is coming in there so graciously and is gonna give new emotion and meaning to that song, as a result of what Dave said to set her up.

EDDIE VALK (Stage Manager): He loved the music. During the music, I would stand with Dave and count back how much time was left so he knew when to cross over and thank the guests. I would stand next to him and say, "1 minute, thirty seconds, etc." I would give hand signals for thirty seconds down. I was never too aggressive with them. You could read when he was in that emotional zone. You learn to navigate where and when to be aggressive, and when to let a moment go. I tried not to be a thorn in his side.

SHERYL ZELIKSON: I knew this was the song he sang for Harry. He wants someone that's going to make it special, emotional, and there's certain artists that just connect that way. Tracy has, besides her beautiful and unusual voice, a very strong and emotional connection when she sings.

Chapman is the highlight of this episode. Her performance puts the lyrics front and center for this tender moment between Dave and his son. For a musical artist to guest on a show not to promote themselves, but to fulfill a wish for the host, is rare in modern television.

WORLDWIDE PANTS TAG:

"Stop calling me."

"FROM AN ARTIFICIAL CORAL REEF MADE OF DECOMMISSIONED SUBWAY CARS..." IT IS EPISODE 6,005 APRIL 17, 2015

"And now . . . with a personality derived totally from caffeine . . . David Letterman." Dave comes out to another extended ovation. The monologue touches on proms, the Country Music Awards, and the Iowa Caucus.

The Top Ten List is "Other Courses Offered by the Vatican." After the list Dave asks Paul what the last show should be. Paul isn't sure. Dave says, "If we knew what to do with the last show, you think the previous 6,000 would look the way they looked?" He plays a best-of montage that compiles Paul Shaffer's comic moments from skits. The clip package plays to "It's Raining Men," which Paul co-wrote. The video shows the times Paul has taken hits from cars, sandbags, food, and baseball bats. All of the clips appear to be from the CBS era.

LEE ELLENBERG: We stopped doing Mailbag in 2004, and we didn't do as many pretapes. There wasn't a ton of pretape stuff with Paul for us to use. A lot of the stuff from Mailbag was from years ago.

BILL SCHEFT: Paul was underrated comedically, and I think he is no longer underrated comedically. Supervising producer Kathy Mavrikakis put the montage together. She used the database that Rick Scheckman and her maintained that documented every event in every episode.

KATHY MAVRIKAKIS: In the eighties, we decided that we needed to have a database of what we had done so that we could always refer back to it. I was one of the people with Rick that developed the database and kept it. I never gave that job up. I would look at what happened on the show and then type it all in, so that we would be able to say, "Paul did this, Paul did that," and find the clip.

RICK SCHECKMAN: Kathy and I built the original database from the old show. Kathy then built a new database from the new show that had the monologue, the topics, and all that stuff. So she was one of the go-to people for that information, along with Walter Kim and Jay Johnson, people who had been around a long time.

KATHY MAVRIKAKIS: When it came time to do the Paul montage, I searched the database and found the pieces I wanted and built it. Paul didn't see it beforehand. I didn't work with him on that one at all. It was sort of our tribute to him, so it wasn't something that we wanted to share ahead of time. Barbara Gaines, Jude Brennen, Matt Roberts [all executive producers] saw it. I think Dave may have seen it. I am not 100 percent sure.

Dave's first guest is Alec Baldwin. He comes out and shakes Paul's hand before walking over to see Dave. They talk about Baldwin's podcast (*Here's the Thing*), discuss being older dads, Baldwin's latest run-in with the media, and Tony Bennett.

At the end of the interview he gives Dave two presents for his retirement: a bag of alarm clocks and a loofah glove. Dave shoots back, "You've been spending time in the dollar store." He throws one of the alarm clocks through the "glass" windows behind him. This is the last glass-break sound of the series. The baseball card picture of Baldwin is from November 17, 1982.

MIKE BUCZKIEWICZ (Segment Producer): When Dave announced his retirement he said, "What I don't want is retirement gifts because we won't be able to talk about things." I think it was Baldwin who emailed me after the pre-interview and said, "I got an idea. I am gonna bring a gift." How do you tell him no, but at the same time, I have to go upstairs and tell Dave he has a gift for you. It worked out fine in the end. Alec was a great friend to the show and Dave. Dave loves Alec.

JAY JOHNSON: There were certain guests that Dave just seemed to have a natural bond with. I think that Alec Baldwin is one of them. They had an easy way of communication with each other. Anyone who knows Dave knows that wasn't always the case with every guest. Alec is a great storyteller. He was always willing to play along.

Musical Guest

"This is going to be special" is how Dave starts off his next introduction. He pauses for just a moment before saying "special." He truly means it. What viewers are treated to for the next eight minutes and fifty-six seconds is a highlight of not just the week, but of the thirty-three years of Letterman hosting a television show.

Dave continues, "He is doing us a huge favor. We asked him, 'Would you be interested in performing this song?' He said, 'Well, I got to get in some road work. I got to get in shape. It's kind of a beast, but I'll give it a shot.' He is going to do it for us tonight. Ladies and gentleman, performing, along with Paul and the kids in the band, 'American Pie,' here's John Mayer."

Director Jerry Foley staged John Mayer's "American Pie" where viewers could see the audience, the screen, and John. Drawing by Wayne Barnes.

Following the Chapman performance by one day, this tour de force appearance is the second in a musical one-two punch in which the norms of the musical guest on a talk show are shattered. CBS devotes nine minutes to a musical performance of a rock 'n' roll classic from 1971. This isn't what talk shows do. John Mayer doesn't even perform the song on any of his albums. The song isn't posted on iTunes moments after the show airs to try to bilk another $1.29 from every viewer. This song is being performed for one reason: because David Letterman wants to hear it. He wants to remind us about the day the music died.

Everyone rises to this momentous occasion: Mayer by owning this iconic song, Paul and the band with their perfect accompaniment, the staff by making sure there is enough time on the show for it, the network for changing its normal commercial pattern. Typically the back end of an episode is heavy on commercials; that isn't possible when you are presenting a nine-minute song. Jerry Foley's direction is magnificent. He changes shots continually, framing each shot differently, keeping the visual from growing stale. Amazingly, in the final seconds of this performance he finds a shot that he hadn't used at all in the entire song. At one point he has it framed so that viewers can see Mayer's back (he wore a *Late Night* jacket), with the band, the studio audience, and Mayer's face on the monitor mounted over the audience. It is a perfectly captured shot from a master director.

With the final chords still lingering, the audience leaps to its feet, clapping and cheering. Dave asks Mayer, "Do you need to sit down?" The audience, now fully lighted, is screaming and smiling. Mayer looks like a tennis player who just broke a legend's serve at Wimbledon. Dave is absolutely beaming. "Thank you. Paul, thank you. Everybody . . . really, really very nice of you. God bless you, sir. That was fun. It's John Mayer." Honestly, I could talk about this performance all day. What I learned was, so could the staff. Almost everyone singled this performance out as a favorite musical moment of the final six weeks. Only one other guest would get more praise than Mayer for his "American Pie" segment (stayed tuned to find out who). This performance meant the world to the staff—even if they didn't understand it at first.

BRIAN TETA: I thought it was the dumbest idea I had ever heard. Dave wanted to hear "American Pie." Really? "American Pie"? And I was WRONG.

SHERYL ZELIKSON: I was a little perplexed at the time, I was like, "Oh, OK . . . that's an interesting choice." But I think with the songs he choose, Letterman was trying to tell people a feeling.

RANDI GROSSACK: I think some of us at the theater thought it was such a long song, but when John did it, it was brilliant.

BILL SCHEFT: I can just hear people before they saw it thinking, "It's a forty-year-old song," but it was an ideal choice.

SHEILA ROGERS: Dave requested the song, but I think it was Sheryl Zelikson's idea to have John Mayer do it.

SHERYL ZELIKSON: You start to write a list of who can sing that song. At the top of that list is John Mayer. I remember calling his publicist and saying, "Hey, Dave wants to hear this song. Will John be willing to do it? He wants to hear all nine minutes."

RANDI GROSSACK: John did our Thanksgiving show a couple times. He had been very generous to the show. I think he wanted to be on the final shows and Dave asked specifically for him to play that song.

SHERYL ZELIKSON: It didn't take too long for John to say he'd love to. "Can he sing it in this key?" And that was the end of it. It was an instant yes, and he just did it. And I remember reiterating, "He knows it's the full song?" They responded, "Not a problem." John Mayer is an amazing talent, and he did a bang-up job. I don't think he overthought it.

JERRY FOLEY: John Mayer isn't doing a gig at the state fair. He knows that these are historical shows winding down to the conclusion. He also has been requested, not by someone shouting out in the audience but by David Letterman, to cover "American Pie." Now John Mayer is invested in ways he might not be in a typical way. Paul Shaffer is invested because anyone playing in front of his band was of paramount importance to Paul. He took pride in his musicianship and his band's ability to cover any song ever written. Then the song, as John will tell you, is a real challenge for a vocalist who is also playing guitar. John was concerned and wanted to rehearse and get it right. I guess you could say that when all those elements come together, everybody is bringing to it the best that they can possibly come up with.

SHERYL ZELIKSON: I can't remember if we gave him a little bit of extra rehearsal time. But I'm sure Paul and John worked out a lot of it on the phone. We ran a very tight ship at Letterman, and rehearsal times are set and we rarely go beyond them if we can avoid it. It really does change the whole working schedule. John and Paul had worked together before, so they were familiar with each other.

BILL SCHEFT: After rehearsal between shows, a friend of mine's mother-in-law said to John, "It has too many stanzas!"

BRIAN TETA: The whole staff was watching that in rehearsal. Those were special performances. Whenever Darlene Love was on, you'd look in the audience and it would be all the staff sitting there at 2:00 in the afternoon. We were all doing that for Mayer. I loved that he wore the *Late Night* jacket. That was fantastic.

RANDI GROSSACK: I watched it recently on YouTube and I thought, "This guy did it better than Don McLean." The way Jerry Foley shot it was spectacular.

JERRY FOLEY: What I have told people over the years is that the most compelling moments behind the camera are usually driven by compelling elements in front of the camera. So rather than being in a conversation about my authorship of these moments, I am the recipient of these moments. You have a TV icon closing out his CBS career. He has this tremendous wealth of respect and goodwill within the creative community, which draws in a guy like John Mayer. Dave asked for it and he, as you will find, engineered this almost inexplicable devotion among the people who worked for him and knew him. All these factors come together. John Mayer is up there on the stage; the lighting and camera people are caught up in this moment knowing we are not gonna get to do this again.

BILL SCHEFT: I think that Jerry is humble in the sense that— the best definition of humility I ever heard was the ability to be inconvenienced. Being a director on that show, all that happened in the last minute, it was nothing but inconveniences, and he just rolled with it.

KATHY MAVRIKAKIS: It was beautiful. Jerry had a bunch of things up his sleeve that I think he thought Dave might not have the tolerance for at a normal time. He was like, "Hell, what's the worst that can happen? I am not gonna get fired." So he might as well try every trick he always wanted to try. His creative touches were amazing.

JERRY FOLEY: If you are shooting something for nine minutes, the picture would have grown stale if he is center stage. But if you shot him so you could see John, the audience, the TV screen, Paul, you had options.

RICK SCHECKMAN: Jerry was integral to all of the final months. He is incredibly great at directing music. That is what he has been doing lately. He did that Tony Bennett at ninety special at Radio City Music Hall.

@LETTERMAN

BILL SCHEFT: Mayer said he didn't realize the effect it would have on people. He couldn't believe it. The fact that he wore his *Late Night* jacket was great. Jerry loved shooting music, and you can tell. To Hal Gurnee [the previous director], it was just another act.

JERRY FOLEY: I think that when you spend as much time in the theater as I did, you were constantly in search of a different angle, presentation, approach to complement whatever was in front of you. For John Mayer to stand up and sing an American anthem, which is inclusive of the entire stage, show, and history, and have a song that familiar to so many people of a particular generation, that is a bigger moment and doesn't belong center stage. John wasn't the only one playing. That orchestra was adding to the song, so they are as much a part of the story as anything else. I hate to attach any kind of false importance to it, but instinctively you know there are plenty of people in the audience that have their own personal history with that song. It would be a crime to not get those faces as a part of the story. There's a practical situation. He is going on for an extended period of time. You need to spread it around, you need to include as many elements as you can. That theater is a very special place to showcase as much of it as you can, and to make it as beautiful as you can is an obligation and opportunity. All those things kind of factor in. I didn't write it down on a page and say, "These are the areas I want to address." It is all instinctual and comes together without a lot of discussion.

SHERYL ZELIKSON: That's a pretty in-depth song, but it went off, like, beyond expectation. Yes, Letterman could see things that other people can't. Everyone kind of knows the song. They've heard it on radio, but Letterman knows how special that song is. He wanted everyone to hear all of it. I thought that was kind of brilliant.

BILL SCHEFT: John Mayer has no idea what he did. It is not an easy song to survive and an impossible song to make your own. Man, did they get the right guy.

JILL GOODWIN: I thought the John Mayer performance was great. He really showed up for Dave. Just the fact that he did that, and nailed it, and wanted to do a good job for Dave. I guess it was asking a lot. It seemed really hard. I felt the pressure for him.

WORLDWIDE PANTS TAG:

"Are you still up?"

4

Stand in the Fire

THE MONOLOGUE

THROUGH THE YEARS, a multitude of writers had a hand in the monologue that began Dave's late-night programs. During the final six weeks of the *Late Show*, the bulk of the monologue jokes were written by Mike Barrie, Jim Mulholland, Bill Scheft, and Steve Young. It was up to them to come up with five new six-minute sets a week. Barrie and Mulholland had written Johnny Carson's monologue starting in the early 1970s. When Johnny retired, they started writing for Letterman, but kept their Los Angeles residence.

> I'M RETIRING. FOX NEWS IS REPORTING IT AS ANOTHER JOB LOST UNDER OBAMA.

BILL SCHEFT: Steve Young and I were the co-head writers of the monologue. He did the clerical work and brought the raw material together. My job, in addition to writing jokes, would be to run through them with Dave.

STEVE YOUNG: The weird thing about my job of running the monologue was that I didn't write many jokes. I mostly organized what Dave picked and asked for more jokes from the various writers. Some days, if things were desperate, I would sit down and write a few jokes where we needed them.

BILL SCHEFT: Mike Barrie and Jim Mulholland contributed the vast majority of Dave's jokes at the top of the show. They are prolific, hip, and have changed their tone over the years as the show's sensibilities changed. They have always been the innovators in self-deprecating jokes about Dave. Hard to pick a favorite joke of theirs, although I loved this line: "People ask, 'Are you going to miss the laughter and applause?' Hell, I'm missing them right now." If anyone else but Letterman does that joke it is disingenuous.

MIKE BARRIE: I think anyone can do that joke. It may have Dave's personality, but it has a setup and a punchline. Theoretically Carson could have done that joke.

BILL SCHEFT: Who else could do that joke? In the hands of anybody else it is a gratuitous plea for sympathy; with Dave it's a fact.

> MOM CALLED TODAY AND SAID, "I HEAR YOU'VE BEEN FIRED AGAIN."

MIKE BARRIE: Jim and I wrote from L.A., so my day started very early. I got up at 4:00 a.m. and met with Jim at 6:00. We would meet at one of our houses.

JIM MULHOLLAND: We would fax our work to Dave around 8:30, and he would check the ones he wanted to do and fax them back to us. On a good day we would get a lot of checks, but sometimes it would be two. We really struggled in the beginning. The first day we wrote for him, we faxed eight or nine pages. We had spent several days writing these to make a good impression, and he checked only one of them. It was a joke about Roseanne Barr getting divorced. We thought we were gonna get fired.

MIKE BARRIE: Then you would hear back from Steve Young, who would say, "Dave only checked one joke on that topic, so we need a few more." Dave always liked to have several jokes on a topic.

STEVE YOUNG: Every day they would send in their pass of jokes to Dave. I would see how many jokes he picked. I usually spoke to Mike and would say, "Dave picked nine; we need more on this or that topic. I saw one good one from this area, if you can try a couple on that."

MIKE BARRIE: Steve was the guy who was in charge of the monologue. Steve is a very funny writer.

JIM MULHOLLAND: For many years they were looking for the big closer joke. That could be frustrating. It was a struggle to find the closer. Also, we were sending in the stuff so early that often news would break. Something would happen at 11, and you would have to throw out the stuff you did.

MIKE BARRIE: We set for ourselves a minimum of four to six pages a day, seven to eight jokes per page. During the course of the day, Letterman would become too familiar with the jokes, and he would start tossing them out. You could be driving on the freeway later in the day and get a call that he needs more on a topic. It was a lot of hours and vastly overwritten to get fifteen jokes that Dave liked.

STEVE YOUNG: Jim and Mike are very professional and prolific. Being thousands of miles away and being a voice on the phone is very different from being in the writers' room. They had been doing this for many years.

JIM MULHOLLAND: Someone once said to me, "You know, there are these two mysterious guys. They write all of the jokes, and no one has ever seen them." He didn't know I was the guy. No one ever saw us because we were never in the office. I didn't want anyone to see us getting older and older. We were like these shadowy characters. "Who are these guys sending these jokes everyday?"

IT'S 68 AND FOGGY. LIKE ME.

BILL SCHEFT: Dave would start the monologue with a "Hi, how are you?" joke about himself or New York City, and then we would try to pair up jokes on topics.

JIM MULHOLLAND: Bill suggested we write New York City jokes, which we started doing. We were good at that because we did them for Johnny when he was in New York. That was how we got our footing on the show, with the cab drivers, subway, or rat jokes—all exaggerated nightmare versions of New York City which no longer existed. It was more like the New York of the seventies. Dave loved that stuff, and that got us going.

STEVE YOUNG: There was a certain rhythm to it that he grew to feel was right for him. "Here is something about the weather" or "I was walking on Broadway on my lunch hour"—something not deeply topical, to dip our toe in the water with something harmless.

BILL SCHEFT: From 1995 on is when the monologue became more topical. He realized if you do topical stuff you don't have to take forever to set something up. If it's in the ether all you have to do is say, "Here is news from the O.J. trial," and they know where you are. You can go right to the punchline.

JIM MULHOLLAND: It didn't look like we were the right fit for him, but as it went on I think we had an influence on him to do more topical stuff.

BILL SCHEFT: I remember a great joke in the middle of the Bill Clinton scandal. I wish I had written this: "Clinton claims that oral sex is not sex; if that is true there is a hooker who owes me $75." That is a kind of joke that none of the other hosts did. Dave would take a global topic and the joke would be about him. That is when he was at his best.

> IT'S A NEW STAGE OF LIFE FOR ME. MY SON WILL BE SAYING, "WATCH IT, POP, THERE'S A STEP."

STEVE YOUNG: Dave didn't want anything to go beyond one cue card. It was minimal—a few words, a phrase and a setup. He would then, depending on his mood, improvise off that. He might have thirty seconds of off-the-cuff conversation leading into a joke that was not on the cue card.

JILL GOODWIN (Non-monologue Writer): When I started working as Barbara Gaines and Jude Brennan's assistant, I would see that the mailroom guy would get monologue jokes on the show. I started asking around, "So anyone can submit jokes?" They said, "Yeah, go up to the fourteenth floor and give some jokes to Bill or Steve." One of my jobs at that time was processing the payments to freelance monologue writers. If a joke aired, they would get $75 or something. That was attractive to me. I can try to write jokes, and if they air I can have a little money for the bar. Everyone was supportive. Once they saw your name on the monologue joke sheet that went around, Barbara would say, "Hey, you are writing jokes. Do more."

BARBARA GAINES: We were so proud. We didn't want to lose her as an assistant because she was fantastic, but we wanted her to succeed. We loved Jilly because she was so funny. She would make fun of us, and we liked that.

JILL GOODWIN: They were very supportive. Bill Scheft was so nice. He would say, "This is funny, but it needs to be twenty words shorter. The punchline needs to be here." He would mentor me.

BILL SCHEFT: When I got the job with Dave, I asked if there was advice he could give me. He said, "Don't write a joke more than four lines. I don't care how good it is, if it is longer than four lines it won't fit on a cue card." The jokes on *Late Night* were all three and four lines. At the *Late Show*, most of the jokes were two lines.

MIKE BARRIE: You'd write "retirement," and he would say whatever he wanted. The second sentence was written out on the cue cards. That doesn't mean it was always told that way.

> BY THE WAY, AFTER THE SHOW . . . IF YOU GIVE ME A GOOD ONLINE REVIEW, IT MIGHT HELP ME FIND OTHER WORK.

BILL SCHEFT: The show was on NBC for eleven years. The sensibilities in the eleven years, maybe, changed twice. In twenty-two years at CBS I think the sensibilities of the show, in terms of the content, changed half a dozen times, because he got older. He deserved to be the kind of host he wanted to be. When we first came to CBS he doubled the monologue, doing eight jokes, but on eight different topics.

JIM MULHOLLAND: It was hard to do a lot of material. As the years went by we got him to do more. When we started with him on the CBS show, it was just a handful of jokes, so you couldn't really get into it.

BILL SCHEFT: The thing that changed that was the O.J. verdict. When the verdict came down, he said to me, "I think we should do the whole monologue on O.J." We did that. It really worked, because if you are doing eight jokes on eight topics, it's just going from joke to joke. That is when the monologue became more like stand-up. Don't confuse being a stand-up with doing a monologue. With stand-up you work ten years on a routine. A monologue, you have one shot on one night.

JIM MULHOLLAND: He was doing a longer monologue. Maybe it went from six to ten jokes.

BILL SCHEFT: At NBC he would do three jokes. Then, after Johnny left, he went from three to four jokes. When he went to CBS, he went from four to eight. So for the first ten years at CBS it was eight jokes, no videotapes. Then it changed to eight jokes and two taped pieces at the end of the jokes. Then the monologue, which had been considered, unfairly, his weakest quality, started testing very high. So he decided to double it.

BARBARA GAINES: The monologue was just Dave. That was his piece. Bill worked almost entirely on the monologue, so it was extremely important to him. It often got criticized, so he would defend the monologue. Bill's place there was much more than just the monologue. He was Dave's friend. That was his place in history, as Dave's comedy friend.

BILL SCHEFT: I stood under the stairs. My title was writer, but my job was entertaining the man during his own show. I would keep him loose. I was a corner man. We didn't talk about the show. We talked about nonsense. I would remind him of an old comic's bit or something on a previous show.

BARBARA GAINES: Bill would interject during a desk piece or have an answer. Bill is a Harvard boy. He is a good person to lean to the left and talk to. He could lean to the left and talk to me and I got nothing.

MIKE BARRIE: Bill is hilarious and a brilliant writer. He has written novels and is very funny on his feet. He is the last person to see Dave before he goes on, so he can give jokes to Dave in the last five minutes. I think they had a rapport that worked for both of them. Bill's humor is smart and hip, and so was Letterman's. I think they fed off each other. It was a good marriage.

> I CALLED MY ACCOUNTANT TO TELL HIM THE SHOW WAS ENDING. HE SAID, "DON'T WORRY, DAVE, I'M SET FOR LIFE."

BILL SCHEFT: Let's say of the twenty-four jokes on cards that Dave had personally selected, he looked at a hundred jokes. Steve and I looked at 200 to 300 jokes on an average day. The monologue had sixteen elements: thirteen jokes and three short tape pieces, a live interrupt or a prop.

JIM MULHOLLAND: He wanted to do nineteen, twenty jokes, which he did for a while, which was very exciting, but then it sort of evolved to the cutaways and videos, so it wasn't as much.

STEVE YOUNG: I couldn't micromanage too much because most days during the show I was going down to the edit room to edit a fake commercial. The monologue was probably twenty-five percent of my time and energy.

JOE GROSSMAN: You have monologue writers, and other shows would call them "sketch writers," but at Letterman you were not allowed to use the word "sketch." There were four monologue writers, and the rest of us would be writing everything else, which included those videotaped pieces or interrupts in the monologue, which we called "extras."

STEVE YOUNG: That was an evolution. I think we became aware that other shows started doing that. It did seem like the natural thing to do. Part of the reason we hadn't done it in the show's history was the technology had improved so much. It was more practical for us to produce seven or eight videotape pieces per day and let Dave choose three he liked. When I started on the show in 1990, if you wanted to put together a videotape piece it would be so technically challenging. We would produce one thing a week, but by 2015 we could produce seven or eight a day.

> ### WELCOME TO THE LATE SHOW'S "WE'VE LOST OUR LEASE CLEARANCE SALE."

JOE GROSSMAN: In terms of videotaped pieces, I would say they started showing up during the monologue roughly around 2006-2008. Before that they would be in Act 2 . They were called "extras," because they were little extras to throw in the Act 2 desk piece. Then we started moving them into the first act.

BILL SCHEFT: The last three or four years we realized because we're doing so many more jokes, that we thought it would be better to weave the tapes and interrupts within the monologue. That is the way we did it. Ideally we closed with the strongest tape.

STEVE YOUNG: I don't remember when there was a greater turn in the monologue to the retirement jokes.

JIM MULHOLLAND: We had a year to do retirement jokes with him. I loved that. You look for anything when you are a monologue writer. We did jokes about him sitting in his robe watching *Ellen*, stuff like that. "Tonight I am interviewing Oprah and next week I'll be hanging out at Ace Hardware." We had jokes like, "I am leaving the show, but I'll be back at CBS in the fall and I'll be solving murders."

All the jokes highlighted in this chapter were written by Mike Barrie and Jim Mulholland. They graciously shared pages of their jokes for the book. Just for old-times' sake, I checked off only a portion of them and sent the rest back.

5

Five Weeks Left

EPISODES 6,006–6,010

"FROM THE MOST PHOTOGRAPHED
COVERED BRIDGE IN VERMONT..."
IT IS EPISODE 6,006
APRIL 20, 2015

"And now . . . what you need, when you need it . . . David Letterman."
Dave's monologue topics are the New York Mets, the TSA, and the
presidential campaign. Writers R.J. Fried and Joe Grossman interrupt to
present a best-of montage of their own appearances.

JILL GOODWIN: Some of the writers thought the walkouts were
too jokey, but some were really good. Our younger staffers made
the show seem a little younger. I didn't mind it as long as it wasn't
every night.

JOE GROSSMAN: I never would have asked to be on the show.
If I had, that would have meant I would never be on the show.
The other writers were amused by my awkwardness and lack of
telegenic qualities. It was always built around the idea that "here
is someone who is uncomfortable on camera." I grew up watching
the show. So the fact that I got to actually be a footnote in the
show's history—I wasn't quite Chris Elliott, but maybe I was the
show's Tommy Newsom.

Photo courtesy of Paul Shafer.net.

The desk piece begins with Dave talking about the previous weekend's Rock 'n' Roll Hall of Fame ceremony. Dave implores the hall of fame to induct Paul and the band. He asks, "Who has been responsible for more rock 'n' roll over the last thirty-three years than this group right here?"

RICK SCHECKMAN: That was a very good band Paul put together. He had the best session musicians in New York—Will Lee, Sid, and all those guys. Tom "Bones" Malone is a great arranger. Paul would have those musicians up in his office all day working on arrangements. He worked very hard. I don't think Dave could do the show without him.

BRIAN TETA: About two months ago, Paul was on tour with the band, and a bunch of the producers went to see him at Westbury Music Fair. It was such a fun night because that music was a part of your life everyday and you take it for granted.

RANDI GROSSACK: Aside from being very funny and talented, Paul is a nice, warm guy. He would always hang out and chat with you. He showed up at parties and funerals. He is a mensch.

BARBARA GAINES: Paul *is* a mensch. He went to my mother's funeral and shiva, and let my nephew be his intern. He's a great guy.

The best-of clip is from February 1995, when Dave played May We Press Your Pants Please? Dave looks for a random person on the streets outside the theater. He picks a "Rolex salesman" who ends up selling Dave a watch. No Top Ten List on this episode.

The first guest is John Travolta. Paul Shaffer, only moments after Dave had lauded him as a musical genius, displays exactly what a genius he is. The song he plays to score Travolta's walk-on is "I Can See Clearly Now." Only Paul and the CBS Orchestra could have come up with that song. I'll give you a moment to see if you can make the connection.

BARBARA GAINES: Paul asked Jude and I, "Can I play this song for Travolta's entrance?" We said, "It's OK with us." I don't think people are musically versed enough to know that his play-ons are genius. He thought about the songs he picked.

MIKE BUCZKIEWICZ: I think if you are going to highlight the creativeness that is Paul, that is a perfect example for it. It speaks to who Paul was creatively, but he also didn't trumpet it.

He was like, "I am just gonna put this out there and if people pick up on it, great, and if people don't, I know what it is." He would do that time and time again.

BRIAN TETA: The staff would try to guess what song he would play. We didn't usually know what it was gonna be. Sometimes it was a very ethereal thread to try to figure it out.

EDDIE VALK: I would sit with the other stage manager, Frank Comito, and watch how they would workshop the music for the guest. Someone would shout out a song and they would work on it. Every time, they just nailed it. It was crazy to see their creative process in such a short time. Paul was always doing something. He never had down time.

RICK SCHECKMAN: I love Paul. He is also a very serious man as a father and husband. He always bought into that Jerry Lewis Vegas-comedy style. He can come up with intro music to someone's walk-on. If a guest brings up a song, he is ready to go.

BRIAN TETA: My first job at the *Late Show* I was Paul's intern, in 1997. That was a thrill for me. It's not something that people who watch once or twice might know, but when you watch the show on a regular basis, you see the respect that other musicians have for him.

Figure out the song connection, yet? In March 2015, HBO telecast a documentary critical of Scientology called *Going Clear*. John Travolta is a Scientologist. Paul played "I Can See Clearly Now."

John Travolta says that October 11, 1989, was the first time he was a guest with Dave. He was on to promote *Look Who's Talking*. "You have been kind to me for twenty-five years," he says. They discuss flying and then Travolta brings out his son Ben. Ben has been in the green room with actress Kelly Preston (Travolta's wife). Ben changes his mind about coming out once he approaches the stage.

The second guest is Amy Schumer. This appearance is before her hit movie *Trainwreck*, so Schumer is not the big star she will become later that year. She does jokes from her stand-up act about a recent breakup. Amy says her mom is a speech and hearing therapist for the deaf. Then she repeats loudly and slowly, "SHE IS A SPEECH ..." Dave says, "I am not afflicted." Amy responds, "This is the last time I am going to be here; I can do what I want, Dave." Dave is excited by this prospect: "Well, now we are talking. Let's see what you have in mind." While the audience laughs, Amy sincerely whispers to him, "Thank you for having me here."

Amy is doing exactly what she should. She is killing it with comedy and paying respect. This is only her second appearance on the show, so a big, emotional farewell would not have been earned.

BILL SCHEFT: Let me say this about Amy Schumer: She's got it. Comedy Central likes to breathlessly hype the un-hype worthy, but this is not the case. This was the second time Amy had been on the show, and she has played it deftly both times. She's funny, quick, and incredibly economical with words, which is something people who are trying to get Dave's approval never are. At one point she said, "I would never lie to you out here, Dave." She is also accessible. She reminds you of someone you know. Jill Goodwin met her before the show, and I hope she said to Amy what she said to me about Amy, which is, "She's like everybody I grew up with."

BRIAN TETA: Dave was really tickled by her. She had a lot of respect for him. She got nervous beforehand, but she was absolutely 100 percent "press play and let her go," because she is hysterical. There were a couple of people that just connected immediately and were instant favorites for Dave. Jennifer Lawrence was one of those. Like, first appearance out, you're like, "Where is this person from? Let's get them back here."

Dave wraps up the interview by saying, "Since we probably won't be on the show together again, do something now that you'll regret." Amy stands up and slowly pulls up her skirt to reveal a scar on her upper thigh. Dave asks, "What is that?" She immediately answers, "That's my vagina." The band punctuates it with a bass note.

Dave puts his hands on his forehead and shakes his head; the audience laughs and claps. "Well, I asked for it, didn't I?" Dave says as the laughter starts to end. She assures him it is a surfing scar and says, "My vagina is right where it is supposed to be." Dave grabs the microphone on his desk and slams it down and screams, "OK!" They both laugh, and Dave kisses her hand and says, "Great job."

BRIAN TETA: In 2005-2006, I was on the subway and someone came up to me and said, "You were on Letterman last night; you were so funny." I used to appear in bits on the show, occasionally. I was like, "Oh, this nice lady is complimenting me." We started talking and it was Amy Schumer before she was *Amy Schumer*. She told me she was a stand-up and would I have any tips for getting on the show. We exchanged emails and became Facebook friends. She grew up on Long Island, where I live now. We became very friendly over the years. I didn't help her in any way, to my chagrin. I was looking through old emails when I was cleaning up my outbox, and I noticed I sent her a very nice, patronizing letter about "hang in there, kid, you'll get to be on the show." So when she became the biggest female comedian on the planet, I got to produce her that night. We would laugh about that earlier exchange. Dave liked her immediately. The first time she was on, she killed.

Musical Guest

The Waterboys from the British Isles are the musical guests. They make their network television debut with their performance of "The Girl Who Slept for Scotland." When they finish Dave walks over and asks what the title means. Mike Scott explains, "If you knew someone who talked a lot . . . she could talk for the Olympics?" Dave says, "I see, so she was good at sleeping."

WORLDWIDE PANTS TAG:

"Pants, the other white meat."

"FROM THE VISITOR'S DUGOUT AT FENWAY PARK..."
IT IS EPISODE 6,007
APRIL 21, 2015

"And now . . . rough and tough and strong and mean . . . David Letterman." Dave receives a standing ovation as he makes his way to the stage. The monologue opens with Dave asking the audience to pick up around themselves so he can get the deposit back on the theater. This is the first time he begins the show with a retirement joke. Topics include New York, Todd the intern winning the Pulitzer Prize, and an "extra" comparing Senator Bernie Sanders to Larry David. This is months before Larry David would first play Sanders on *Saturday Night Live*.

JILL GOODWIN: I watched a few of these episodes before we talked, and I wondered if someone from *SNL* was watching the show and thought, "Hey?" It isn't a crazy leap to make. We were doing that first.

STEVE YOUNG: We do get points for being there ahead of the curve, but history has proved that it was sort of a piece of low-hanging fruit.

The Top Ten List is "Things Overheard at the Latest Secret Service Meeting." The best-of piece is a spoof of *The Shawshank Redemption* with Alan Kalter trying to escape the theater through a tunnel.

BILL SCHEFT: We showed a classic remote in Act 2. It first aired February 24, 2006. In November 2007, when I was moderating a *Late Show* writers panel at the Paley Center, my longtime colleague Lee Ellenberg, who wrote the piece with his frequent collaborator Jeremy Weiner, introduced it as "an example of the kind of thing we can do at the show when we have the time and the resources."

JEREMY WEINER: Lee wrote the *Shawshank* one. I worked with Alan Kalter a bunch. When I was working as a segment coordinator for the writers, I would bring down scripts to Alan and have to talk to him about what he would have to do on the show. It was so fun to see his initial reaction to what he would have to do. Alan was great.

LEE ELLENBERG: I mentioned the idea in passing to Eric and Justin Stangel [head writers] and they said, "That's funny. Write it up." That was the whole thing. Of all the pieces I was responsible for, that one was, by far, the most involved. Because we could only shoot when we had a spare moment, which wasn't often, it took about a month! I think Spielberg shot the D-Day scene from *Saving Private Ryan* in less time. But our director, Jerry Foley, somehow managed to carve out slivers of time in the schedule so we could grab a shot whenever possible: during rehearsal, before rehearsal, after the show, etc. To be honest, the idea itself and the writing are . . . fine. Rather, it's a testament to our crew and production staff that they managed, in the limited free moments we had, to pull this piece together and make it look as good as it did. The head of our scenic department, Jason Kirschner, designed some really beautiful props, like the tunnel that Alan crawls through. Editor Steve Hostomsky did an outstanding job editing the piece.

STEVE YOUNG: Alan Kalter was such a pro and so entertaining. He had a terrific ability to just be the announcer guy, but with shading of weird darkness and desperation underneath. I would write all the weird lines that Alan would say going into commercials. Once in a while he would call me up and ask, "How do I pronounce this odd word?" He was quite game. I would see him in the elevator and he'd say, "That one last night was so bizarre. I loved it."

JEREMY WEINER: Alan was such a pro. He was just really fun. We would do these screen bits where it was him and his brother Rick. They would do duets together. It was great.

RICK SCHECKMAN: When Alan Kalter was hired, it energized the show. We didn't know he'd be great in comedy pieces. We lucked into that. He was hired for his professionalism and then we found out he could do that stuff.

This episode includes the Piedmont Bird Callers, a bit that was carried over from *The Tonight Show With Johnny Carson*. Dave announces that this appearance marks the fiftieth year of the Bird Callers appearing on late-night television: a group of high-schoolers from Piedmont, California, making different bird calls in groups. For the viewer, it's bittersweet, knowing this is likely the end of a fifty-year run.

BRIAN TETA: It was important to Dave to continue that tradition. We all assumed that Ellen Degeneres or someone would pick it up. It is sad. It was a fun tradition. Dave enjoyed teasing the kids. I am not even sure the kids had seen the show before they showed up. I know more about these birds than anyone should ever know.

SHEILA ROGERS: Peter Lassally, who had worked at *The Tonight Show With Johnny Carson*, was integral in bringing them on our show for twenty years. It was the last hurrah of the bird callers, which is ridiculous, but fun.

The first guest is Paul Rudd. He tells a funny story about how he inadvertently invited all of Kansas City to his mom's house. He also promotes the upcoming *Antman* film, then pays tribute to Dave. Rudd says, "I am so happy to be on the show before it ends. I know how much you hate compliments. Thirty years ago I joined the David Letterman Fan Club." Dave says, "It had nothing to do with us."

As a fan club member Rudd received a pin, a collapsible cup, a sponge, a back scratcher, and a balloon. He shows his pin, and a never-used sponge that says "I'm a member of the David Letterman Fan Club" on it. They put the sponge in water, as it is supposed to grow. If it does, it doesn't grow very much. Rudd wipes the desk with it. "I never thought I'd clean your desk with it," he says.

BRIAN TETA: Paul Rudd is one of those people we have known forever. He is a tremendous Dave fan. He had the fan club sponge. He had pitched this for years. Jonah Hill, Seth Rogen, and Paul Rudd—we never let them talk about how much they loved Dave. Dave didn't want to be fawned over. Now at the end, we were able to let Paul pay tribute.

Musical Guest

Chaka Khan performs a song that Paul Shaffer co-wrote with Paul Jabara, "It's Raining Men." Paul and the band accompany her. The band is set up on stage with Paul playing the electric piano center stage.

SHERYL ZELIKSON: It was a great tribute to Paul. Still to this day people don't know that Paul Shaffer wrote that song. It was a lot of fun.

RANDI GROSSACK: Paul was very involved in rehearsal. It was a huge production. It seemed pretty wild to us in the tape room. Chaka Khan performed on the show the first year and then sent a painting, a large portrait of herself. It hung in the writers' room for a while.

WORLDWIDE PANTS TAG:

"Hey look . . . canaries."

"FROM THE ILLINOIS STATE FAIR POULTRY BARN..."
IT IS EPISODE 6,008
APRIL 22, 2015

"And now . . . the last man to set foot on the moon . . . David Letterman," begins an Earth Day-focused monologue. Even the first joke begins with Dave announcing he is doing the show with no energy. Dave, in his later years on the show, was deeply interested in the environment and global warming. His first television project after the end of the *Late Show* was the series *Years of Living Dangerously* (2016), in which he travels to India to explore solar energy.

BILL SCHEFT: I think Dave is remarkably self-taught. He had a lot of interests that he developed late, and he pursued them. The planet was one of them.

RANDI GROSSACK: He is so smart. I learned just listening to him talk sometimes in the later years, when he became so involved in the environmental stuff and feeding people.

The desk piece is a best-of video of astronaut Buzz Aldrin at the 2000 Daytime Emmys. The Top Ten List is "Things You Don't Want to Hear from Your Receptionist." It is Administrative Professional Day, so the list is read by Worldwide Pants receptionist Art Kelly.

Bruce Willis is the first guest. This is his sixty-first appearance with Dave. His normal bit was to come out with some sort of comic hairpiece. Tonight he arrives dressed as he did on his first appearance, on December 9, 1985. They found the same shirt and vest and a wig to match that David Addison hair he had back in '85. Bruce Willis was always loyal to the *Late Show*. His sixty-one appearances prove that. He was always game to do a pre-taped bit, usually tied to a fad of the moment.

Brian Teta, Bruce Willis, and Mike Buczkiewicz. Photo courtesy of Brian Teta.

BRIAN TETA: Bruce is always one of those guests you get nervous for. Maria Pope [former executive producer] and Matt Roberts did most of Bruce's segments. I started doing them the last couple of years. This was Mike Buczkiewicz and I working together. There is just a high bar and expectation level for a Bruce segment. The idea of doing the last one was intimidating. Bruce was game for anything, to his credit. He went for the idea of re-creating his first appearance right away.

JOE GROSSMAN: There were some guests who would come on and want some prepared material, like Steve Martin, Bill Murray, Bruce Willis, Tom Hanks, Ben Stiller, Jim Carrey. The writers would pitch some ideas, and the segment producers would pick the ideas that they hoped the guests would pick. One of the better Bruce Willis pieces was him pretending to be an intern for a day at the show, and it was done as an action movie. I think Lee and Jeremy wrote that, and it was a very good piece.

KATHY MAVRIKAKIS: We needed a big lead-in time for Bruce, because usually a wig needed to be created. Usually a suit needed to be purchased, some unusual prop or an exploding thing.

Jim Gaffigan is the second guest. A fellow Indiana comedian, he answers questions from Dave that allow him to do bits from his stand-up routine. Gaffigan would appear on *CBS Sunday Morning* three days before the end of the *Late Show* to explain how much Dave meant to him.

Musical Guest

Dawes is the musical guest. Dave introduces the group's performance of "Things Happen" with: "If you are looking for a rock 'n' roll band, this is all you want." That is the song that aired on the show, but they also performed a bonus song for an online exclusive for CBS.com and YouTube.

> **RICK SCHECKMAN:** Dave would often ask a musician to play a bonus song if it was one he liked. Then it would only be aired on the internet.

Dawes's bonus song is a song written by one of Dave's favorite songwriters, Warren Zevon. Dave takes his suit coat off and stands in front of Dawes and addresses the studio audience about how much the late Warren Zevon meant to him. This video was posted on YouTube.

Dave says Dawes "is doing a huge favor for me. I can't thank you enough, because this is very meaningful to me and Paul. Warren would come on when Paul was off for holidays. We grew fond of his music.

Warren became ill . . . He was nice enough to come on our show before he died. And he said, 'What songs would you like me to do?' I asked for a couple. . . . The one I really wanted to hear, but was uncomfortable pressing Warren for doing nine or ten songs, was called 'Desperados Under the Eaves.' Dawes said, 'Hell, we can do that for you.' This is for Dawes, myself, and Warren Zevon. Thank you."

The song starts with a beautiful strings arrangement played by Paul on the synth. The lyrics are heartbreaking, as the narrator of the song watches the world come to an end in a hotel bar in California. Understandably, there is only so much that can be fit into an hour of broadcast television, but this is a performance that should have made the on-air cut.

SHERYL ZELIKSON: Dawes had a new album to promote, but Dave wanted to hear "Desperados Under the Eaves." Sometimes he just wanted to share with the audience. So they were kind enough to do the song.

JAY JOHNSON: We had digital exclusives peppered in there. Sometimes Dave would ask a band to do a specific song, and they would agree to do it if they could do it as a bonus song for digital. It was always great when Dave would do an intro like that for the bonus songs. He would kind of wing it. I always enjoyed seeing Dave do something off broadcast.

SHERYL ZELIKSON: Dave really appreciated Warren's songwriting abilities. Dave was sharing his view of what people should be watching. That's the best part about music: you get to see it for the first time, and get to share it, and see people react.

BARBARA GAINES: Dave loved Warren's music and he got Warren to fill in when Paul was out. Warren had a quirky sense of humor. They developed a relationship. Dave really loved him as a musician and a person. Warren never got the props he deserved.

Warren Zevon on his last appearance on the *Late Show*, October 30, 2002. He died eleven months later of lung cancer. Photo courtesy of @Letterman, CBS publicity photo.

As the song says, "Heaven help the ones who leave." After the song, Dave finishes his tribute to Zevon: "The last night Warren was here, it was beyond an emotional evening. I didn't know what to do except try to enjoy what we had there with us. I went up to his dressing room . . . He opened his guitar case . . . Here is a guy who is getting on the bus and not coming back. He puts the guitar in the case and snaps it closed, picks up the case, hands the case to me, and says, 'Take care of this for me.'" The audience gasps and applauds.

WORLDWIDE PANTS TAG:

"Which one's Dave?"

"FROM SOMEWHERE ALONG THE CONTINENTAL DIVIDE..."
IT IS EPISODE 6,009
APRIL 23, 2015

"And now . . . here to share the moonlight . . . David Letterman." Dave's topics are garbage in New York, the Pope, and South Carolina Senator Lindsey Graham. The desk piece is a best-of from November 1995, when they broadcast from L.A.—Fun in a Car. Dave drives around town in a car filled with 1,200 tacos and smashes things at a local Midas. No Top Ten in this episode.

The first guest is Robert Downey, Jr., who is promoting *Avengers: Age of Ultron*. The baseball card shows Downey from August 1, 1990. The second guest is Sirius XM sports host Chris "Mad Dog" Russo. He has been on the show thirty times, starting in 1991. Dave loves to talk sports with Russo. He thanks Dave, saying, "You've been great to me. I'm a little radio guy. Thank you."

JAY JOHNSON (Media Content): We had this ongoing feature online where we asked guests to write on these white cards anything they wanted to put on our social feed. On the later days of the show, they started to write things on their cards that were very heartfelt, sweet, and funny. That was an effective way to wrap things up digitally for us.

BRIAN TETA: I produced Chris Russo's segments for eleven years because I was the sports booker. He was a bigger deal in New York than anywhere else. Dave just enjoyed his mannerisms and how worked up he would get. He made Dave smile every time he was on. He was someone who would come at the last minute if we had an opening. This is someone we wanted to put in there because he had been good to us.

Musical Guest

The musical guest is Elvis Costello. His baseball card is from August 23, 1982. Costello, in his twenty-seventh appearance on the show, performs with the Quills a cleverly themed medley: "Everyday I Write the Book," his own composition, and "When I Write the Book," by Nick Lowe.

SHERYL ZELIKSON: Elvis Costello has a longstanding history with the show. Sheila booked Elvis and is very friendly with him. It was somebody that is on the no-brainer list of who you would want on the show, with their history.

WORLDWIDE PANTS TAG:

"Nice shoes big shot."

"FROM THE EMPLOYEE BREAK ROOM AT THE LARGE HADRON COLLIDER..." IT IS EPISODE 6,010 APRIL 24, 2015

"And now . . . a man hopped-up on placebos . . . David Letterman." Monologue topics include garbage in New York, *People* magazine's "Beautiful People," and the Vatican's thoughts on climate change. The Top Ten List is delivered toward the end of the episode. It is "2015 Prom Themes."

The desk piece is a best-of tribute to stage manager Biff Henderson. Dave invites Biff to sit in the chair. Dave says, "Biff Henderson and I have been together in television since June 23, 1980." He speculates that the idea of not seeing Biff, Paul, and the staff every day is going to be like "suddenly great chunks of your family have left the country." Biff responds, "It is just about half my life." Before rolling the clips, which seem to cover only the CBS era, Dave says, "Biff has been a real fixture on this show, and like so many other fixtures on the show, is more beloved than me." (See Chapter 10 for more coverage of Biff Henderson.)

The first guest is Jerry Seinfeld. As he walks to center stage to begin his stand-up routine, he says, "This is not happening. It is not happening." This is Jerry in denial, refusing to acknowledge the end of the *Late Show*. He talks about weathermen, braces, and the fattest man in the *Guinness Book of World Records*. The audience loves it. After Jerry completes his stand-up set, Dave walks over and whispers to him, "Was that from the old show?" It was. Without any mention to the audience, Seinfeld performs a 1982 comedy routine. And it kills.

BILL SCHEFT: Jerry Seinfeld came out and did the same set he performed his first time on the old show in February 1982. He had to monkey with some of the bits to keep them relevant, but it was essentially the same set. When he came off, he said to me, "That was really hard," which, when you consider how effortlessly he does stand-up, is a statement he has probably never made.

BRIAN TETA: Jerry had the idea to do his original set over again. I wish I could take credit for it, but it was all Jerry. It held up incredibly well. Some of the tonal things have changed. There was maybe a fat joke that was a little rougher. It was amazing to see how polished that set was and how well it still played in 2015. He is hysterical in any time.

BILL SCHEFT: He closed the set, as he did in 1982, with a bit about Bob Hughes, the fattest man in the world: "Fourteen hundred pounds. The man has really let himself go. . . . " He did about three-fourths of the bit, but as he admitted to Dave, you can't just haul off and make jokes about fat people the way you could thirty-three years ago. I reminded him of a tag he used to do after the "let himself go" line. He would say, "Bob, have a salad. Get the small cone once in a while." He remembered the salad part, but forgot about the small cone. To me, the brilliance is in the phrase "once in a while." That fake sympathy.

RICK SCHECKMAN: We had to find the original tape. That was one of the things I would do. We pulled it for the segment producer to watch it. On Jerry's first appearance, we bumped him. It was 1982; he was the last guest and he got bumped. We were bumping comedians left and right in those days.

BILL SCHEFT: I've known Jerry Seinfeld a long time. For him to come out and do that stand-up set, as a gift, was uncharacteristically sentimental and the kind of tribute only a comic would give to another comic that he admired.

Most times when Jerry sat down with Dave it was structured so that Dave could tee up bits from Seinfeld's act. Even if Dave would try to ask Seinfeld a "real" question about how things were going or about his family, Seinfeld would pivot toward giving a response from his stand-up act. Not this time. This is Jerry Seinfeld's best Letterman guest spot because he doesn't talk in recycled routines, but talks about Dave leaving television.

Seinfeld asks Dave about running across the stage. Seinfeld says that he can't run like that anymore. "Let's go," says Dave, and the two of them walk over to one side of the stage. Dave walks Seinfeld through the routine. He explains that "when you feel it," tap Biff twice on the lower back and take off. Dave runs across the stage. Seinfeld taps Biff twice and runs across the stage.

Director Jerry Foley cuts perfectly to the typical shot as we see Seinfeld running, after Dave. Dave cheers him on, "Come on. Come on," begging him to pick up the pace. (Seinfeld even runs funny.) We can hear Jerry and Dave talking off camera, stage right, laughing about the run. "That was a thrill," chuckles Seinfeld. Seinfeld is so happy he got to do this. "That was FUN," he says, gesturing with both arms as they make their way back to the desk. Seinfeld allows fans to live vicariously through him. Who wouldn't have wanted to run across the stage with Dave?

BRIAN TETA: That was a lot of fun. That happened in the moment. Jerry was tickled by Dave running across the stage when it happened beforehand. The running was not a prepped bit in any way. Some comedians would want to do a lot of prep and some would want to do not so much. Jerry got on the phone and did a pre-interview, but in the end you are gonna let Jerry Seinfeld do what he wants to.

When they return to the chairs, Jerry informs Dave that Dave has never been a guest on the *Late Show*. He asks Dave if he would like to know what it's like. Seinfeld then sits on the back of the chair so his eyeline is above Letterman's. Dave asks if it really is that bad. They switch places so that Seinfeld sits at the desk and Dave in the guest chair. Seinfeld offers to switch back, but Dave declines.

Photo courtesy of @Letterman, CBS publicity photo.

JERRY FOLEY: Your first assignment in those moments is: Don't screw it up. Don't throw away your game plan because all of a sudden two guys switched chairs. We've got to be better than that. It does change the dynamic a bit. The center of the Earth is the guy behind the desk. When you do something as simple as switch chairs, you have two suns that you have to give equal weight to. Dave is a different guy when he is sitting there. He has done it infrequently, but you do have to make sure that it doesn't become Seinfeld's show.

JOE GROSSMAN: Other people have done it before: "Let's switch places. I'll sit at the desk and you sit in the chair." But in this case, Seinfeld actually had some good questions for Dave. "Why are you retiring? You have nothing else you want to do in real life. This is what you want to be doing." You can tell that was a real conversation between two life-long comedians. It wasn't just some shtick there. I thought that was actually really good.

Dave compliments Seinfeld on *Comedians in Cars Getting Coffee*, and tells Seinfeld he could continue doing that show for years. Seinfeld brings it back by saying, "You could do *this* for years. This whole quitting idea is the stupidest idea I ever heard." The audience screams with applause. They have been waiting for someone to say this. Here is where Seinfeld's true personality shines. He is always no nonsense. Dave can't argue and agrees it is stupid. "Tell me what you think you are doing by quitting and what the hell you are gonna do." Dave blames his wife and family. Seinfeld asks, "Do you think you are going out on top or some nonsense like that? There is no top." They close out by talking a bit about family, and Seinfeld takes over throwing the show to commercial as they shake hands.

JERRY FOLEY: Sometimes you forget you had work to do because you are watching TV, which is the worst thing you can do as a director.

Musical Guest

Jason Isbell & Amanda Shires sing the Warren Zevon song "Mutineer."

BILL SCHEFT: "Mutineer," the last song Warren sang on his last appearance, when Dave devoted an hour to him.

SHERYL ZELIKSON: Jason was someone that Dave put on my radar. He's another great songwriter. I couldn't think of anyone better to represent Warren Zevon than Jason. Two great songwriters that Letterman really introduced to people. "Mutineer" was a very specific song that Dave wanted to hear.

WORLDWIDE PANTS TAG:

"That's just fine."

6

Looking for the Next Best Thing

THE TOP TEN LIST

THE TOP TEN was one of the few comedy bits that Dave never discarded over the run of both late-night shows. It became what the show was best known for. In the *Late Night* years the list was read only by Dave. When the show moved to CBS, politicians, surprise guests, and even animated characters occasionally delivered the Top Ten.

It was a simple concept. Pick a topic and have the eight or so writers come up with ten jokes. Turns out it wasn't that simple. Coming up with those ten jokes took all day and all hands on deck. Sometimes someone outside of the writing staff even landed a joke on the list. One of the perks of working at Worldwide Pants was that anyone on the staff could submit jokes for the Top Ten. When Jill Goodwin started as the executive producers' assistant, she got a joke on the Top Ten. A few years later, she graduated to full-time writer on the show.

JILL GOODWIN: Around May 2006, while I was working as Barbara and Jude's assistant, I got a joke on a Top Ten. It was: "Gas is so expensive Britney Spears's baby is driving a Prius." I don't remember what the story was, but that was one of my earliest. It was really exciting when you could go home and watch the show and tell people, "That was my joke."

JEREMY WEINER: We would always get together in the morning and come up with a topic in the room. We tried to keep it as topical as possible. My favorites were the ones that were silly or random, like the top ten words that kind of sound like "peas." I remember pitching that the final Top Ten should be a sequel to that—top ten other words that kind of sound like "peas."

JOE GROSSMAN: I wrote thousands and thousand of Top Ten jokes through the years. We would pitch topics in the morning. The head writers would pick a topic that they hoped Dave would go for. Then, depending on how busy you were with other things, you would sit there and try to write Top Ten jokes.

JEREMY WEINER: Once we got the topic, it was just grinding it out and getting as many jokes as possible. You would work on as many versions as possible. There were days when maybe I wrote upwards of as many as fifty jokes for a topic. Then you wait with bated breath to see if you got on the list at the end of the day.

JOE GROSSMAN: I might write anywhere from twenty to forty jokes on a typical day. I think I once had to write ninety jokes because I was the only writer who wasn't busy with other stuff that day.

LEE ELLENBERG: There were days, because you are just writing Top Tens, you could write a hundred jokes by yourself. I got progressively lazy with each pass. I think by the end I would be typing random words together.

JILL GOODWIN: I loved writing the Top Ten because I like short jokes. I like punchy and punny. It was something that was, after a while, easy to crank out. I never felt that my tenth pass was gonna be better than my first pass. Do you want to go back and read the first pass again? You knew what Dave's favorite references were. If it made Dave chuckle, that was the best part. All day you are kind of chasing that.

LEE ELLENBERG: That was what I loved about working on a show that you do every day. When the time hits 4:30 the camera starts rolling. I loved having that deadline. Comedy writers can debate about what is funny till the end of time, but having that hard deadline every day just was the universe's way of saying everyone has to shut up now.

JOE GROSSMAN: On a bad day you would have to do pass after pass after pass. It was rare that after your third page of jokes you are gonna come up with your best stuff. Then sometimes at five minutes till showtime you would hear that Dave just killed number four, so everyone scrambles to try to come up with the best stuff you can because he is gonna do the list in fifteen minutes. So while Dave is doing the monologue, we're still writing jokes.

JEREMY WEINER: The craziest moments were when during the show you get a call and they say, "Dave doesn't like the list; we are gonna write one right now." We'd be in the conference room pitching ideas to the head writers over the phone as they are typing them up to get them out in the next two minutes.

LEE ELLENBERG: It really was a process that continued throughout the day. We just kept writing pass after pass. There would be changes and writing up until showtime. There were many times where Dave would look at the completed product and say, "No." We would have to write a new one in five minutes. I always loved those the best. We did it in no time at all. So it was amusing to me that we would spend six hours on the first one and fifteen minutes on the new one.

JEREMY WEINER: The ones we sort of cranked out turned out to be fun and exciting—flying by the seat of your pants. When you spend all day working on it, sometimes it makes it better and sometimes not.

JILL GOODWIN: While the show was taping the writers would sit around in the conference room and eat dinner together. If you would get a little chuckle out of one of the writers, they might say, "Whose was that?" You might feel good about yourself, but it was a tough room to get a laugh out of. Mostly it was groans. The fun part was to write something that was super weird.

EDDIE VALK: I did hidden camera Top Ten Lists that we recorded on the street. I would be dressed in some sort of costume—Elvis, Santa, a horse. We would film them on a Friday when the show wasn't in production. We would go on the streets of New York and set up a hidden camera in advance. I would have lines that were sent to me from a writer and an assistant director. There were twenty lines I would have to say to different people. It was so crazy to see how many people in New York could care less.

LEE ELLENBERG: A lot of times the Top Ten was a promotional thing. If it was for a movie, those were pitched to us. For *The Transformers*, they had asked us to do it, we wrote a list, and they voiced it. They got Optimus Prime to do it and animated it themselves.

JOE GROSSMAN: The celebrity Top Tens were always difficult because they had to be approved not just by the head writer, producers, and Dave, but the celebrity and usually a publicist who saw the jokes before the celebrity. You just knew that so much good stuff was gonna be killed by one of those people. That is just part of the job. For the most part, we felt that the celebrity Top Ten Lists were not the best ones. It makes for a good viral video, but the jokes don't usually hold up as well.

EDDIE VALK: I would be the stage manager for Dave's camera. I would be telling Dave when he was back on camera. I was the safety valve for Dave. The other stage manager, Frank, was next to the camera where the Top Ten presenters were. He would cue them when to step forward, when to speak, when to say their line.

JEREMY WEINER: Rob Burnett [executive producer] at one point said number six needed to be a really strong joke because that is where the turn was on the graphics page, so you needed a big laugh.

LEE ELLENBERG: The funniest entry was always at number two. The second-funniest one was at number six, because you wanted the laugh to cover the page turn. That is when we wiped the screen. For the number one, we usually picked the shortest joke. You wanted something punchy that the band can kick in and take us out of the segment.

BILL SCHEFT: The third-funniest joke is at number ten. The funniest one is number two. Number one is a throwaway, but Dave and I disagree about that. The second-funniest one had to be at number six, because that is when you turned the Chyron on the old show. So you had to have something that would carry over when they cleared the screen. Even though that technology was not used at CBS, we were still thinking that way. We started to put the audience callback joke at the number-six slot.

LEE ELLENBERG: In later years, we did that number-six audience joke almost every night. Bill Scheft or the head writer wrote number six because they were out there for Dave's Q&A session before the show. I understood it logically, because it got the audience going. As a viewer when I was younger, it was kind of cool that you weren't in on the inside joke. It made it seem like it was just as much fun to be in the audience as it seemed to be.

JAY JOHNSON: Dave always did a short audience Q&A before every show that would typically last three to five minutes. I think we always recognized that he was taking ordinary questions and creating really fascinating answers to them. He is a great storyteller. We always admired what he was doing with the Q&A.

JERRY FOLEY: It is a reminder for all of us that the show starts well before the cameras are recording. It became a very important part of our day. When he went out and did that warm-up, you were aware that those callbacks could be part of his monologue or at any time throughout the whole evening.

BILL SCHEFT: For years Dave's warm-up was ninety seconds every night. But for some reason when Alan Kalter started doing the warm-up, Dave felt like he could talk with the audience much longer. He would stay out there maybe ten minutes—it didn't matter anymore when the show started. I think the longest he stayed out there was fifteen minutes, just yacking with them.

JAY JOHNSON: In the final year of the show, we ended up shooting the Q&A with our studio crew, since our camera operators were already in place to do the show. We recorded all those camera angles, and Walter Kim and I would edit them into a Q&A piece for digital content. As we got closer to the end of the show, Dave started going longer and longer with the Q&A's. I think he was really enjoying it. He was probably realizing he was going to miss it. Knowing that the end was coming, he was just kind of soaking it in. People loved it, because they were seeing Dave in a way that they hadn't seen before on broadcast.

JERRY FOLEY: No script, no TelePrompTer, no briefing from Dave that he is likely to do this or say that. It was one of the things that I have come to appreciate as Dave is deconstructed. He was out there without a net. It made it difficult, but exhilarating, because we all had this tremendous creative autonomy. We weren't locked into a script. We could pivot and change direction with him.

BILL SCHEFT: I was always out there for the Q&A. We started adding that joke to the Top Ten in the last year or so. We went down to the stage with ten entries, but Matt Roberts and I would always try to put something in from the Q&A. It would be something that the audience would get. We stumbled on it by accident, and I said to Dave that we should do it every night. He would do the Top Ten in Act 2. Matt or I would point to six on the card, which was the new entry that Dave had not seen. He would either OK it, change it, or add something new.

JERRY FOLEY: In the warm-up, we would create a little narrative, and it was familiar what was likely to happen. On occasion you could motivate him to go back to someone he spoke to in the audience. It was challenging and it didn't always work, but Dave was really dedicated to having a conversation with the camera and the audience. You just can't do that if you are a slave to a script. Yes, he had introductions on cue cards, but he really made it as difficult as he could for himself in pursuit of the conversation, and he certainly succeeded more than he failed.

BILL SCHEFT: We could add a joke because we had so much more to work with, rather than a minute and a half of someone asking him for a canned ham. That is why we could put them in every night. He loved it.

LEE ELLENBERG: I think the only thing was when it started to be every day I wondered, "Are we doing it just to do it?" They would find a way to shoehorn it into the Top Ten. Then you have to retype Dave's card and get it to graphics for them to put in the new entry. Nothing is easy on a talk show. Even the slightest change sends a half a dozen people scurrying.

JOE GROSSMAN: The Q&A was not miked, so we could barely hear it in the conference room. It was something the audience would recognize and get a laugh whether it was funny or not. I think a lot of the writers thought it would have been nice to put an actual joke in there instead of something the audience said, but that's OK.

Photo courtesy of Rick Scheckman.

BILL SCHEFT: The longest single laugh of the show was during a Top Ten in February 2012. It was the thirtieth anniversary of the show in late night, and we did the longest-tenured staffers. Jude was number seven, and it was "Things I have always wanted to say to Dave." Jude said, "I refuse to be berated like this. Go fuck yourself," and the place went crazy. [See photo above.]

JEREMY WEINER: I always tell people that I wrote number seven. Whenever they ask—number seven was mine.

7

Four Weeks Left

EPISODES 6,011-6,015

"FROM THE VIP LOUNGE AT APPLEBEE'S..."
IT IS EPISODE 6,011
APRIL 27, 2015

"And now, a practitioner of vibration energy medicine . . . David Letterman." The monologue topics are New York City coyotes, the presidential campaign, and Dave's retirement. He says he better start using up his sick days before his time is up with CBS. Rock 'n' roll legend Todd Rundgren sits in with the band. The desk piece, a best-of, is a clip montage of the best celebrity Top Tens (see Chapter 6 for more on the Top Ten).

> **STEVE YOUNG:** I spent some time with the Top Ten montage. We started with our celebrities that came out with Top Ten Lists. I watched a lot of them and picked the jokes that went over very well. Half of them I could discard because they were a forgotten topical angle that wasn't going to work anymore.

The fun part of Act 2 is that over the weekend Letterman's racing team, Rahal Letterman Lanigan, finished second at the Honda Indy Grand Prix of Alabama. Since Steak 'n Shake is one of the team's sponsors, everyone in the audience gets free shakes. In a flash, the entire theater fills with staffers passing out 400 milkshakes. The audience smiles and sways to the CBS Orchestra. We may be a divided country, but everyone loves free ice cream.

Photo courtesy of @Letterman, CBS publicity photo.

BARBARA GAINES: We were going to show "The Strong Guy, the Fat Guy, the Genius" clip, then Dave gives out shakes to the audience. What are you gonna do? That is what happens. For a second you would be like, "But we planned . . . .." Then it was, "Whatever." A year later Dave asked me, "Why didn't we show 'The Strong Guy?'" and I say, "I don't know. We ran out of time." I didn't say, "BECAUSE OF YOU!" [Laughs]

RICK SCHECKMAN: The thing with the shakes was decided probably an hour before taping, so we have that all ready to go. But there were some times when he would come up with things that were an impossible demand and he would demand them. One time, I think, he was looking for a Taco Bell and there was no Taco Bell in the neighborhood. What we planned on doing was not what ended up airing on television.

KATHY MAVRIKAKIS: He would definitely come up with things on the fly, and then expect within an hour you could get them.

One time he wanted Eskimo Pies. Immediately we pick up the phone and the back deck of the control room is trying to find our props person to try to get her to go to Gristedes to see if they have the Eskimo Pies brand there. He asked for pizza to be delivered from Brooklyn. We sent somebody to Brooklyn. I was like, "There's no way they are getting back here in an hour." Dave's like, "They will." He never got that pizza.

The first guest is Scarlett Johansson. Paul plays the Neil Diamond song "Red Red Wine." Scarlett/Red, Paul is always clever. She begins by saying, "I am so honored to be on one of your very last shows." The first time she was on the show was for *The Horse Whisperer* in 1998, when she was thirteen years old. She says, "Coming on this show is like you've made it." She also mentions that she kept the canned ham Dave gave her until she was about twenty-five. Dave shows a picture of her entering the theater moments before, and says that is what a movie star should look like.

Scarlett Johansson arrives on 53rd St. Photo courtesy of @Letterman, CBS publicity photo.

Dave's second guest is John Mellencamp. Paul plays Mellencamp's hit "Crumblin' Down" as the walk-on music. This is apropos, because the walls of talk show norms are about to come tumbling down. Wall number one: Letting musical guests talk instead of just sing. Wall number two: Smoking on network television. The final six weeks often evoke the Carson era, when the focus was on conversation and the guest's priority would be to entertain the host. Maybe nothing recalls the Carson era more than a guest smoking while talking to the host. Mellencamp smokes throughout the interview. Dave, just as Carson would, has a one-liner he shoots out immediately. Dave starts writing on a blue card and slides it over to Mellencamp: "Here is the surgeon general's number."

Mellencamp, like his cigarette, is completely unfiltered. He talks about having "real" doctors in Indiana, jokes that Paul shouldn't be in the Rock 'n' Roll Hall of Fame, and discusses the heart attack he suffered in 1994. Dave responds, "And then the doctor said, 'When it was all done, whatever you do, don't stop smoking.'" John says, "Smoking is my strong suit. I am not a doctor, you know that, right?" Dave, lightning fast, responds in disbelief, "I didn't know that. I was told all day long that you were a doctor."

All of this chatter is off the cuff, and is not wrapped in an ounce of political correctness. Once again, the musical guest becomes the highlight of an episode. The uninhibited conversation is a breath of fresh air, even if it is filled with second-hand smoke. The fade to commercial depicts Mellencamp on the show from October 26, 1985.

SHEILA ROGERS: There is the Indiana connection between John and Dave. I remember John went to Dorothy Letterman's house for a comedy bit there. I think it all started with being Hoosiers. I produced those segments because my background was in music. John put a lot in it. He was so unguarded—just said whatever he wanted to say. He's smoking! [Laughs] It was real.

BARBARA GAINES: They had been friends a long time, Indiana boys. That seemed to make sense to me.

SHERYL ZELIKSON: John does what John wants to do, but he was very happy to do the show. I loved his storytelling. Another person who's a great songwriter. I just loved that he was doing this song for Dave.

Musical Guest

Mellencamp moves to center stage to perform "The Longest Days." He dedicates this song to Dave. "You know, Dave, my grandmother lived to be 100 years old . . . She gave me some good advice . . . John, life is short even in its longest days." He sings the folk song about looking back at life and savoring every moment as it happens. A perfect sentiment for the final six weeks. After the song, Dave shakes his hand and says, "Thank you, my friend. Lovely."

Photo courtesy of @Letterman, CBS publicity photo.

WORLDWIDE PANTS TAG:

"More pants, Chester."

"FROM THE SENATE CLOAK ROOM..."
IT IS EPISODE 6,012
APRIL 28, 2015

"And now . . . a working stiff on the night shift . . . David Letterman." The show begins with costume designer Sum Hum giving an audience member a handful of Dave's ties. (If you are that woman, call me, I want one. Please and thank you.) Dave does his annual Tony Awards joke—the show is the biggest waste of a Broadway theater. A man comes out to ask for the cue card from that joke, since Dave has told it every year for two straight decades. They want to put the joke in the Smithsonian. He takes the card and throws it away in the dumpster on 53rd Street. This joke is sadder now because that is exactly where the set will end up (see Chapter 15).

The Top Ten List is "Things I've Always Wanted to Say to Hello Deli Customers." Hello Deli owner Rupert Jee delivers the list. In the banter between Dave and Rupert Jee we learn that the best-selling sandwich is the Paul Shaffer, which sells for $7.95. Dave suggests that for the rest of run he sells it for a buck. Jee declines (see Chapter 10 for more on Rupert Jee).

The first guest is actor Michael Keaton. Paul plays "The Bird" for the walk-on music. Dave and Keaton talk about meeting in the 1970s, plus Keaton's Oscar nomination and subsequent loss for *Birdman*. Keaton says he has saved his Oscar story for the *Late Show*. He explains that he was expecting to win until the Oscar lunch, when an older man shook his hand and said, "Sorry, illness always wins."

Keaton then launches into his tribute. "Thank you for all these years. You are just gonna have to sit back and hate this. Bear down. When [Dave] showed up in Los Angeles, everyone knew it. This guy was so funny and fast. It was so clear how bright and funny and [he had] that great Midwestern thing. We have become friends. Look, you had a paper route, right? And look at this [Keaton moves his arm across the stage, the band, the audience, displaying all that has been in Dave's eyeline for decades]. And look what you have now. Thanks for what you did for comedy. Thanks for all the stuff you did for me. I can't tell you how much I am going to miss this. I kind of hate being here." The audience applauds this tribute from one old friend to another.

Dave replies, "Michael is the kind of guy that you wake him up in the middle of his sleep and he will have something funny to say. He's always funny and the right kind of funny." After the break Keaton tells a story about the time he and his mother met the Pope.

BRIAN TETA: That was the first time I had worked with Michael Keaton. He did the entire pre-interview on a run, doing it through a Bluetooth headset. He was pretty steady. It wasn't like he was laboring in any way. I thought it was very impressive. He had the idea to retell the Pope story. We never let people retell, but in this case, he wanted to go to the greatest hits. It really killed. I was proud of that appearance.

BILL SCHEFT: Michael told a story about meeting the Pope that was too long for a YouTube clip, but was note perfect in energy and build. I know Michael Keaton is a movie star, but he will always have a stand-up's heart.

MIKE BUCZKIEWICZ: Keaton is great because he is such a peculiar guy in all the right ways. I think if you just pulled him off the street and sat him next to Dave and said, "Go," it would be funny.

For the third act, Dave says, "I am sorry we don't have time to show the embarrassing videotape." Dave wishes, but doesn't get his way this time. The staff worked hard to convince Dave to roll this clip. Michael Keaton and David Letterman were cast members on the variety show *The Mary Tyler Moore Hour* (1979).

BRIAN TETA: I had been trying to get the Mary Tyler Moore thing on forever. The idea that Dave was doing stuff like that musical number was just mind-boggling. When you watch it, you can see what is going on in his head: "There is no way I am doing this." I had tried at least four times to try to get it on the show. He always killed it.

MIKE BUCZKIEWICZ: Keaton had been around Dave for so long that the comfort level was there. Not many people had that. When you get into that rarefied air it just takes the interviews to a whole new level. Keaton, Seinfeld, Clooney all have it. They call Dave out when they need to. They will poke fun, but there is a deep mutual respect on both sides of the ball.

RICK SCHECKMAN: Michael and Dave are two guys who go back to working on the Mary Tyler Moore show without competition. Dave is doing stand-up at The Comedy Store when he is on the variety show, but it is not what he wants.

Before the clip is played, they reminisce about working on the show together. Wednesdays were choreography day, and Dave dreaded it. He says, "It was the worst day of my life for an entire summer." He then reveals an interesting fact: "For a while the people at *Saturday Night Live* were nice enough to invite me to host that program. Because of that experience that we had [on *The Mary Tyler Moore Hour*], I said, 'No dice.'"

BRIAN TETA: The funniest thing is Dave's revelation that that was why he would never do *SNL*. I had no idea that was coming. I don't think Michael loved the idea of showing the clip either. I said, "The staff wants to do this, we are gonna get Dave on board. You've got to do this." Then he got behind it and was game to do it.

RICK SCHECKMAN: We had the clip from the show in our archives. We carefully edited the clip that we had sent up to Dave. I am sure he has never seen the entire hour. He doesn't revisit these things.

We see the clip of the two of them singing and dancing to the Paul McCartney song "With a Little Luck." The other dancers are giving it their all, but Dave has no energy and is not committing. This is not the Letterman we have seen mocking the world for thirty-three years. When we come back, Dave is hiding under the desk.

BRIAN TETA: He was hysterical, hiding under the desk. During the segment, I am looking at the clock and I am thinking, "We are not gonna have enough time." He is delaying. He doesn't want to show it. Then he looks to the podium and says, "That's it. We're done?" We yelled, "Got to show the tape!" Then he begrudgingly did it. Barbara or Nancy was timing the show and we went three segments.

Musical Guest

Future Islands, fronted by Samuel Herring, performs "The Chase." A year ago they had made their first appearance on the *Late Show* and had thrilled Dave. Musical booker Sheryl Zelikson recalls Future Islands's first appearance.

SHERYL ZELIKSON: Dave was talking about having Future Islands on. I had listened to the album and wasn't really getting it. I remember seeing how kids were going nuts about them, so I called and said, "Let's book it." If you listen to that first appearance, Samuel has a very guttural way of singing. I was in the song engineer's room when the performance was happening. I was watching them like, "Oh my God." He was so amused by it. People look to his reaction. So if he enjoyed it this much, then other people will enjoy it. It reminded me of some of the stuff from the NBC show. The show was viable all the way up to the end. Front to back, not just the music.

Dave introduces this 2015 appearance by saying, "We have been waiting for them to come back and be on the show." Herring dedicates the song to his hometown of Baltimore, where a riot had just occurred over the death of Freddie Gray, an African-American who died unarmed in police custody. "This song is gonna go out to the people in Baltimore. Let us not discount their voices—or the voices of all the people in the cities that we live and love." Paul Shaffer, Will Lee, and Felicia Collins join the band at the end of the performance. Just like he did the year before, Herring dances and rocks the studio audience. Dave tells the band, "You are welcome here anytime. I won't be here, but you are welcome here anytime."

WORLDWIDE PANTS TAG:

"Yours in pants."

"FROM THE SWEDISH COTTAGE MARIONETTE THEATER IN CENTRAL PARK..." IT IS EPISODE 6,013 APRIL 29, 2015

"And now . . . collector of rotary phones and shiny objects . . . David Letterman." If the theme to the *Late Show* sounds a bit different on this episode, it's because harmonica player John Popper from Blues Traveler sits in the with the band. Dave receives a standing ovation. He begs the audience to stop, saying, "When you stand up, the audience at home feels they need to stand up." The monologue jokes are about Central Park, New York City Mayor Bill de Blasio, and a clip of "Animals Versus Humans." Dave introduces Popper, who thanks him "for starting our career." The Top Ten is "Future Nik Wallenda Stunts."

The desk piece is a best-of clip with Paul and the band called Pedestrian Theme Songs. The band would write songs for people walking on the streets of New York. An example is a woman walking while Paul sings, "No one can tell I drank at lunch." The woman trips and Paul sings, "Everyone knows I drank at lunch."

The first guest is "Jungle" Jack Hanna, director emeritus at the Columbus Zoo in Ohio. Dave announces that Jack ranks third in appearances among all guests, at 102. Ranking second is Marv Albert (126), and the top spot goes to Regis Philbin, at 150 appearances.

When Jack is called to the desk, he's visibly sad. He walks slowly and purposefully to Dave. The audience gives him a well-deserved ovation. The dynamic between talk show host and animal expert has a long tradition in late night, whether it was Joan Embery on Carson's *Tonight Show* or the spider wrangler on the fictional *Larry Sanders Show*. But as usual, Letterman made it his own. The banter between Dave and Hanna typically topped the actual animal appearances. Hanna even started to do comedy bits on the show.

BILL SCHEFT: There was a piece of tape that Dave and I watched dozens of times. It was sometime in the 2010s. We showed a videotape the day after Jack was on. Dave says, "Something odd happened after Jack's appearance last night." A clip cuts to this van out on 53rd Street. The door to the van bursts open and a guy in a bear suit opens the back door and runs down Broadway. Jack turns to his helper and says, "Let's get out of here." They jump in the van and drive off. Dave and I couldn't stop watching it. I don't think I ever laughed harder at one piece of tape. That's my favorite Jack Hanna story. By the way, is any of this helpful? I don't think it is.

BRIAN TETA: I got to work with Jack a lot over the years. As a producer, you want to know every detail of what is going to happen, and it is methodically planned. Not a Jack Hanna segment. They would say, "We have a jaguar, a lynx, and an eagle is gonna fly down." Then the animals would come. I would go out to the van and it would be entirely different animals than I was expecting. But those guys were so good and professional. Dave took an actual interest in these animals and wanted to know more about them. It is a great late-night tradition, and I don't think anyone is better than Jack Hanna. I think Dave really appreciated how often Jack did the show over the years. They were always high rated.

Hanna gives Dave a lifetime membership to the Columbus Zoo and tells him they have named a baby rhino Letterman. Dave asks when he can pick the baby rhino up. Hanna also gives Dave a shirt that he has worn on every continent. "Thank you for everything, Dave." Dave introduces a best-of clip montage of Hanna's visits with, "You've been so generous and so giving." The montage is scored to the classic song "Wild Thing." After the montage, Hanna is wiping tears from his eyes. The final shot is a baseball card from his first appearance, on February 14, 1985.

BILL SCHEFT: Jack had trouble saying goodbye, wiping his eyes repeatedly. Who can blame him? As valuable and indelible a guest as he has been, Dave has brought tremendous attention to the Columbus Zoo and his brand.

BARBARA GAINES: It was fun to put that segment together, to show Jack just being Jack. That retro, which I think was like six minutes, could have probably gone on forever, because there were so many fun clips. Jack is delightful in his nonsense. He had a good gig with Dave. We loved him.

SHEILA ROGERS: The beloved Jack Hanna. He has been on the show for as long as I can remember. We were loyal to him and he was loyal to us. When Jack was available we would get a call and we would always find a spot for him. Not that it is about ratings, but he always did well.

BRIAN TETA: I had my kids come in so they could play with the animals. You would go out on the street and the staff that had children were all petting leopards on 53rd Street. I have a six-year-old daughter who has held a kangaroo and lions. That is an amazing thing. I have a distinct memory of listening to John Popper playing "Run Around" with the band in rehearsal while we were petting the animals.

EDDIE VALK: I am an animal lover, so it couldn't be cooler to me. I got to pet a baby tiger. I would never imagine that I would have done that. Before they went on to the set, you can see the animals up close.

BILL SCHEFT: They used to set up food for the animals. One time there was a bowl of really bad-looking grapes on the desk and Jack asked Dave to hand him the grapes and Dave said, "No, those are for the guys from CBS. They will be over here any minute." So whenever Jack was on the show and they would pre-set the food, I would lift up the lid and say, "The guys from CBS are gonna be here any minute." That is the kind of stuff I would do during the break.

JERRY FOLEY: Jack was somebody I did get to know over the years. Jack's got this persona of being goofy and in the moment, but was professional enough to know that the animals will be better if they have some familiarity of the environment. They alway came early to get the animals on stage. That gave us all an opportunity to size up what may happen.

EDDIE VALK (Stage Manager): We have to coordinate which animals are gonna enter from which side of the stage. If there were any flying animals, we would have to block where we wanted the handlers. Who was gonna release the bird? How it was gonna fly? Where would it land? Where would Dave sit? I always felt like I was at a safe distance from the bigger animals. That was more intricate for me more than when the president would visit, which is crazy to think of, but logistics-wise anything with moving parts and not formulaic to the guest was more work for me. We would have to figure out which camera he would be looking at to throw to commercials. It was a little more demanding.

JERRY FOLEY: By the time we got to the final Jack appearance, the camera crew had this comfort and familiarity. So you can go after the fun moments. I think Jack and Dave grew into something really amazing over the years. Jack knew his role as being kind of the absent-minded, goofy guy. Dave was energized by that and genuinely amused by it. They became a great one-two combination. In the middle of it would be unpredictable animals—sometimes menacing and sometimes adorable. Put all that together and maybe it defines circus. It was a delightful circus.

Musical Guest

John Fogerty is the musical guest. He plays a medley of Creedence Clearwater Revival hits, "Travelin' Band," "Proud Mary," and "Fortunate Son."

WORLDWIDE PANTS TAG:

"Worldwide Pants."

"FROM THE EXACT MIDPOINT OF THE CHUNNEL..."
IT IS EPISODE 6,014
APRIL 30, 2015

"And now . . . here to fool you once again . . . David Letterman." Dave comes out with a call back to Monday's show, starting with, "There will be no milkshakes." Topics include New York's subway, Michelle Obama, and, in a videotaped piece, "Bernie Sanders: 60 Words per Minute."

> **JILL GOODWIN:** Bernie's hand motions looked like a typewriter. So we added the sound effects of a typewriter. We didn't have packets of videos of the top news. Any story you could find you could use. Everyone else was watching a debate to hear about the policy, but I was watching the news for a very different reason.

The Top Ten is "Complaints About the Apple Watch." The best-of clip, "Pop Up to Short," from 1997, is Dave running to Yankee Stadium to take a swing at bat for the home team, with music from the Randy Newman score for *The Natural*. It is all about the build-up, and then Dave hits an easy out.

> **RICK SCHECKMAN:** The close-ups of the crowd are all staffers and were shot in the theater. It must be a Rob Burnett piece, because his wife is holding his daughter on her lap in the close-ups.

The first guest is the First Lady of the country (at the time), Michelle Obama. She receives a standing ovation as she heads over to greet Dave. Dave starts the conversation on a typical topic for the two of them—parenting. He asks about Malia and Sasha. Michelle talks about Malia learning how to drive and going to parties. Dave says, "It is virtually impossible to raise normal kids anyway, but when you are raising them in the White House that makes it a billion times more pressure." Michelle responds, "We treat them normally. We don't let our circumstance become an excuse for them." Dave follows up with, "See, I do. My son thinks he's being raised in the White House." They continue talking about the perils of parenting teenagers.

MIKE BUCZKIEWICZ: You go to the green room beforehand to greet the guest, walk them through their pre-interview, and spend a little more time with them to get an idea of how the interview will go. The First Lady was wonderfully attentive and receptive to talking about the segment. I had worked with her several times. She makes you feel like you are the only person in the room. I said, "We will touch on this and we have a couple questions for you on that.'" Then she looked at me and said, "And then we get to the point of the interview where I am Dave's therapist, right? And he turns to me for parenting advice?" I shut my folder and said, "Exactly." She said, "He is going to have a thousand parenting questions for me." I said, "Who better to ask than you?" She doubled over with laughter. She said, "I am well prepared. I am ready to help him."

In the second segment, they talk about Michelle Obama and Jill Biden's initiative, Joining Forces. The program, celebrating its fourth anniversary, helps veterans get the training and resources they need to transition back to civilian life. The First Lady says, "When leaders ask the country to step up on behalf of our men and women in uniform, they do." She also talks about the number of veterans who are homeless and how this program assists those soldiers who defended the United States in times of need. She continues, "I hope that whoever is in the White House next sets the bar higher even higher than we have. This can never be a problem in this country again."

[*The website was shut down in 2016, only hours after the president who followed Barack Obama was sworn into office.*]

They discuss the importance of a college education, with Michelle Obama noting that while athletes are lauded for signing with a college, academic students who make it against great odds aren't celebrated in the same way. Dave asks how people can help; she suggests mentoring and helping students perform tasks like filling out financial aid forms. She says, "If you've gone to college, you can help a kid in your area get to college." Education, homeless veterans, parenting . . . these are the topics covered in this interview. The topics are not female centric. They cover general American politics. Dave is not asking the First Lady to dance, lip sync, or play a game. This is another intellectual conversation laced with one-liners at just the perfect time.

JERRY FOLEY: I share with Dave a sincere affection and respect for tradition and the service of the military. The sanctity of the office of the president and the importance of government, tradition, and patriotism—that runs through Dave's veins, and I share that with him. With the Obamas, there was a genuine affection that they had for Dave, and to everyone associated with Dave. That was a big factor in our lives, people who appreciated Dave appreciated us. That was a pretty charmed existence for a long time.

EDDIE VALK: He still has a close relationship with Michelle Obama. I think she was at the Mark Twain Awards. He always seemed like he had a fondness for her and President Obama.

MIKE BUCZKIEWICZ: The First Lady has a unique ability to switch gears from something serious to lighthearted. It is almost a trick on the audience, where they learn something on the way, but they have fun doing it.

BARBARA GAINES: I am a woman, a gay woman, a parent. I love the Obamas, so you are gonna get a slanted idea from me. I am going to be for them. Dave loves them, has a fondness for them, and has done things for them since we went off the air. They are lovely and funny people. Michelle came on for the Joining Forces Initiative. What isn't to like?

BILL SCHEFT: Look, forget the ideological trappings of the internet. I have met Michelle Obama three times, and I find it fascinating that someone as bright, independent, and modern as her could put up with the First Lady gig, which still carries with it a lot of nineteenth-century hostessing.

Michelle Obama has a surprise for Dave. She says, "I'm here because you are leaving. You have been a tremendous support to me and my family, but mostly to our men and women in uniform and our veterans. You have been such a huge supporter. So we decided to pay tribute to you. We have here with us today The President's Own United States Marine Band. In honor of you, David Letterman." A drum major with a huge bearskin hat comes through the back doors of the Ed Sullivan Theater. He is carrying a mace on a five-foot pike as he leads the band through the back doors. They stream through the audience, which leaps to its feet, clapping as the band fills every inch of the stage floor playing "The Marines' Hymn." When the song ends, Dave says, "Thanks so, so much. Couldn't have been anything better. Absolutely lovely." They embrace on stage, with The President's Own behind them.

MIKE BUCZKIEWICZ: I remember asking, "How long is this song? Are we going to run out of song before they get to the stage?" The musical director very nicely said, "We have done this before. We can fill if we need to. We have to keep playing until the president walks out. We can do this." Then I remember, "Oh, right, you guys are really good at what you do."

EDDIE VALK: Dave always had a special space for Marines and serviceman. That was incredible to see all that. It was chaotic to block and see which moving parts were gonna move in from which section. You can see Dave was touched by that kind of stuff. It was pretty emotional to see that.

JERRY FOLEY: For those musicians to be on stage, that pageantry, that tradition, for all of that, I feel sorry for anyone who didn't observe it.

MIKE BUCZKIEWICZ: The First Lady wanted to do something special for her last appearance. We had known "The Marines' Hymn" and The President's Own was near and dear to Dave. He had been at the White House for an event, and he came back and would not stop talking about The President's Own. The First Lady's office said, "We could do The President's Own. We know Dave really likes that." I said, "Do that." [Laughs]

JERRY FOLEY: The dealings we had with the Obama administration were very collaborative and creative. I think the Obamas did know Dave well enough to have the sense of what kind of gift he would appreciate. Dave's appreciation for the military has been a part of the CBS show from the beginning. Every year during Fleet Week we would have representatives of the Navy in the audience. Dave interviewed many Congressional Medal of Honor winners. We did demonstrations with the Navy SEALs. We did a very ambitious project with the Army when they were in Bosnia. Dave, Paul, and Biff did trips to Iraq over the holidays that were underpublicized.

BARBARA GAINES: We had done things like that in our history. It was meaningful to Michelle to offer that up to Dave. The Obamas liked Dave, and he very much liked the Obamas.

BILL SCHEFT: Michelle Obama brought the Marine Band with her to serenade Dave for all he's done for servicemen since 9/11. It was a nice touch. When he received the Kennedy Center Honors and went to the reception at the White House in December 2012, we snuck upstairs after and Dave said, "Let's see if we can get them to play 'The Marines' Hymn.'" I asked, they stand up and play it. Dave was stunned by that. The irony was we had to wait until they finished playing the *Late Show* theme.

JERRY FOLEY: The Obamas knew optics. I don't think you roll that out for a small-town mayor. It was a big deal. That is an amazing front-row seat that I get to be a part of for a couple of minutes on a given day. It was thrilling. As a director, you have this theater and technology and skilled people and you are looking at a band that you've seen on television your entire life and you're collaborating with them and interacting with them. It is this giddy party thing—"Aw, man, I get to be part of this."

BILL SCHEFT: Dave loved the military, and it's the type of love that you had for the military right after WWII. His weeks off were sacrosanct for him and yet he went to Afghanistan, went to Iraq. So it was a big deal when she brought the band. It meant a lot to him.

MIKE BUCZKIEWICZ: They came in from D.C. early that morning for rehearsal. We were trying to think of a way for them to enter in a grand fashion to try to surprise Dave. We decided on the back of the house and have them walk through the aisles, get up on stage, and play. The drum major's hat is a huge headpiece. There was a long conversation of whether that hat would fit through the door. We were concerned he was going to clip the doorway and chaos would ensue. It went off without a hitch. Dave was as pleased as punch to be able to pull that off. Look, you have the First Lady, The President's Own, you've got Dave there, I think it was something that he remembers. It was nice to have a small part in that.

Musical Guest

Hootie and the Blowfish are the musical act. They return to sing their hit "Hold My Hand." In Dave's introduction, he reminds viewers that they made their television debut with this song in 1994.

SHEILA ROGERS: Hootie was so closely associated with the show. We had them on so much in the nineties. They made their debut on the show and then they were so widely popular in the era. We thought it would be an interesting nod to that period. We certainly had played a part in their initial popularity and attention.

BILL SCHEFT: This was a great touch by Sheila Rogers and the talent department. Dave had them on a good half-dozen times to promote their debut album, *Cracked Rear View*. When you write the history of the *Late Show*, and the music it discovered, you must lead with them.

SHERYL ZELIKSON: As you hear certain artists, it becomes a soundtrack to your life. I remember the Hootie phenomena; every guy had his baseball cap on. It was a timestamp for me. Knowing the ages of people that grew up with Letterman, they would remember when they were in college.

BRIAN TETA: I was a big driving force for the Hootie and the Blowfish booking. I think I had to convince some people to get Hootie on our list. As a fan of the show, I remember in the nineties that was the first place I ever saw Hootie and the Blowfish. They became such a big deal. In interviews, Darius Rucker has attributed the success of the band to appearing on the *Late Show*. I begged Sheila and anyone who would listen, "You've got to have Hootie back on doing one of their original songs." They had broken up at this point. For fans of a certain era of the *Late Show*, this is meaningful. The staff was excited about it. I wanted Hootie and John Popper to come back and they both did.

EDDIE VALK: They had something on their drum kit that had our logo on it. They might have done that the first time they came on. I remember people being excited about that. To see it up close while we were setting up was fun.

WORLDWIDE PANTS TAG:

"Dear sweet pants."

"FROM THE WORLD'S 3RD LARGEST BALL OF TWINE..." IT IS EPISODE 6,015 MAY 1, 2015

"And now . . . a man who can wear stripes with plaid . . . David Letterman." As soon as Dave hits center stage he takes his shoes off. A person in the audience is shown laughing. If you are a longtime Letterman fan, this face is familiar to you. But amazingly at this moment, the face is not yet familiar to Dave . . . stay tuned. Monologue topics include spring in New York, the presidential campaign, and the Kentucky Derby.

The Act 2 desk piece has a Top Ten List of "Guys Bernie Sanders Looks Like." The number-six entry is "The guy who lets strangers handle his shoes." The audience member is shown again. There is still no recognition from Dave as to who this person is. The best-of montage is clips of the many guests who have appeared on the show. Dave gives the statistic: 105,000 total guests. Paul quips, "That you have spoken to and pretended to be interested in." This clip package is something you would assume would be on the final episode. It has all of his most famous interactions: Madonna, Drew Barrymore, Joaquin Phoenix, Hillary Clinton, and more.

After the clips, Dave announces who has been in the audience. Dave points out the woman is Colleen Boyle. She was in a remote from *Late Night* on NBC. The reason that Dave hadn't mentioned this, even though he had called on her and Matt Roberts had added her to the number-six spot of the Top Ten, was because no one had recognized her. That was until Bill Scheft saw her in the Top Ten.

BILL SCHEFT: I had to make some last-minute changes to the monologue, so I missed Dave's warm-up. When the joke in the Top Ten came, there was a giant cutaway shot of Colleen Boyle in the audience. I mouth to her, "Colleen?" and she nods, "Yes." She was in one of the most famous remotes at the old show. There she is sitting with her husband not looking a day older. Before the show, Dave walks out and takes questions from the audience. She raises her hand and asks, "Who helps you select your shoes?"

Dave misses it and doesn't see the connection. I told him that was Colleen. We got a still from that tape from NBC.

RICK SCHECKMAN: I sat in the control room on the back deck. In the middle of the show Dave would ask for something. Randi would say, "We want the clip XYZ." I would punch that into the computer. If the clip was on the seventh floor, I would tell an intern to go get tape 1652 and bring it to the tape room. I could do it in a commercial break.

BILL SCHEFT: All this jumped off a period of maybe fifteen minutes. None of it had been planned for the show, but there is was. This happens more than anyone gives us credit for. A lot of people's hands go up when Dave asks if there are any questions. But he picked a woman he assumed was a stranger. It was a beautiful confluence of *Late Night* and *Late Show*—and more evidence that there are no strangers.

The first guest is Steve Martin. His first appearance with Dave goes back to the morning show, September 30, 1980. Dave welcomes him and says, "A lot of people come on the show and keep the cab running. Run in, run out. But you have actually come and helped produce things and made things better." Martin responds with, "When I heard you announced that you are retiring, I thought, 'He's got to be joking.' Then I remembered, 'Wait, you're not funny.'" Martin mentions that when Johnny Carson retired, he invited him to be on the last week of his shows and now Dave has asked him to be in his last month, sort of.

MIKE BARRIE (Carson writer): On the last couple weeks of *The Tonight Show*, Steve came on and did The Great Flydini, which was classic. It still holds up. He was young enough then to also be on Dave. He was very funny. I never saw Steve come on the show without an original thought. He always came prepared.

Martin talks about touring with Martin Short and his upcoming Broadway musical, *Bright Star*, and continues to skewer the fake Hollywood relationship between Dave and himself. Martin says, "I was on the morning show, but that doesn't make us friends." Dave says, "There is show business friends and then there is actual friends." Steve Martin says, "And we are neither." He has brought a video clip of Dave's life that boils down to this: He had one show and then he had another show. They also play the classic clip of "Dave and Steve's Gay Vacation" from October 2, 1998. Martin thinks that some of his funniest moments have occurred on the show.

BARBARA GAINES: "Gay Vacation" played differently in 2015 than it did when it originally aired. In 1998, the audience couldn't breathe they were laughing so hard. When we replayed it at the end, I think this new crowd wasn't sure how they were supposed to take it.

RICK SCHECKMAN: Steve Martin worked very hard on his segments. They might start working on it two, three weeks early. Steve was one of those people that would say, "What do you want me to do?"

KATHY MAVRIKAKIS: With Steve Martin, probably they ran a bunch of ideas by him, he chose ones he wanted and then maybe rewrote them. We worked very closely with people who were comedians so that they could create the segment that represented what they wanted to be on the show.

JEREMY WEINER: Steve would come with things ready to go, and he was also great about asking if we had any ideas. Sometimes the writers would present a few things and he would pick ones he liked. One week I worked with Steve where he teased his appearances the entire week leading up to being a guest on the show on Friday. You could always count on him to know what was going to work.

BRIAN TETA: Steve was one of the more intimidating people to produce because he is a legend. That was the first time I worked with him. He had usually worked with Maria Pope or Matt Roberts. It was me and two writers from our show that we're working with Steve on this. There was a lot of prep for that. I did very little on the content of this particular one because he was working on it for so long.

Musical Guest

Steve Martin, Emmylou Harris, Rodney Crowell, Mark O'Connor, and Amos Lee perform the gospel classic "Will the Circle Be Unbroken?"

SHERYL ZELIKSON: I think that Steve Martin was scheduled as the top guest and Dave wanted to hear the song. We picked people that had a history with the show. It was meaningful for the audience and for Dave.

BRIAN TETA: I thought it was a crazy idea. I am the worst person to ask about this stuff. "Will the Circle Be Unbroken?"?? But, it was fantastic.

WORLDWIDE PANTS TAG:

"Is your name Connie?"

8

Johnny Strikes Up the Band

CARSON & LETTERMAN

ON NOVEMBER 24, 1978, David Letterman walked through those iconic colorful curtains onto the stage of *The Tonight Show With Johnny Carson* and his entire life changed. His stand-up set inspired Johnny to call Dave over to the couch to chat. Johnny Carson calling a comic over to the couch was the seal of approval in the comedy world. Is there a comparable moment to that in show business today? Would it be like getting a retweet from a Kardashian with a million followers? Seems trite in comparison, doesn't it? Dave would go from guest to guest host of *The Tonight Show* to host of his own show, which followed Carson. For Dave, Carson set the standard.

> *"He created the template for that show and everybody else who is doing a show, myself included, we're all kind of secretly doing Johnny's* Tonight Show.*"*
>
> —DAVID LETTERMAN, JANUARY 31, 2005, *LATE SHOW*

JERRY FOLEY: Johnny Carson was a mantra for several of us when Dave was unsure. What did Johnny do? How would Johnny handle this?

VINCENT FAVALE (CBS Executive of Late Night Programing): Dave grew up watching Carson. He was a small-town guy, just like Dave was. Forget his love as a fan, he gave him a huge break. You get booked to do stand-up on *The Tonight Show* and you feel you won the lottery. *Late Night* was produced by Carson. He had total say in what followed him. Dave invented 12:30. It existed in a Tom Snyder way, but not in a comedy way. *Late Night* couldn't book the same guests. They couldn't do a monologue or it had to be abbreviated.

BILL SCHEFT (Writer): The directive when he got *Late Night* was, "Don't be *The Tonight Show*." That is why the monologue was three jokes long. That is why there were no mega-celebrities. Whatever you do, don't do it like *The Tonight Show*.

VINCENT FAVALE: He had to have different guests from *The Tonight Show*, and his band had to be smaller. Dave was fine with all that.

MICHAEL BARRIE (Writer for Carson and Letterman): When Dave was doing *Late Night* it was a parody of a talk show.

JIM MULHOLLAND (Writer for Carson and Letterman): Letterman didn't really do a very long monologue in those days. It was sort of a throwaway. He just did a few jokes. He memorized the stuff, as opposed to Carson, who put it on cue cards. Carson had a horizontal board, and he would look at the jokes. He did eighteen, twenty. Letterman did half a dozen.

Johnny Carson delivers a Top Ten to Dave when the Late Show was in L.A. Photo courtesy of @Letterman, CBS publicity photo.

MICHAEL BARRIE: Carson had a different cue card system than Letterman. Carson had a long easel that was about fifteen-to twenty-feet long. It was in front of him on the floor, and the cue cards would be stapled left to right, maybe eight to ten cue cards, with the jokes more or less written out. Johnny liked to jump around. He was very good at hearing the audience. If he did a topic and the first joke died, he might feel they are not into this topic. So, he wouldn't want to be locked into three more jokes on that topic. He wasn't locked into some guy flipping cards, whereas Bob Hope and Letterman had a guy holding stacks of cue cards and flipping them one at a time. If the audience didn't like a topic, they were stuck with it. Dave would sometimes say, "Go to the next one." Johnny didn't have to do that.

JIM MULHOLLAND: We met Dave through *The Tonight Show* in 1978. Peter Lassally [executive producer at *Tonight*] said, "You should also write for Letterman." They were sort of grooming Dave to be the next guy. We went to see him at The Comedy Store on Sunset Boulevard. Most of his act was interacting with the audience, so we didn't know how to write for this guy. We met with him and asked if he had any ideas for material. Dave is a very quiet guy. He said, "No, whatever you want to do."

MICHAEL BARRIE: Dave had a different personality. He was more of a character who was more ironic, offbeat. He liked to talk about himself maybe more than Johnny would in jokes.

JIM MULHOLLAND: They made him the first permanent guest host. We were writing his monologues then. I could never get a handle on what he wanted to do. It wasn't like he was a monologist. He was more from the Steve Allen school of "Just make it up on the spot" and was good with people. He didn't last because he got the morning show in 1980. Then the guest host became Joan Rivers.

BILL SCHEFT: Dave was not topical, he was personality driven. He was very sort of Will Rogers Midwestern. Johnny had it in him too, but he became famous, wealthy, and was doing this long monologue. Johnny loved the monologue; that was his favorite part of his show. The monologue for Dave was something to get through and settle everybody down. Johnny would do the monologue and then do the desk piece, which was all written out. Dave did more conceptual stuff throughout the show. Johnny had seventy-five percent of the writers working on the monologue. At *Late Night* it was the exact opposite. If you had twelve writers, you only had two or three working on the monologue.

MICHAEL BARRIE: Letterman didn't like long setups. There was a line we wrote about retirement for Dave that went, "Well, it is over, and I wanted to keep doing this until it was sad." That is a Letterman joke—sort of a sarcastic remark, although that doesn't quite explain it. I don't think Johnny would do that one. In the hands of somebody else, it wouldn't even appear to be a joke.

JIM MULHOLLAND: Dave had a different point of view, and I could never quite get a handle on what it was. With Johnny anything was an open target. It was a little more narrow with Dave. It was a struggle for me to find what topics appealed to him. He seemed to be more interested in the topic than the joke.

Johnny was peerless in the art of getting out of a joke that bombed. Even Dave was in awe of this.

"The best part about Johnny was when a joke would not go well. He would look at the audience and give them that look like he had just bought them drinks and nobody said thank you."
—DAVID LETTERMAN, JANUARY 31, 2005, *LATE SHOW*

MICHAEL BARRIE: Carson would have fun with bombing. I don't think he wanted to bomb, but if a joke wasn't working he would tap on the microphone or go into his soft shoe. He just had fun with it. Most comics don't have that.

BILL SCHEFT: Johnny was so good at it, you almost thought maybe he wants this to happen so he can get out of it. As a viewer you started rooting for stuff to bomb. You would see him do the soft shoe. You just would love that. You knew there would be a good joke coming along.

MICHAEL BARRIE: Johnny didn't want to bomb. He wouldn't do a sketch where he had to play a character that would build to something. He wanted a series of jokes, like in vaudeville. So he could jump around. Sometimes you would hear Johnny say, "I am in it, and I can't get out." That was his worst fear.

JIM MULHOLLAND: Today, you don't see these late-night guys bomb very often. For one thing, these audiences are so amped up they just applaud when the comic stops talking, whether there is a joke or not. So it is rare to see a comic bomb today. Johnny might tell six jokes in a row that would die. It was more of an honest thing. Today, it is a little more polished. They rehearse the monologue. All of them have that safety net there. Letterman rarely went into the tank.

MICHAEL BARRIE: Letterman was more chagrined when a joke died. Johnny kind of made the audience feel like they were in it with him.

VINCENT FAVALE: Their affection for each other was so apparent over the years. Then they probably bonded over Dave not getting the 11:30 show when Carson retired. Carson wanted Dave to get the show.

JIM MULHOLLAND: Johnny liked Dave a lot, He wanted him to take over *The Tonight Show*, but no one ever asked for his opinion.

VINCENT FAVALE: Before Carson died, he was submitting monologue jokes to Dave. It was a secret, and Dave thought it was kind of cool. Johnny was like a little kid.

JIM MULHOLLAND: Sometimes Steve Young would fax a list of jokes back to us and some of Johnny's jokes would be mixed in with ours. I would say, "Whose jokes are these?" and here it was Johnny Carson's material. I am sure what happened was he was sitting out at his house in Malibu and was going through the paper and saying, "I could have had some fun with these." So he started writing them and faxing them to the *Late Show*. One time we had lunch with Johnny and he said, "I wrote a great joke about Liza Minnelli getting a divorce and Dave didn't do it." He sounded like one of the writers. He was pissed off he didn't get the joke in the show. I said, "Now you know I how I feel." It was so funny to hear Johnny Carson pitch a joke and not get it in. He did that right up until he died. He wanted to keep his hand in. He was a great joke writer.

Photo courtesy of @Letterman, CBS publicity photo.

Johnny Carson died on January 23, 2005. Dave was in reruns the following week, but when he returned on January 31, he aired a tribute episode to his mentor. The entire monologue consisted of jokes Carson had written over the years for the *Late Show*. Dave's guests were Peter Lassally and Doc Severinsen. Doc, Tommy Newsom, and Ed Shaughnessy (all members of *The Tonight Show* Band) played with Paul Shaffer and the CBS Orchestra to perform Johnny's favorite song, "Here's That Rainy Day." It is a beautiful instrumental version of the song that Carson sang with Bette Midler on his penultimate show.

9

Three Weeks Left

EPISODES 6,016–6,020

AT 9:30 PM ON MAY 4, with three weeks to go, CBS aired *David Letterman: A Life on Television*. It was a prime time compilation special that covered Dave's career on both NBC and CBS. It began with a music video compiling the classic moments from over thirty years of Letterman's television career set to the R.E.M. classic "It's the End of the World as We Know It (and I Feel Fine)."

VINCENT FAVALE (CBS Executive of Late Night Programing): I produced the prime time special much against everyone's wishes. I knew I wanted to start with a bang. R.E.M. made their debut on *Late Night with David Letterman* in 1983. I wanted a montage of every great, iconic moment of when Dave did something big and stupid—jumping on the Velcro board, snowboarding on 53rd Street, all that stuff. It wasn't chronological. It was any visual thing that he did that was larger than life.

The host of the special was Ray Romano. He was the perfect host, as viewers knew how important Letterman was to Romano's career. Worldwide Pants produced *Everybody Loves Raymond*.

VINCENT FAVALE: We needed someone to guide us through it. We couldn't shoot on the *Late Show* set. It was a really sensitive time. So we re-created Dave's desk as a backstage set and we filmed it all in California. Having Ray was a big part of it, because it gave us credibility. Ray is the guy.

RICK SCHECKMAN: When Vinnie got the OK from Worldwide Pants, they put that special together in like a week and a half. I think it was a very good overview of Dave's career. Vinnie flew out to California to film Ray. It was well done. They didn't have a lot of time to put it together.

Photo courtesy of @Letterman, CBS publicity photo.

The special highlighted guest moments (Drew Barrymore, Madonna, Joaquin Phoenix), Dave flirting with actresses (Dave kissing Gillian Anderson—it made me jealous, in 2002 as well as today), montages of Top Ten Lists, and serious moments through the years (September 11, Dave's heart surgery). Some of these clips were also shown on the late-night show during the final six weeks. This double dipping became a point of contention between the network and the *Late Show* staff.

BARBARA GAINES: They wanted to do their own special. They wanted to use the same clips and they were going first, so I felt in competition with my own show against my own show. It was stressing me out to no end.

VINCENT FAVALE: Barbara Gaines, and I say this lovingly, and I butted heads because they didn't want to do a prime time special, because they wanted to save these look-back moments as packages within the context of their final shows. I was like, "There is room for both. These clips are iconic. We can put it in prime time, where there are more people watching, and grab America by the throat and remind them that this guy is leaving after thirty some-odd years." I just couldn't get anyone to agree to that notion.

BARBARA GAINES: I need that kind of added stress for them to put on their show? I needed support for us. I feel that we would do it or don't do it at all.

VINCENT FAVALE: I partnered up with the CBS news organization because they are used to getting things done quickly. I had to call my boss for help, for her to call the head of NBC to say, "Trust us."

RANDI GROSSACK: That was all CBS News. I would have been happy to have been involved, because I had all these reels and could have helped them with some of it. I thought for people who weren't involved with the show, they did a nice job. We would have done it differently, but it was a nice thing from CBS. For something done that quickly, they deserve credit for it.

KATHY MAVRIKAKIS: If you were to see the documents that I had to create for any time we had to do a clip package. I did the document for the CBS prime time show, basically tracking every single clip and who needed to be paid for it and what date it originally aired. Every single person in all of those clips gets paid. All the writing teams from all those clips have to get paid again. If there are different directors on different segments, they get paid again.

Photo courtesy of Vincent Favale.

VINCENT FAVALE: I wanted Dave jumping in the cereal bowl. I wanted Cher calling Dave an asshole. I wanted all those moments. Barbara wanted them too. I was like, "Whatever you don't use, I'll use." To me it didn't make a difference if we both used the same clip. When you are winding down, you can watch these classic clips a million times. Emotions were running high, and I was sensitive to what they were up against. For me, life was going on, but for Barbara she was out of there.

BARBARA GAINES: I wanted our show to be special and unique. I didn't want it to be, "I just saw this clip last Monday at an earlier hour." Everything is all on the internet anyway. It felt too saturated. They felt that they were promoting the 11:30 show.

VINCENT FAVALE: I was saying, "I'll trade you an Andy Kaufman clip for a Cher clip." It was really intense, but I wanted to honor Dave and the people that worked for them. It was their hard work, too. I wanted more people to watch it than were watching the nightly broadcasts. The prime-time special ended up doing a large number [8.14 million according to tvbythenumbers.com]. It helped the 11:30 show, because people realized he was leaving.

BARBARA GAINES: I thought the show was OK. I didn't feel we needed it. It didn't add to my enjoyment of the last weeks.

VINCENT FAVALE: I ended the special with David Bowie's song "Changes," about how Dave had changed over the years—not just physically, but with his child being born. I wanted to celebrate Dave's three-decade relationship with Howard Stern, Tom Hanks, Jerry Seinfeld, Julia Roberts, and Bill Murray. Ultimately, I think Dave liked it.

Later on that evening . . .

143

"FROM THE WOODWIND SECTION OF
THE NEW YORK PHILHARMONIC..."
IT IS EPISODE 6,016
MAY 4, 2015

"And now . . . center fielder for your Go Go White Sox . . . David Letterman." Dave begins this week with a few retirement jokes. He mentions that he just got a call from his mom saying, "I heard you were fired." He teases tonight's appearance by President Obama by joking that with Obamacare, employees can lose their longtime jobs and still have health care coverage. To his staff he says, "You're welcome."

Someone in the audience starts talking, and the camera pans out to the audience to see Will Ferrell dressed as baseball announcer Harry Caray. This imitation may not be Will Ferrell's most popular one, but it always tickled Dave when Ferrell was a guest.

BILL SCHEFT: Will Ferrell interrupting the monologue as Harry Caray? Absolutely note perfect. I can't think of anyone that plays the camera with more skill or confidence. I got to see him in the airlock after the taping and he said to me, "There's nothing better than standing next to Dave and seeing him laugh at something you do. And not just laugh, giggle." I added, "And not just giggle, turn away and giggle, like he doesn't want to spoil the bit."

There is no comedy bit for Act 2. Dave welcomes then-sitting President Obama. Paul has rented timpani for the occasion, and "Hail to the Chief" reflects this with the roll of the timpani. Obama ribs Dave for liking Michelle Obama better. Obama says, "I assure you, you are not alone. But I'm not gonna let her have all the fun. Mainly, I came by to say goodbye to Biff and Paul. But they said I couldn't get on the set unless I also spoke to you." Dave thanks him for sending The President's Own with the First Lady. Obama explains, "They are not just playing music. They're serving in all kinds of ways." Dave says, "A guy in a huge bearskin hat brings them out and then they have a whole different conductor." Obama gets the last laugh before the commercial break with, "Yes, they do. You were really paying attention. That's good."

RICK SCHECKMAN: When you have the president as a guest, there would be a sweep of the building. Kathy Mavrikakis would be meeting with the Secret Service for over a week before the visit. How are they getting him in? Where are they entering? All that kind of stuff. Secret Service would be in the back of the house in the theater.

KATHY MAVRIKAKIS: Basically having a huge political guest meant dealing with Secret Service. I also supervised the audience. We would have to get to every audience member and let them know to come faster and earlier in the day than they normally would. We would try to get extra music to play for them because they had to sit in their seats earlier because everyone had to be wanded and checked more thoroughly when the Secret Service was involved. The staff had to wear their IDs; they had to come in a different entrance.

RICK SCHECKMAN: I would stay in my office on those days. At about 11:30 the stage was cleared so the bomb-sniffing dogs and Secret Service could come. Then we would have our badges, but you could only enter through the lobby, where there were metal detectors. There were sharpshooters on the roofs across the street.

JEREMY WEINER: We are given a heads-up in an email saying, "There is going to be a lot of extra security today, so if you don't have to be backstage, steer clear." You would try to avoid those areas. It was fascinating to see Secret Service hanging out.

KATHY MAVRIKAKIS: Once the Secret Service locked down the side entrance where the president would come in, you couldn't use it again. For a sitting president it is much more intense than for a former president. The government paid for the Secret Service. It only affected our budget if I had to bring in extra security that day.

JEREMY WEINER: One time Vice President Al Gore was on the show. My job that day was to shepherd Calvert DeForest [Larry "Bud" Melman] through his live walk-on during the monologue. As part of that, I had to take Calvert around to the dressing room. He told me he had to go to the restroom. I took him down to the basement to go the restroom, and I am waiting outside. Al Gore comes down with his Secret Service detail, and a serviceman just opens the bathroom door. Calvert didn't lock it. I see the Vice President of the United States of America walk into the bathroom, and I heard Calvert DeForest yelp, "Oh my God!" I am sure Al Gore has never been the same.

The second segment takes a more serious tone as they discuss the recent riots in Baltimore. They discuss racism, poverty, slavery, and Jim Crow. To see a difference in how the world has changed since 2015, here is a direct quote from the president of the United States that night. Notice the complete sentences and intricate thoughts expressed, tempered with concern for other human beings.

"This country, our democracy, works because ordinary folks, well-meaning people, each and every day are trying to make it a little better. And we are teaching understanding to our kids, and when mistakes are made we acknowledge them, as opposed to try to cover them up. And most importantly in my mind, we think about not just our own kids,

but we think about all kids, when we say to ourselves that that child in Baltimore has tough circumstances but that child is worth, in the eyes of God, just as much as my child. We need to make sure to make an investment in them. When we get to that point, then not only does that child do better, but the country as a whole does better. And that requires the kind of sustained commitment that I'd like to see."

—PRESIDENT OBAMA, MAY 4, 2015 *LATE SHOW*

The audience applauds and Dave asks, "Is this the first country you have presidented?" Obama responds, "It is, I suspect, the first and last. Unlike late-night talk-show hosts, I am term limited."

JERRY FOLEY: When you talk about Obama and Dave talking about a shooting in Baltimore, it starts with this native intelligence you can't fake, and the two of them share that. I think they both realized that words count. Once you have drawn people into the intensity of their conversation, you are obligated as host and president to open the door so people can see the exit and go forward and have hope. I am not saying Dave thinks about all that before he starts the show. It just comes naturally. He is a conversationalist, and he is an intelligent guy. He is not one to leave the conversation in darkness and despair. He wants to end it on an up note.

MIKE BUCZKIEWICZ: When Baltimore happened and we knew we wanted to discuss it, I think the president's office was game. They looked at our show as one of the few places that you can have a conversation that wasn't three minutes of a cable news hit or a *Meet the Press*-type show. We can have fun and a good conversation. We never put preconditions on an interview, and this went for anybody. My pat line was always, "We don't put conditions on an interview, for the simple fact that I can go to Dave and say, 'We can't talk about X, Y, and Z,' and he will go out there and the first three questions will be about X, Y, and Z." President Obama could take a punch, and Dave knew it. Dave could needle him, and Obama would needle him right back.

JERRY FOLEY: Dave, like any other comedian, will do anything for a laugh. But if you go back to several moments of national crisis, Dave's humor was comforting. It was defusing and hopeful, that in the middle of an intelligent dissertation about a variety of topics he could find the lighter note that would make you feel better and feel like we have quantified how horrible the situation is, but here is this guy to find the perfect time to punctuate these moments with humor. I found it to be comforting and really kind of bold of him. Who makes a joke in the middle of a Congressional Honor recipient's recalling a firefight they were in? Dave would find the perfect moment to interject something clever, lighthearted that would take you back to the present and set you up for the future. It is only a very high level of intelligence that can do that. You can't fake it or script it. There were so many moments like that over the years. You kind of stick a finger in your ear and shake it a little bit and say, "What did he just say?" That is surgical work.

In the next segment they discuss the Free Trade Agreement and then talk about retiring. Obama suggests that they should play dominoes together. When Obama asks Dave what he is going to do in retirement, Dave responds, "I plan to teach law at Columbia."

MIKE BUCZKIEWICZ: At the time, there was a question of what the president would do after he leaves office. I had told Dave that morning that in the paper there was speculation that Obama was going to go back to Columbia law and teach. And Dave was like, "Really?" Then flash forward to the exchange at the end of that interview when Dave asks, "What are you gonna do now?" and Obama says, "What are you gonna do now?" Dave deadpans, "I am gonna teach law at Columbia." You could see in Obama's face that he just lost it. Dave had that uncanny ability to retain little pieces of color and then pull them out at the perfect moment.

Photo courtesy of @Letterman, CBS publicity photo.

As the interview wraps up, the president of the United States thanks David Letterman for what he has given to the country. This is something that Johnny Carson didn't get during his last days on the air. "We've grown up with you. The country has—after a tough day at the office or coming home from work—knowing you've been there to give us a little bit of joy and a little bit of laughter. It has meant so much. You're part of all of us. You've given us a great gift and we love you." Dave tries to change the subject by complimenting Obama. The president says, "I meant what I said. We love you."

SHEILA ROGERS: I can't take credit for booking Obama. That was Mike Buczkiewicz. Mike would just say, "I think Obama is gonna be available." And I'd say, "Where did you want him?" Mike, who now works at *Morning Joe*, was our political person. We had great relationships with the Obamas and Bill Clinton from previous appearances. When we got the date of the end of the show, as I was reaching out to the A-list stars, Mike was getting in touch with the Obamas. He really organized all that.

MIKE BUCZKIEWICZ: Trying to get a president to come on is no small order. It was cool to call and say, "This is our final show date, we would love to have the president come on before the final show," and for them to say, "Sure, let's find a date."

BILL SCHEFT: When Dave got the Kennedy Center Honor, I went with him to the White House. Barbara, Jude, and I went. We were on the receiving line. I hear Obama say, "Hey, Letterman, you in my house now. We keep it a little warmer here." I think Obama was fond of him.

BARBARA GAINES: My Obama story is, my mother, may she rest in peace, would always ask, "Who did you meet? Who did you talk to?" She would be very upset because she wanted to tell her friends that I stood next to a lot of famous people. But I never talked to the celebrity, only to Dave. That was my policy. No one told me to do that. So even if the president was on, I only

Photo courtesy of Barbara Gaines.

talked to Dave. When I eventually left the podium and went to the control room and the president was on, I wasn't even on stage. So I clearly wouldn't see him. This would be the last time I would ever have a chance to be near the president of the United States—my president. I said to Jude, "We have to meet this guy." She said, "That isn't gonna happen." I said, "We have to be on the welcoming committee." She said, "We can't. We are up in the dressing room with Dave going over the show. There is no time for us to be on the welcome committee." I said, "It's May 4. The show is ending in less than three weeks. So what if we leave the makeup room? We are going." So I get us on the welcoming committee. The talent department told us what to do, since we had never done anything like that in thirty years. They said, "You have to say, 'Hello, Mr. President, thank you for coming. This is the green room.'" I said, "We are grown women. We know what to say and how to do this." The president walks in, and like two ninnies, it was like we saw The Beatles. We screamed, "Oh my God, it's you." He said, "Yeah, it's me." Just as cool as can be. We hugged him. That was our president of the United States.

Musical Guest

The Avett Brothers and Brandi Carlile are the musical guests. Dave promotes Brandi Carlile's newest album, *The Firewatcher's Daughter*, but the song they perform is not on that album. It is an old country standard, "Keep on the Sunny Side."

SHERYL ZELIKSON: I think Brandi might have been booked, and then I found out that Dave wanted to hear "Keep on the Sunny Side." I would listen to the song, and then I would start to write a list of people that have been on the show that I think can perform the song and make it special. I knew Brandi had an album coming out, and the Avett Brothers are one of my favorite bands that can do everything. And they know Brandi. It was like the stars aligned. They knew that Dave wanted to hear it. I think it was nice to see these artists sing this song, which was a little outside their box, and take the time to learn and make it a very special performance. I loved that. Dave definitely wanted to hear that song.

WORLDWIDE PANTS TAG:

"Do you know where your pants are?"

"FROM A SUBMARINE CRUISING BENEATH
THE POLAR ICE CAP..."
IT IS EPISODE 6,017
MAY 5, 2015

"And now . . . clicking virtuoso on the castanets . . . David Letterman." He begins again with a retirement joke, "Between the psychiatrist and the daytime drinking, I'll be fine." He talks Cinco de Mayo, John Boehner, and Hillary Clinton. The Top Ten List is "Signs You're at a Bad Cinco de Mayo Party," and all the numbers on the list are cinco. The best-of clip is Dave having fun with delivery guys from 1997-98. He talks through a speaker at an apartment building and has birds, singing telegrams, and more delivered to the door.

The first guest is Reese Witherspoon, who is on to promote her new movie, *Hot Pursuit*. Reese shows a picture of her teenage daughter and says she was born just after Reese's first appearance on the show with Dave. Dave makes a face and the audience reacts to the implication. Reese doesn't catch on to what she just implied. Dave laments, "It is the furthest thing from her mind." Reese's first-appearance baseball card is shown as March 2, 1999. mind."

The second guest is Nathan Lane. Paul plays Nathan Detroit's theme from *Guys and Dolls*. Nathan Lane always comes prepared with one-liners, which he doles out one after another. He references the retirement, saying, "This is a very sad time in show business and not just because Netflix is bringing back *Full House*. All the characters you loved only now old and bitter. No, we're very sad because of this premature retirement of yours. And if you decide to stay on Broadway I think you would make a wonderful Hedwig. It's a great part, and you wouldn't have to wear as much makeup."

Lane moves to center stage to sing a song to Dave. This song was written with Marc Shaiman and Scott Wittman. Shaiman also plays the piano, as he did for Billy Crystal. The song is about Nathan Lane being "Dead Inside," and that Dave is as well. The only mention specific to Dave is a shingles reference. Nathan receives a standing ovation for the performance.

BILL SCHEFT: I've know Nathan for at least thirty years, when he used to hang out at The Improv after a day running around on auditions. For years, after I got the gig at NBC, Barbara Gaines and I tried to get him booked on the old show. We knew how great he'd be. When he finally got a shot, he quickly became one of Dave's favorite guests. He'd showed up with plenty of material, a lot of it written with Matt Roberts, and could memorize all of it in the twenty-four hours before he came out.

Musical Guest

Mumford and Sons perform "Believe." Dave mentions that the band made its network debut on the *Late Show*.

WORLDWIDE PANTS TAG:

"Aren't pants nice?"

"FROM NASA'S JET PROPULSION LABORATORY IN PASADENA, CALIFORNIA..."
IT IS EPISODE 6,018
MAY 6, 2015

"And now… the first to run the sub-four-minute mile… David Letterman." Dave begins with, "Tonight I am giving my two-week notice." The monologue covers Hillary Clinton, Bernie Sanders, and "Deflategate" (a "scandal" involving Tom Brady and the air pressure of a football—2015 was a different time). In the middle of his monologue, he is interrupted by Cher. She says, "On the first show I called you an asshole." Dave says, "That was twenty-nine years ago. I took it with a grain of salt." Cher says, "I really mean this from the bottom of my heart. I really love you and I am gonna miss you." They hug, kiss, and hold hands. She ends with, "You're still an asshole."

SHEILA ROGERS: I went to Liz Rosenberg, who works with Cher. Cher wanted to do something.

RICK SCHECKMAN: Cher called at the last minute, so we gave her a walk-on comedy piece. At that point everyone wanted to do the show one last time, but we only had so many slots. In one of the production meetings, we were all asked to list our ten favorite guests. I don't know how far the list got, but basically who we would want in the last ten shows.

The desk piece is a best-of package from September 1993, Fun With a Car Phone. Dave drives around the city calling radio stations and businesses causing trouble.

The first guest is Martin Short. He says, for his last time on the *Late Show*, "Thanks for remembering," as he unbuttons his suit jacket and spreads his arms wide to soak up his standing ovation. He has done this for every entrance for the last twenty years or so. Martin Short always arrives as a completely prepared guest. He also always begins the interview by insincerely complimenting Dave on his appearance. He says, "You look sensational. I wonder, are you getting younger looking or are you just asking your staff to dim the lighting?"

> **BILL SCHEFT:** Others will give you their opinion, and others may be their favorite, but the fact is that Martin Short is the best guest we've ever had. There are a lot of very strong people who command the chair, but they line up after him. He works the hardest on his spot and gets the most consistent laughs. Sure, there is a tried-and-true formula (fake fawning over Dave, a couple of show business stories, and then a thoroughly original song parody written with Matt Roberts), but the energy and joy he brings is singular and hardly formulaic. He coughed up my single favorite fake compliment years ago. He had been out about a minute and said to Dave, "Can I just say something? I applaud the decision you've made to wear your suits tighter."

Martin Short mentions he has been coming on the show for thirty years, with his first appearance on December 3, 1982. He explains that on that night Dave did a bit where he rolled the credits pretending the show was over, but then said there will be more. Short explains that all his friends turned off the TV, so no one watched his first Letterman appearance. Short then launches into a story about having to follow singer Tony Bennett and then forgetting the words to the song. Throughout this masterfully told story, Dave is truly laughing. It is a full-on laugh, not a talk-show laugh. Dave sends the show to commercial break while still laughing. As he delivers, "We will be right back," he turns to Martin Short and says, "This is the kind of thing I will miss, stories from you. That was delightful."

I highlight this statement because it is the only time Dave ever says he will miss anything about the show, excluding the live music, which Dave doesn't view as having to do with him. Dave has told jokes about how retiring was all a big mistake. He has picked songs that, in retrospect, tell us that he will miss the show. But this off-the-cuff utterance, "This is the kind of thing I will miss," is the only full admission Dave makes in the final six weeks that he, like us, will miss all of this.

Martin Short is a great talk-show guest. I have seen him on many other shows—it isn't the same. Dave's reaction to his stories lift the stories themselves. This is similar to Johnny Carson. When Johnny laughed at a stand-up, the stand-up became a contender. Dave is a storyteller, when he laughs at a well told story, the story becomes legend. When I watched this episode for the first time in May 2015, that small sentence made everything real for me, as a fan. It was my first realization of what I was losing. All the tributes didn't mean as much as actually hearing Dave admit he would miss the moments at the desk, talking to Martin Short.

In the second segment they discuss Martin Short's movie *Clifford*. He tells a great story about accidentally exposing himself to the hairdressers. Short mentions he has been on the show over fifty times. He says, "I want to thank you for allowing me to promote all the things that rarely opened or worked. I do think it is a testament to you, Dave, of how hard all the people with any merit wanted to work [to prepare for the show.] Steve Martin has, through the years, phoned me up and said, 'Tell me if you think this joke is funny.' And I'll pretend it is. 'I got Letterman in three months.' I want to thank you and your staff and the writers and Paul Shaffer." Dave says it all starts with people like Martin Short, Steve Martin, Tom Hanks, and Bill Murray, who prepared for the show. Short turns it back to Dave, saying that Dave set the tone with a high bar for comedy and broadcasting. It is nice to see two comedy legends paying respect to each other, especially when it is well earned.

As he always does, Short offers to sing his song on the desk right to Dave. In the past, Dave has always declined this offer. However, tonight Dave says he should go ahead and sing it on the desk. Short declines, and makes his way over to center stage to sing a song he says he wrote for Dave's funeral. He kicks off the song by saying, "Wish me luck on the top note, Pappy." This is a parody song set to "Rockabye Your Baby With a Dixie Melody."

BARBARA GAINES: I love Martin Short. The summer after we went off the air, I worked on the show *Maya & Marty.* It is the only thing I would have possibly done after Dave. They had a twelve-week series. It was fun to work on. It was fun and weird to be back at the same studio where the NBC show was taped.

MAY 6, 2015

BRIAN TETA: Matt Roberts [head writer] had a very good relationship with Marty and went on to do *Maya & Marty* afterward. Matt was much more involved with breaking that song with Marty. He comes prepared with his stuff. You are basically just writing it down. Paul works on the arrangements with Marty and Matt on those amazing parodies.

Musical Guest

Norah Jones performs her hit "Don't Know Why." She performed this back in May 2002. Dave says, "She will performing the very first song she sang on this show, thirteen years ago."

This performance was a peronsal highlight for me. I had seen Norah Jones perform this song thirteen years ago. I now own all of her albums. Watching Martin Short kill with great stories and then Norah singing a slowed-down, sparse version of "Don't Know Why," I felt the very real loss of something that had shaped not just my comic sensibilities and my storytelling, but my musical tastes as well. I had discovered many artists through watching Letterman over the years and that was all ending.

SHERYL ZELIKSON: When you are booking the show, you don't know the impact the music has on people. Norah is a very special artist. We had Hootie and the Blowfish, Dave Matthews Band, and Norah Jones come on and sing the song they first did when they debuted on the show. These were certain artists that went on to have very big careers.

BILL SCHEFT: Dave was crazy about Norah Jones, and she is so ethereal. That was a big deal. Maybe it was just the piano and guitar, but it was so quiet in the theater.

WORLDWIDE PANTS TAG:

"Flip the switch, froggy."

"FROM THAT RED SPOT ON THE PLANET JUPITER..."
IT IS EPISODE 6,019
MAY 7, 2015

"And now . . . your citric tonic to ward off scurvy . . . David Letterman." Dave starts with a retirement joke about no longer wearing makeup. He also jokes that after the last show they will have fifteen minutes to get out of the studio before the wrecking ball. (Remember this joke when we get to the final episode. This is pretty much what happens to the staff.) If the third joke, about Dave not wanting to hold hands with his girlfriend, seems a little strange, it is, because it is a call back to his Q&A with the audience earlier in the evening.

> **BILL SCHEFT:** The first guy Dave called on said, "I used to be a stand-up comic. I always wanted to get on the show but I couldn't, and now I want to do a line from my act and try to make you laugh." So he tells Dave this bit about his then girlfriend not being affectionate. She never wanted to hold hands. And then one day, they were walking and she slipped and fell. When she got up, she asked him why he hadn't put his hand out as she was falling. He said, "Sorry, not in the mood." The bit predictably gets a tepid, good-sport applause from the audience and a sympathetic chuckle from Dave, who listened intently as the guy did it. Now the show starts, and midway through the monologue, Dave repeats the bit verbatim, but with all the energy of a comic doing a spot on his show. It gets screams and the guy gets a shot on camera basking in his glory. Sure, Dave got a giant laugh because he's Dave, but he also got the big laugh because of the thing I have mentioned in the past: commitment to the material.

The Top Ten List is "Surprising Facts About Sesame Street." The best-of clip is "The David Letterman Story" from February 1997. This episode was supposed to contain a best-of montage of on-screen appearances by the staffers, but it was cut for time, much to the sadness of the people who created it. The five-minute montage was released as an internet extra.

It is a fun montage illustrating how much the staff contributed on screen throughout the years.

> **JEREMY WEINER:** It aired during a taping, and we were so over it got cut from the show. Gianes asked me to start to put that together back in March. It was initially gonna be just the best of Pat Farmer, Alan Kalter, George Clark, and some of the staffers that had been on the show the most. Then we kept adding people. I would have to email Gaines and say, "I can fit in six more people if I cut thirty seconds of this Biff section." So we would do that. We had like fifteen versions of this video. The idea went from six or eight staffers to maybe over seventy in it. It was quick bursts of some of their highlights.

> **LEE ELLENBERG:** I probably spent a large portion of the last six weeks creating some of those compilation packages with Jeremy Weiner. We did one with the whole staff that was pulled from the show.

> **JEREMY WEINER:** I would ask people to give me all their appearances. It was one of my favorite things that I worked on. I think at one point they wanted us to put the names up of each person, but it got a little too busy. All the clips are now taken down from the *Late Show* YouTube page. Maybe Don Giller [Letterman archivist] might have it. It was such a fun thing to work on. It was long and they had to chose that or a classic remote that everyone remembers.

Paul plays "Unbreak My Heart" for Tina Fey as she walks over to be Dave's first guest. She is the creator of *Unbreakable Kimmy Schmidt*. Fey comes out in a blue cocktail dress hemmed at the knee with quarter-length sleeves and black lacing around the body. She compares Dave's impending retirement to the end of *30 Rock*, another show she created. She informs Dave that going forward, he will not be able to use his show as an excuse to get out of going places. He will have to attend weddings and parties and host galas. She talks to him about going to the Metropolitan Museum of Art's costume gala in New York City. She thrills Dave by saying the event is full of every jerk from every walk of life. She calls it a "jerk parade" of people. Dave repeats this phrase many times in the interview.

In the second segment they discuss her upcoming movie *Sisters*, *SNL*'s fortieth anniversary special, and parenting. Dave compliments her look, saying, "Forgive me if this is indelicate, but you look wonderful." Fey says, "I have been here twenty times, because I live nearby and people cancel a lot. I realized when you retire I am never gonna wear a fancy dress on a talk show again. Because it is very hard work. I don't know if you are aware of the contraptions that are under here. It's almost medical. I'm terrible in heels. I dress up like this for respect for you."

Tina Fey stands up and models the dress, turning around and strutting in front of the chairs. She says, "Because this is my last time wearing a fancy dress on a talk show and conforming to gender norms out of respect to you, my gift to you is that I want to give you the dress. You can keep it." Dave unzips her and Fey takes off the dress. She is left wearing a bra, leotard, and spanks. The leotard has "Bye Dave" printed across her abdomen. Printed across her rear is "#LastDressEver." Dave and the audience go wild.

Dave moves around to the front of the desk and asks, "Can I hug you in this?" Tina screams, "Goodbye, America." Dave tries to settle the audience down so he can say, "I am told now we have time for another segment." She laughs and as she stands in her skivvies, she whispers to Dave, "This is what we do for you." The baseball card shows her first appearance as October 8, 2001.

BRIAN TETA: It was all Tina's idea. She had come with another idea that didn't kind of work initially that we were kind of on the fence about. Then she came up with the dress idea, and we immediately loved it. It was genius and fantastic. None of us ever saw the undergarments. We didn't know exactly what she had on underneath until it actually happened. We were all kind of holding our breath a little bit. "What is exactly going to happen here?" I have worked with Tina a bunch of times. She is one of my favorite guests—so relatable and funny—and Dave had so much respect for her. She worked really hard at what she was doing here.

JERRY FOLEY: These people know what they are doing. One of the connections I feel Dave and Tina have is a construction of a joke. Dave had this relationship with a couple of people. He can say those odd things in a heavy talk with Obama, but he also constructs jokes and agonizes over them. When the joke is over, did it take too long to get the joke? Tina is the same way. So when she comes in with this idea that she is gonna strip down, you are dealing with experts, people who know how these things can go right and more importantly how they can go wrong.

BRIAN TETA: You are really holding your breath waiting for her to strip down. This is Tina's idea. You have faith in her. You know she is funny and can make it work, but it's a leap of faith and you approved it and Dave is looking to you: "Is this going to work?" I trust Tina Fey as one of the funniest people on the planet and it's gonna work, and it did. I was concerned at how long was it gonna take for her to get stripped down. I didn't know it was gonna say "#LastDressEver" on her rear. I think she avoided telling me that on purpose in case we were gonna censor that. The reason it works so great is that it was sincere. Big actresses and comedians got legitimately nervous coming on the show because Dave meant something to them and they wanted to do well.

JERRY FOLEY: Brian was probably closer to the circumstances that led to Tina doing what she did, but I can assure you, Tina went into that with all confidence in the world that it was going to come out like it did. I don't really recall anyone being nervous about it. If there was any nerves it was wanting to get to it right. I was just excited to have it happen. I was very confident in that moment going well.

Musical Guest

The musical guest is the folk duo First Aid Kit. This is another request from Dave. This is his introduction to the performance: "A couple of weeks ago Tracy Chapman was here. She sang 'Stand by Me.' We had that on because it was one of the songs that I used to sing to my son, because I remembered it and it's a wonderful song and it is sort of applicable to a relationship for a father and son. He would not want to hear the same song every night. The other song I would sing was by Simon and Garfunkel, 'America,' because I remembered it when I was a kid in high school and college. Tonight First Aid Kit is going to do 'America.' The last time I sang this to my son, I read him the story and I put him in the crib and I said, 'Harry, which song do you want to hear tonight?' and Harry said, 'No song.' And that was it. So here now completing the old musical one-two punch from his early days on the planet, please welcome First Aid Kit."

First Aid Kit consists of two sisters from Sweden. They sing a beautiful version of the sixties classic "America." A string arrangement accompanies the guitar. When the song is completed, Dave comes over and says, "That was sweet, very nice. That means a great deal to me, and congratulations. And we can't pay the strings."

SHERYL ZELIKSON: Of course the first thing you do is reach out to Paul Simon and Art Garfunkel. I don't remember the exact situation, but I reached out to Paul Simon's people first and he just wasn't available to be on the show. So that's when I start to do my research, and again it's just luck that I'd been having conversations with First Aid Kit. I've watched some of these performances again to refresh my memory, and they are one of my all-time favorite bands. I just think they are incredible. Their harmony is just like Simon and Garfunkel.

The songs Dave chose were starting to tell a story. It was the story of how Dave chose to say goodbye to his viewers. Dave was never someone to pour his heart out openly on camera, and yet you always knew how he felt about a situation. That is because he was a master at communication. (They don't just give away those degrees at Ball State University.) Here are the titles to the songs he chose to be sung during these final weeks: "Keep on the Sunny Side," "Desperados Under the Eaves," "May the Circle Be Unbroken," "Stand by Me," "America," and "American Pie." Dave was saying goodbye through the songs he was choosing. One by one, the artists were coming in and rising to the challenge. They weren't worrying about selling their latest record; they were paying tribute to a fellow music lover. If the viewer pays attention, Dave, through the musical guests, was passing on thoughtful, wise words to live by.

WORLDWIDE PANTS TAG:

"Cute pants sister."

"FROM A POINT JUST BEYOND THE HORIZON..."
IT IS EPISODE 6,020
MAY 8, 2015

"And now . . . this year's grand marshal of the Jerk Parade . . . David Letterman." The Tina Fey line resonated enough that they appropriated her "jerk parade" for the next show. All Friday shows were taped ninety minutes after filming the Thursday episode, so the "jerk parade" is fresh in everyone's mind. Dave begins this show with a New York City rat joke. He tries to do a joke about *Fifty Shades of Grey*, but stumbles over the wording. Paul interjects, "There are only nine episodes left." Dave then realizes he has the setup completely wrong. Bill Scheft calls out from the side, "The nurses are stealing my shoes." After they play a clip comparing Dave as the Lone Ranger to Christian Grey, the bit doesn't go over very well. Dave says, "That's like driving all day, you get to the Dairy Queen, and it's closed." But these are the moments that fans love: a bit that goes off the rails and the interactions between Dave and his staff—that is what Letterman fans tune in for.

Act 2 features Top Ten Things "You Don't Want to Hear During Mother's Day Brunch." Since Mother's Day is the upcoming Sunday, the best-of montage is a tribute to Dave's mom, Dorothy Letterman. The montage shows her with John Mellencamp, Top Ten appearances, at the Olympics with Hillary Clinton, cooking segments, and the Thanksgiving-pie guessing segments. This was my personal favorite bit Dave and his mom did. She would bake pies for Thanksgiving and then he would guess which pies she made over a live satellite feed to her home in Indiana. Thanksgiving just isn't the same without it. (Don't get me started on how Christmas isn't the same without Darlene Love and Jay Thomas.)

LEE ELLENBERG: I loved when Dave would say to his Mom, "You didn't make any of those trick pies did you?" It is such a Dave thing, the notion that there were trick pies. It makes me laugh. During the last few weeks, Barbara would send us an email saying, "How about a clip package for this person or that person?" Then Randi Grossack would get us the footage and we would get to work with the editors. Dan Baggio and Andrew Evangelista were great editors. They cut a lot of that stuff with us.

BARBARA GAINES: Dave was the one who decided to make his mother a character. Dave and his mom were two different people. She was so quiet and proper. I would not use "quiet and proper" to describe Dave.

LEE ELLENBERG: It wasn't that difficult of a montage to put together. She had appeared on the show less than people like Paul or Rupert, so we knew what most of it was gonna be—the Olympics, when she interviewed Donald Rumsfeld, her in England, throwing the inbound pass during a Pacers game. That was almost easier because you knew what the footage was gonna be.

The first guest is Ray Romano. He walks on with the weight of the world on his shoulders. The entire interview is emotional, starting even before Romano takes his seat. He is sporting a beard and prophetically tells Dave that soon he will grow one as well. Dave says he is looking forward to it. Dave thanks him for hosting the prime-time show earlier in the week. Romano tells a comical story about his son running out of gas on the freeway. This story is masterfully told, with the skill of a comedian who knows how to excel at the desk with Dave. Dave laughs at each bit. Having completed the comedy portion, Romano moves to the sentimental, emotional segment of the appearance.

Romano says, "I'm a little emotional since this is my last night here. I don't think most of the audience knows what this show has meant to me. Twenty years ago was my first spot. I did stand-up right there [points to the center of the stage]. I was doing stand-up for eleven years. I had three little kids, struggling. I came here, did a spot. The following week Worldwide Pants, Dave Letterman, your people, call me up. They say, 'Dave likes what he saw. He wants to develop a sitcom for you,' and that sitcom became *Everybody Loves Raymond*." The audience gives an extended applause. "The credit is all yours, my friend," Dave responds.

JERRY FOLEY: As Ray was establishing himself in stand-up, he got what is the modern-day equivalent of being on the Johnny Carson show. He got a spot on Letterman. As a result of that stand-up performance, Dave signed Ray to a development deal. As you see in that interview, what Ray is trying to get across is, from that stand-up performance came everything.

Romano continues, "You're like me. You don't think anything you do is worth anything. I want to prove to you how wrong you are. I want to show you what my world became *because* you existed." Ray Romano picks up a stack of pictures and goes through step by step how David

Letterman changed his life. He starts by showing his family in 1995, when he had three kids. He goes through how *Everybody Loves Raymond* allowed him to have the money to have another child, get another dog, and kiss Patricia Heaton (his wife on the show), and Lauren Graham on *Parenthood*, and how his agent could have more kids, and so on. To Romano, all of these good things happened because of Letterman.

Dave doesn't want to accept these things. He says, "It's very nice to hear you say those things, but everybody loves Raymond. You are Raymond and that's why there was a show." Romano says, "The biggest night of my life was here." He goes on to say that he got emotional watching John Mayer sing "American Pie." "I just saw him at that spot where my life changed and my family's life [his voice starts cracking because of the emotion] . . . because of the lyrics. 'The day the music died.' For me that is what is happening here. For me on May 20th, that is the day the comedy dies, as far as I'm concerned." Dave invites Ray to walk over to the stand-up center spot one more time. Ray walks over and stands there. Paul and the band play "American Pie." Emotion overtakes Ray Romano. Dave hugs him. Ray says, "I lost money on the hug." They fade to his baseball card showing the first appearance, from March 23, 1995.

BRIAN TETA: Ray is someone who clearly owes Dave his career. Dave doesn't want to hear it and take credit because Ray is so funny. Ray would have been a star no matter what. I was glad that Ray was able to do this—have Dave sit there and take it.

JERRY FOLEY: Ray is a decent enough guy who honors that and remembers it and can't ever let Dave forget that his success was a direct result of doing stand-up on the *Late Show*. Ray had a lot of appreciation for his professional life being connected to Dave and Worldwide Pants. Ray was a friend of the show and had been on many times over the years. He had a lot of guest segments. There was a personal connection as well.

BILL SCHEFT: That is not easy for Ray. Doing that show was really important to him, and it didn't have to be. He had made it by then. Some shot on Letterman after he has *Everybody Loves Raymond* isn't gonna help or hurt him, but it was really important to him. He wanted to be out there longer, and he would check his watch at how long his segments were. He was obsessed with that.

JEREMY WEINER: The thing I loved about Ray is that he timed his segments. He wanted to know how long each of his appearances would be. He was always so thrilled to be on the show.

SHEILA ROGERS: Ray was another favorite guest. People who came on to talk to Dave and were not there to promote themselves or sell something were the best interviews. That was the majority of the guests during the end.

Dave introduces Brian Regan, who has been on the show twenty-five times. Before starting his set he says, "This is that magic spot. It's an honor to be here. Thanks, Dave."

Musical Guest

Dave introduces the Dave Matthews Band with, "This is a great night. Twenty years ago, they made their TV debut. They are back here. They will be performing the song they debuted on network television twenty years ago, 'What Would You Say.'"

BILL SCHEFT: Dave Matthews Band then did a webcast in the theater in the continuing quest of CBS to make sure there isn't a dollar left on the table they haven't grabbed. Let me just say this about the Dave Matthews Band: their drummer, Carter Beauford, is one of three guys I've seen Anton Fig stand to watch when they play.

SHERYL ZELIKSON: We started the series called *Live on Letterman* I believe in 2003 with Pearl Jam. And as usual Letterman was ahead of the curve. We live-streamed it on the web, and then they were on CBS radio. It was very powerful to help sell albums. We did seventy of them, and they were very successful. I think that was the last one, and again it was full circle of Dave Matthews, who I believe debuted with the show. And Dave is a big Dave Matthews fan. They performed on the roof of our theater, and performed for us multiple times.

WORLDWIDE PANTS TAG:

"Drive me home, Helen."

10

For My Next Trick
I Need a Volunteer

RUPERT & BIFF

JEREMY WEINER: The reason Dave used Rupert and Biff was because they were genuine. They weren't trying to act or be on the show. The fact that they weren't actors and didn't want to be on the show is what made them special.

RUPERT JEE RUNS THE HELLO DELI in New York City. As Dave was fond of saying, "There are hundreds and hundreds of delis in New York City and the Hello Deli is . . . one of them." With all due respect to Dave's joke, there was one thing that distinguished Hello Deli from the hundreds and hundreds of other delis: it was only a few steps away from Dave's studio. Within a moment, a cameraman could walk out the "Bill Murray Doors" in the Ed Sullivan Theater at 1697 Broadway, take a few steps down 53rd Street, and be in the deli. Inside this very small space, Dave would play games with contestants plucked from the street or just pop in to talk with Rupert. As time went on Rupert Jee become one of the regulars and part of the *Late Show* family.

BILL SCHEFT: We are not even on CBS yet. We were in the conference room and [writer] Spike Feresten said, "You know that guy who runs the deli, Rupert? Let's make him a star." I will never forget that.

RUPERT JEE: Really? I never knew that.

BILL SCHEFT: Rupert could have come and gone. Dave is notorious for getting tired of premises. So the fact that Rupert was on virtually every week for the history of the show says a lot about Rupert and that he did not change.

RUPERT JEE: That is the irony of this whole thing. During the first two weeks, I heard they were doing these segments visiting the neighborhood. When I was in college, I deliberately avoided speech class because I didn't want to be in front of an audience. I told the head writer that they didn't have to come in. I was thrilled they were in the neighborhood, but they could skip me because I didn't want to be on television. But they gave me a surprise visit early on, and my second career started.

LEE ELLENBERG: The writers loved Rupert. There is not an ounce of irony or sarcasm from Rupert. It comes from a sweet place in him. No matter what outrageous thing Dave would say to him, he would just say, "Oh, really?" I would love Rupert segments because I would look over at Steve Young and he would be laughing so hard he would be wheezing. Maybe, as comedy writers, it was those things that made us laugh instead of jokes.

Rupert Jee working in the Hello Deli in 2018. Photo by Scott Ryan.

BILL SCHEFT: I'll never forget when Dave was heckling him to get a Slurpee machine. Rupert breaks down and gets the machine and Dave says, "What do you say, for today Slurpees ten cents apiece?" And Rupert said, "You mean just till the end of the taping?" Rupert was dead serious. "I am not losing money." That was what was so appealing about him. He was money in the bank. It was an inconvenience for him to be on television and to keep his store open past 5:30.

LEE ELLENBERG: We loved writing for him because we loved his flat, unironic, genuine delivery. There is a sweetness that we found hilarious, and not in a mean-spirited way—to be able to put jokes in his mouth with that delivery. Jokes are best when they are told by someone who pretends they are not funny. That was what we were told from Dave. Everything is flat, we are not in on the joke. When I would shoot a piece with Jerry Foley, I would always say, "Let's shoot one more just a little flatter." To me Rupert has that absolute pinnacle of earnest flatness, which sounds like an old-time banjo duo.

BARBARA GAINES: Rupert just answered questions and did what we asked. He was the perfect straight man.

LEE ELLENBERG: That is why in the "Fun With Rupert" segments the joke is really on Rupert. That character he is playing is so moronic. That is what is so great about the piece. Dave is in the van and Rupert is being fed the lines. So you hear Dave say the line in the way that only Dave can deliver it. Then you hear Rupert say the line a second time, and that is what makes the piece so enjoyable: hearing Dave's humor come out again in that earnest, flat tone. As a comedy writer, it is a great to have this vehicle that you can trust. It doesn't matter what I write. If Rupert says it, Steve Young is gonna fall off the chair laughing.

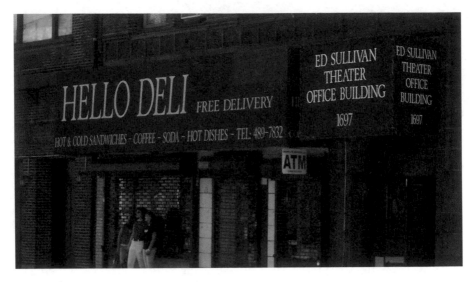

Photo by Scott Ryan.

RUPERT JEE: I called that the suicide skit. I am all wired up with an earpiece and a camera. Dave would feed me these lines to tell people and tell me to do some crazy stuff. I still didn't understand what was going on until we started to execute it. After one hour, I knew it was going to be something special. Rob Burnett and Dave have been around humor their whole lives. I never had seen them laugh or smile at anything. What I thought was funny they wouldn't even laugh at. But I could hear them through my earpiece cracking up in the car. The fact that they were laughing at the whole thing was a testament to me that this would be a very special skit.

LEE ELLENBERG: You don't have to have a killer joke, because you knew coming out of Rupert it was gonna play. I loved writing and shooting with Rupert. Dave is always big on when we were doing pieces that the joke was on us. You aren't the idiot; we are the idiot—which is something that has changed in TV that I am not entertained by.

EDDIE VALK: When I started off as a stage manager, I used to go into Rupert's and let him know when he was gonna be on the air and made sure that the contestant knew what to do. I'd make sure the store was ready, organize the cue cards, and check the lighting—mostly make sure the shot looked good.

JEREMY WEINER: Whenever we went to Rupert's there was always a plan or quick game we could do with a pedestrian outside. The best was when we went out with a plan and then Dave went off script and went with his gut and just rolled with whatever was available out there.

KATHY MAVRIKAKIS: Going into Rupert's deli wasn't a big thing from a production standpoint. We basically had an open-door policy with Rupert. I would work with my production coordinator and make sure I approved any additional crew members that we might need, like a new stage manager to be outside on the street all day. They needed my financial approval to do those things.

LEE ELLENBERG: I would get breakfast there. It was amazing. People go in and buy T-shirts and ask for pictures. And that is who that guy is. I like to think I am a kind, polite person, but here he managed to be this unfailingly polite and kind person to everyone. Every day for two decades someone would come in and they would tell him a story. He would appear to be riveted. That is why we all love the guy. Fame did not ruin Rupert.

RUPERT JEE: It is still ongoing. It's an experience that very few people have. I've enjoyed it. I never expected it. It is fun and time consuming at the same time. You have to accommodate the tourist, but also tend to your business. But, hey, life could have been a lot worse. My only complaint is that Dave retired a little too early. Wait, I don't want to burn the bacon.

Rupert walks away to check on the bacon and begins waiting on a customer who has ordered the Paul Shaffer sandwich.

According to Worldwide Pants records, Biff Henderson was the third-longest-running employee. The only people who worked with Dave longer were Barbara Gaines and Jude Brennen. Over the years Biff went from stage manager to spokesperson for Dave. When Dave cut back on doing remotes, Biff stepped in. Whether it was spring training, Super Bowls, or small-town America—Biff Henderson was the traveling face of the show.

LEE ELLENBERG: I remember Biff and I had to shoot a piece in Wyoming. We had to take a puddle jumper to get there, and we caught the flight at 4 in the morning. We shot in a town that had seventy people. It was really tiny. I lean back to sleep for the ride and I look over and Biff is talking to the guy sitting next to him, because even in this small town, the guy recognized Biff. That was surprising.

BRIAN TETA: I actually spoke to him a couple months ago, which is great. I miss him a lot. Biff was absolutely the exact same guy on TV as he was in real life. He was a stage manager. People forget he was actually working. At a certain point, he became a bigger star than a lot of the guests on the show, which is crazy. Even if you weren't a religious watcher of the show, you knew Biff Henderson. When he walked down the street, he would grumble when he couldn't walk five feet without being asked for a picture, but I think he loved it.

LEE ELLENBERG: Biff, a director, and a writer would go on the remotes. We would go out with two or three pages of jokes. Usually it was questions. It was always supposed to be an honest reaction from people attending the events. If the person said something amusing, then you could scribble something down on a legal pad and Biff could say it. It was a very primitive way that we went about filming those pieces.

JEREMY WEINER: I worked with Biff for many years. I used to travel with him on the "Biff Henderson's America" or Super Bowl spots. Dave sort of transitioned out of doing remotes and that is when Biff sort of became the one that would go out and do "Biff Henderson's Stopwatch."

LEE ELLENBERG: When I'd do a Super Bowl piece with him, there were people everywhere and jumping in the shot. You'd say, "Biff, walk over to that mustard dispenser and do this." You'd be surprised how many times you had to do that, because someone is calling out, "Biff!" or jumping into the shot. When I would shoot those with Rupert it was hard, but when it was Biff, he would be surrounded by people.

RANDI GROSSACK: I was the director with Biff and Dave's mom at the Olympics. I did the Super Bowl pieces every other year. I was especially proud when Biff got to touch the Super Bowl trophy before it got on stage. I got to travel the world shooting stuff. There were two A.D.'s on the show, so we rotated who would go out and shoot things with Biff or Rupert. You can't be thankful enough for that. When we did the Biff montage, there were so many clips that I got to direct.

JEREMY WEINER: Lee and I worked on Biff's montage. I had a lot of firsthand knowledge of things from 2000 on because I was working so closely with him. I needed to rely on Barbara, Kathy, Mike McIntee, and others to help me remember all the other stuff that Biff did. You couldn't screen everything, so it was asking people for their favorites and then looking back at those.

LEE ELLENBERG: Randi and Jessica were in charge of footage and clips. Randi sent us a list of every remote. Jeremy and I checked off the ones that they should load into the Avid. When I got the job at *Letterman*, I was twenty-four. I had watched the show. So I knew who Biff was. He was a celebrity to me.

JEREMY WEINER: Biff was so authentic. That is why he was so great on air. He was a straight shooter. He just had this presence about him and was always so genuine. That was what was great about Biff, Rupert, and all these people we ended up having on the show. They got used to being on camera a little bit, but they never really changed, and that was the best part.

Writer Jill Goodwin with Biff Henderson.
Photo courtesy of Jill Goodwin.

RICK SCHECKMAN: Biff wasn't a trained actor. He was beloved and very good on camera. That is what is so funny. Biff was lightning in a bottle. He would do almost anything you asked. His reactions were genuine, like when he shot that starter's pistol early in the supermarket bagging contest. You would see him flinch. That was real. He is not acting. There was one show when we played "May

We Turn Your Pants into Shorts." He does this triple take because he didn't want his pants cut. You can't script a triple take.

EDDIE VALK: Biff is one of the kindest men you'll ever meet. I got my start as a stage manager because of him. I was a production assistant. I expressed to Jerry that I wanted to start stage managing. I started to fill in when they would write a segment for Biff to be a part of. They needed someone to replace Biff. So if it wasn't for him, I wouldn't have a career. When he was on camera, I would fulfill his duties as stage manager. From there I worked my way up.

BRIAN TETA: My favorite Biff moment was when we had a phone in the airlock where you would page the guest to tell them they had to come down. There would be this massive star and he would say their names completely wrong. He could not have cared less. [Laughs] I would say, "That isn't their name." He would say, "Aww, shit."

11

Two Weeks Left

EPISODES 6,021-6,025

"FROM THE INCENSE STORAGE ROOM AT THE VATICAN..."
IT IS EPISODE 6,021
MAY 11, 2015

"And now . . . a visionary with floaters . . . David Letterman." Dave comes out to an extended ovation. With only eight shows left, the applause is infectious. He opens with a retirement joke, talks about Mother's Day, and plays a video extra about Tom Brady learning his lesson after deflating footballs.

> **JILL GOODWIN:** Some of these jokes are so topical of the time. Tom Brady was going to be forced to sit out games. Poor guy has to stay at his mansion with his supermodel wife, Gisele Bündchen. Tom Brady: ready to learn his lesson.

Act 2 begins with a Top Ten List of "New Fall Shows." For the second time in two weeks, audience members get free milkshakes because Graham Rahal placed second at the Indianapolis Grand Prix. Oprah Winfrey may give away cars, but you have never seen an audience happier than when they are given a free shake.

The first guest is radio host Howard Stern. He comes out carrying the recent *Rolling Stone* magazine with Dave on the cover. This is Stern's twenty-fourth appearance. His first was on May 21, 1984. He gives Dave grief for doing interviews now that the show is ending. He asks why Dave wasn't doing this throughout the years to help promote the show. (Good question, Howard.) Dave has a plausible answer: No one asked him to do interviews. Stern brings Dave's wife, Regina Letterman, a painting that he made for her. This same painting shows up in 2018 when Letterman has Stern on his Netflix series.

Stern then starts in about Dave retiring and moving to Montana all because of a tip from Jack Hanna. Dave denies all of this, but isn't given a chance to respond. Howard Stern is known for being a great interviewer and for being a provocative, entertaining guest with Dave. Stern's bit was always to try to annoy Dave by asking him personal or uncomfortable questions. Trouble is, during these final weeks, Dave is more willing to talk than ever before. A few times Dave starts to give info about his retirement plans, tries to explain Montana, and even tries to mention spending time with his family, but Howard Stern talks right over all of it. There was an opportunity here to get a bit of rare, personal information. Recall that in the Michael Keaton interview we learned why Dave never hosted *SNL*. Wonder what we could have learned here? The interview ends by the two of them moving to center stage and Howard Stern trying to forcibly kiss Dave.

VINCENT FAVALE: Howard was a guy who told it like it was. He was a perfect 12:30 guest on *Late Night*. They had this relationship, and it lived over thirty years. NBC had a holding deal with Dave after the morning show. So Dave had an office at Rockefeller Center on the same floor as Howard Stern. My office was also on that floor, because I was working for NBC at that time. I would see Dave in the halls. There was a glass window and you could watch and listen to Howard Stern on the radio. Dave and I would find ourselves just standing there, looking in, not talking. That was the first seed, I think, of Dave knowing that Howard Stern existed.

BRIAN TETA: I always enjoyed working with Howard. Having him be the subject of an interview is always nerve-wracking. Howard was fascinated by Dave retiring. He kept asking me, "Where are you gonna work? What's gonna happen to you?" He was very interested, because he is one of the few people that has operated as long as Dave on a level like Dave. He has an entire staff working for him. Someday he will retire, and all this kind of hit Howard personally. Howard felt pressure, and he wanted it to live up to one of his best performances. He did do a pre-interview, which he didn't always do. The pre-interview went really well, and then he complained the next day on his radio show that I kept him on the phone too long and made him do a pre-interview. Then I was heckled by Don Rickles—all in the same day.

The second guest is Don Rickles. His first appearance was on September 26, 1983. He has been a recurring guest for Dave for many years. This time, Howard Stern is left out there with Don Rickles. This allows Rickles to take shots at Stern and Letterman. He points to Stern and says, "Where is this guy gonna go with the trick-or-treat hairdo?" He tells Dave that Johnny Carson was always great with Joan Embery and the animals, while Dave was only "so-so" with Jack Hanna.

MIKE BUCZKIEWICZ: Don, true to his craft, would always do a pre-interview. Due to circumstances he did a super-early pre-interview. I remember staying late on a Friday afternoon in a pretty much empty office. People were like, "Why are you still here?" and I could respond, "I am waiting for Don Rickles to call," which is a great thing to say on a Friday afternoon.

BRIAN TETA: We had two lead guests, so the way we made that work was by having Howard stay out afterward with Don. It gives Don another target.

Photo courtesy of Brian Teta.

JERRY FOLEY: Having Howard stick around is a producer decision made by David Letterman. We could float ideas past him that he could accept or reject. On rare occasions a guest would stick around, and that was usually Dave's call. In this case, Dave saw the possibilities there and had Howard stay. Don had been out there many times. Dave revered him. I think a lot of people you talk to will tell you what an honor it is to be insulted by Don Rickles. I was insulted by him. I loved it. You never once felt it was malicious.

MIKE BUCZKIEWICZ: Don was incredibly warm and generous. You walk into the green room to brief him, and he cuts you down to size in such a fashion that you are like, "Wait, what is going on?" Then you realize Don Rickles is basically roasting me and I've been in this room for thirty seconds. He doesn't know me, has nothing prepared, and he just eviscerated me. You wouldn't trade it for anything in the world. I remember him making fun of my last name with a string of classic Don moments.

BRIAN TETA: The heckle that sticks out to me is he asked, "How are you?" I said, "We're doing well. We're having another baby." He patted my stomach and asked, "When are you due?"

MIKE BUCZKIEWICZ: Then you got through that and he was like, "Come here." You sit down and he would tell you stories about Sinatra, Vegas, or doing *The Tonight Show*. To be a part of his final appearance on Dave and him giving me shit about my last name was a treasure.

WORLDWIDE PANTS TAG:

"Ha, ha pants."

"FROM THE INFIELD OF THE TALLADEGA SUPERSPEEDWAY..."
IT IS EPISODE 6,022
MAY 12, 2015

"And now . . . a man who makes you put down the remote control . . . David Letterman." Dave begins with, "Six days left. I sure hope I get that call from the governor." At the desk Dave talks about how he and Paul meet in the makeup room every day before the show and talk. Dave asks Paul to tell him the story from today. The building has added extra security to accommodate tonight's top guest, former President Bill Clinton. When Paul was riding up the elevator with a member of Clinton's advance team in her late twenties, Paul said, "She looks at me and she says, 'You work here?'" Dave responds, "We can't get off the air fast enough . . . thirty-three years, 11:30 every damn night on CBS." The Top Ten List is "Least Popular Thomas Edison Inventions."

The first guest is former President Bill Clinton. The band plays "Harlem Nocturne," with saxophonist Aaron Heick taking the lead. After receiving a standing ovation, Clinton says he always had trouble playing that song. During the first segment he mentions another jazz classic, "God Bless the Child." As they go to commercial, band memeber Felicia Collins sings the Billie Holiday song. The two songs illustrate how adaptable the CBS Orchestra is under Paul Shaffer's direction. They could pick the perfect song for the walk-on and then change in midstream to perform a song mentioned in the interview.

Dave and the former president discuss the saxophone, his new granddaughter, and the Clinton initiative in Africa. They do not talk about Dave retiring, and there is no mention of the show ending.

JERRY FOLEY: The first time Bill Clinton was on the show was one of those electric moments. It was one of the few times that I witnessed someone who slightly intimidated Dave. You have two intelligent guys who were combatants in a certain sense. It wasn't a fair fight. Dave got up there and did Lewinsky jokes like everyone else in late night every night. Then here is Bill Clinton sitting across from the guy who has mocked him. It was a tense and interesting dynamic. Clinton shows up and is confident enough that he can get past it. Dave is an artist, and his commerce is in making fun of the president. It was always a kind of validator for him when someone he has been going to town on in the public eye shows up and sits face to face with him in the same room. In subsequent appearances, it became more conversational and much more fun. They got to know each other a little bit.

MIKE BUCZKIEWICZ: I feel like Dave's interest in politics grew toward the end of the run of the show. They touched on a number of topics. How often do you get to pick a guy's brain like that? I think that is what Dave liked about those interviews. It was nice to see Clinton in that role, because as he got further from the office he was less guarded.

JERRY FOLEY: You saw that with a lot of guests who came on the show. They weren't always as uninhibited as you wanted them to be, because there was a certain sense that when you sat across from David Letterman, you had to have your dukes up. There were people who were overly sensitive to that. Through repeated appearances things got to be more fun. Clinton is a great example of that.

The second guest is Adam Sandler. Paul plays the Warren Zevon song "Werewolves in London" for his entrance. Sandler recorded this song for a Zevon tribute album. Sandler talks about his children and tells a charming story about his grandmother, who is ninety-nine years old. He tells Dave, "When I was on *Saturday Night Live* and we did your show, we thought we were the coolest guys ever—Farley, Schneider, Spade, Norm Macdonald, and Rock. We were all best friends. We were in the same building as you. Every time we went to the other side of the building, where your show was, we thought, 'I think he's better than us.'" The baseball card shows Sandler's first appearance as April 4, 1991.

Before moving to center stage to sing, he says, "I hate going over there. I hate leaving the couch, but I'm going over there." Martin Short, Nathan Lane, and Billy Crystal all tried to sing the perfect tribute song. They tried to use sarcasm, they tried deep-cut *Late Show* references, they tried parodies. Sandler didn't try, he succeeded. The first line is simple and, from Sandler and his generation's perspective, totally true: "There simply is no better man/than our David Letterman." The tune begins as a typical Sandler tune, one that sounds simplistic, but as the song progresses it becomes more rooted in a true acoustic rock song.

The lyrics become less jokey and more heartfelt as the song continues. He hits the classic moments of Dave's career, cracking jokes about Julia Roberts, Stupid Pet Tricks, Les Moonves, and speeding tickets. By the end of the song, Sandler has transitioned from silly to true sentiment, singing that he hopes the cop who pulls Dave over for speeding "drags you back here for thirty more years." He frantically strums the guitar as the music builds, and the audience screams with agreement.

He brings the song back down to say Dave is "the King of Comedy and our best friend on TV." Dave comes to greet him, and while the audience stands and cheers, Adam whispers, "I love you, Dave." It truly is a touching moment. Writing it out doesn't do the performance justice. YouTube it and watch a perfect tribute.

JERRY FOLEY: I can tell you the difference between Adam's song and Nathan's or Marty's. They are more Dave's contemporaries. Given the age difference, Adam Sandler is a true fan. How long had Dave been at it before Adam became Adam? There is a meaning to Adam's song that wouldn't be possible for older performers. Adam grew up with Dave. Bill Scheft had a line for a lot of these younger comedians and performers for a whole generation: "Dave came with the TV." Adam's song was right up there with [the upcoming performance of] Norm Macdonald as being something deeply felt.

BILL SCHEFT: Adam Sandler did an absolutely note-perfect, in-character song for Dave. No matter how many times I try to tell Dave, he refuses to accept or acknowledge the two generations of comics he either influenced or who aspired to make it onto his stage, absolutely refuses to do it. Maybe with the time and critical distance coming up he can.

BARBARA GAINES: We felt bad that Adam came after President Clinton because he only got four minutes for talk and four minutes for a song. He really got no time. President Clinton got fifteen. That was how those shows went. People didn't get their regular time.

SHEILA ROGERS: People were totally cool about that. And that is unusual. Normally you hear they have to be the lead guest. As we got to these last six weeks of shows, people didn't care so much. They were like, "Fine, I just want to be on the show." Adam was fine following Bill Clinton. He did the song and couldn't have been more gracious and wonderful.

BRIAN TETA: When you think of a late-night tribute song, you think of Johnny Carson and Bette Midler, and that is so not Dave. We thought there was gonna be a bunch of songs they are gonna want to sing to him, but they have to be funny. Marty Short is, of course, going to do one. Billy Crystal and Nathan Lane did one. Then Adam wanted to do one. I wouldn't say I was nervous about it, but as soon as I heard it I was like, "We have to let this happen." It was fantastic. I don't think Dave heard it until it aired. Adam did it in rehearsal for us. We knew it was gonna be great. Adam wrote it with a writing partner. It was sincere and it was definitely praising Dave, but it was funny enough that it was OK, and Dave could sit there and take it. I am not even sure I told Dave it was happening till right before it happened: "Adam is gonna sing to you, bye."

WORLDWIDE PANTS TAG:

"Pants are fun."

"FROM A REGIONAL DISTRIBUTION CENTER..."
IT IS EPISODE 6,023
MAY 13, 2015

"And now . . . jumper cables for your humdrum life . . . David Letterman." Dave begins by saying "Tonight, Julia Roberts. Next week I'll be lucky to get a table at IHOP." They also do a bit where the workers in the control room, Alan Kalter, and Todd the Cue Card Boy all fall asleep during the monologue. The desk piece is Top Ten "Things Overheard at the Olive Garden Test Kitchen." Dave also gives out a Letterman jacket to a man in the audience.

The first guest is Julia Roberts. Paul plays The Beatles song "Julia," as he always does when she walks out. Roberts is wearing an older Letterman jacket. They cut to the guy in the audience who was just given a newer version of the same coat. Dave greats Roberts midstage and kisses her hand. Julia wants everyone to know that she was wearing her jacket before Dave gave away one to the audience member. She was cold backstage and says she took the jacket from "sweet Jenny" backstage.

BRIAN TETA: Julia was freezing backstage. She took one of the staffs' coats because she was so cold. I ran into the hallway and grabbed whoever was standing there. I think it was one of the talent coordinators, Jenny Chapin. "I need your coat, Julia's cold." It was a *Late Show* black-and-white jacket. She loved it. She decided to wear it on stage. So Jenny backstage is like, "I can't believe Julia Robert is on TV wearing my coat." Julia ended up taking it home, I think. But we got Jenny a new one.

"I have come here tonight to just find out what the hell is going on here. Someone says we are closing shop around here. I turn my back for a minute. I don't know. It's bullshit, David Letterman." That is how Julia Roberts begins her twenty-sixth appearance. The relationship between Roberts and Dave was always a mixture of playfulness, flirtation, and genuine respect. Watching Julia Roberts be upset that she is losing her "TV friend" helps viewers deal with their impending loss as well.

They discuss her first appearance on November 3, 1989, which was to promote *Mystic Pizza*. She says, "As a fan of the show, I didn't want to come on, because I had seen you absolutely dismember young actresses of my kind of peer group." Embarrassed by this, Dave asks, "What do you suppose was wrong with me?" Roberts sums up his thirty-three years in one succinct sentence, showing she truly is a fan of Letterman. "I think stupid people annoy you."

A compilation video of Roberts and Letterman is played, showing all of the times they flirted and kissed over the years. When the video is over, Dave walks her to center stage and plants one final kiss on her. The audience swoons and the band plays. Dave starts to go to a commercial, but Roberts isn't having it. She says, "Wait, wait, wait, I just want to say, David Letterman, I love you and I thank you for all the joy and laughs and the intelligence you have brought to us for thirty-three years." They hug and Dave says, "I love you."

BRIAN TETA: As a fan of the *Late Show* it is a tremendous amount of pressure to produce a Julia Roberts segment. I had worked with her a bunch of times. Those appearances were so special. She didn't do a lot of talk shows. The rapport they had was real. Because she is Julia Roberts you want to keep her out there as long as possible, so you have to have enough content to keep it going. I thought the best way to handle that segment was to look back on that rapport. So we did a mash-up of all the times they kissed. I was of course hoping that it would lead to another one.

BARBARA GAINES: Julia Roberts, who only got ten minutes instead of her usual twenty, felt like, "That is it?" But these are not your regular shows. These are the-keep-it-moving-to-say-goodbye shows.

JERRY FOLEY: Julia Roberts fits the description of friend of the show, somebody who had a relationship with the show and Dave. Julia Roberts wasn't always "Julia Roberts." She comes off

Mystic Pizza and is doing a big talk show. Among the options is this imposing, ironic, sarcastic David Letterman. That was intimidating for a lot of young actresses. But then like any great challenge in life, if you survive it, there is a certain desire to do it again. That relationship evolved and grew over the years. So to have her cap all that off center stage was pretty magical.

BRIAN TETA: I was hoping he would kiss her, but it wasn't a scripted thing. I maybe planted the bug and said, "If you wanted to, you could kiss again afterward." The walking to center stage was Dave in the moment. It was one of those things he had to feel if it was gonna work or not. They really are friends.

BILL SCHEFT: It took me until her twenty-sixth and last appearance to realize that the band always plays her on to "Julia," the oft-forgotten John Lennon ode to his mother.

RICK SCHECKMAN: Julia Roberts is always good. The show with Julia Roberts where Paul said, "Hey are you getting laid much?"—that was not scripted. That was just Dave asking Paul if he wanted to ask Julia Roberts a question, and Paul just went with it. It wasn't planned.

RANDI GROSSACK: Paul is very funny. He would say things that would make you do a spit take. He would say things out of nowhere that would crack you up. None of that was scripted. The scripted stuff is never as good when the two of them just started to talk.

Speaking of, the second guest is none other than Paul Shaffer. Dave introduces him with, "I have had the pleasure of working with our next guest for thirty-three years. He is a Grammy Award winner, he is our music director, and most importantly our good friend." The band plays Paul's song, "It's Raining Men." The audience gives him a standing ovation as he slips out from behind the keyboard, crosses the stage and takes the seat next to Dave. "We should have done this more often over the years," Dave says.

Paul thanks each member of "the best band in the land": Aaron Heick, Frank David Greene, Tom Malone, Felicia Collins, Sid McGinnis, Anton Fig, and Will Lee. Paul then introduces a music video that Jerry Foley directed. Dave had asked Paul if there was anything else he wanted to do. Paul wanted to make a music video to the song "On Broadway." Paul felt this song represented what it meant to come from Canada and wind up with his name in lights on a Broadway marquee.

SHEILA ROGERS: Paul being a sit-down guest was something Dave wanted. It came from Dave and was a good idea. Paul was a great guest.

MIKE BUCZKIEWICZ: If you ever read the last book he put out it is just jaw-droppingly funny [*We'll Be Here for the Rest of Our Lives: A Swingin' Show-biz Saga*]. You never worried about Paul being in the guest chair.

EDDIE VALK: Paul has a lot going on all the time. He would come in from musical rehearsal and they would show him what acts needed music. He would then work out in about an hour all of the music that needs to be played on the show.

SHERYL ZELIKSON: Paul and the *Late Show* band were really some of the best musicians. They learned everything on the fly by ear. I've never seen anything like that. I remember the day I saw Paul pull out an accordion, and I thought, "Where did that come from?" The level of Paul's musicianship was one of the greatest I've ever seen. He's a band leader, and that's great in itself, outside of just being a musician.

JAY JOHNSON: Paul is great. He is a musical wizard, one of the most amazing musicians I'll ever know. He can do anything, play anything. I love what he brought to the show through his banter with Dave. Any talk show host will be lucky to have a guy like Paul Shaffer as their sidekick.

Musical Guest

Upon returning from the commercial break, Dave sums up what has been proved over and over throughout the final six weeks: "It is obvious," Dave says, "the music on this show is the glue, the mortar, the foundation of this program for thirty-three years, and it continues tonight." He then introduces Ryan Adams, who performs "Starting to Hurt." Ryan's *Late Show* debut was October 4, 2001.

SHERYL ZELIKSON: Sheila Rogers would've booked Ryan Adams. I remember seeing him as a solo artist for the first time and just being blown away. He is still one of those artists that gets me. I saw him recently at the Apollo and I was like, "Wow!" He's got personality. If you've ever gone to one of his shows, it's like Ryan Adams and Shecky Greene. He's just funny.

WORLDWIDE PANTS TAG:

"Nice pants, sister."

"FROM EUROPE'S BUSIEST PORT..."
IT IS EPISODE 6,024
MAY 14, 2015

"And now . . . a man just the right size for his britches . . . David Letterman."
The lead joke: "George Clooney is on the show tonight. Next week at this
time, I'll be in a hardware store watching them mix paint." Act 2 has a
Top Ten List titled "Reasons Max Is So Mad." Dave asks Paul to open up
the list; when the graphics are gone, Al Pacino is standing behind Dave
in the fake windows and cityscape.

The surprised audience starts cheering, and Dave turns around and
welcomes the legendary actor. Dave asks Pacino why he is there. Pacino
says, "I know you've got just a handful of shows left. I was wondering if
you would let me help you out with one of your last Top Ten Lists." He
walks around and takes a seat next to Dave. He says that he doesn't want
to read the Top Ten List. He wants to read just the numbers. Dave starts
to write something out on a blue card and slips it over to Pacino. He
looks at the card for a moment and then reads it aloud, "Say hello to my
little friend." Pacino then proceeds to just say the numbers, as Dave reads
the jokes about the recent *Mad Max* movie.

RANDI GROSSACK: Al Pacino just wanted to say goodbye to Dave. I think he called a couple days before and he wanted to come to see Dave. Him reading the numbers for the Top Ten made me laugh.

SHEILA ROGERS: I think I was trying to book him and he said he wanted to do a Top Ten List. It's not like, "Let's go get Al to do a Top Ten." Al Pacino wanted to do comedy. I'd tell Barbara, Jude, or Matt Roberts, and then it went off to the comedy side. It was all collaborative. Nothing was just one person.

The first guest is George Clooney. He receives a standing ovation as he makes his way over to Dave. Dave tries to ask him how things have been, but Clooney doesn't want to talk about that. He asks to see Dave's wrist. In a flash, Clooney reveals that his left wrist is already cuffed, and he quickly cuffs Dave's right wrist. They are now handcuffed to each other. Clooney tosses the key into the audience. He says, "You're not going anywhere, David Letterman." Dave, now handcuffed to George Clooney, says, "Is this something left over from the bachelor days?"

Clooney continues, "For many years I was not a married man. I was a single guy. I was out gallivanting in the evenings. So I would tape your show in the old days and I would watch it early in the morning. I am a married man now. I am home with my wife. I turn on the TV and now I hear you are not gonna be there? That's not OK. I have been watching the show and all these people coming on the show and how sad it is. This is a terrible thing you are doing to all of us. It hurts." Dave says,

"Speaking of that, what about the circulation in my right hand?" They move on, while still handcuffed to each other, to talk about Amal Clooney, George's wife, and her fight for human rights around the world.

Upon returning from commercial, Dave and George are still handcuffed. Dave says, "Welcome back to another installment of Judge Judy." They discuss Clooney's house in England. He brings the conversation back to Dave's retirement. "I have watched you, Dave, in my underwear. There are not many men I have watched in my underwear. What you have meant to us, all of us, with so many of the laughs and everything, but also the moments like walking us through the times when we didn't know what to do, like 9/11, and where we weren't sure when we could laugh again and all of that. You may be going off the air, but you belong to us for the ages, my friend."

Dave takes a selfie with them cuffed together and slyly puts his hand on Clooney's. Clooney responds, "You had your chance; I'm married." The baseball card shows Clooney's first appearance as February 21, 1995.

BRIAN TETA: We had discussions about what kind of handcuffs we were going to use. Dave had some in his office, but we didn't have a key. I have two souvenirs from the show that I love. I have the Empire State Building from atop the Christmas tree. It's my favorite. My second favorite is I have George Clooney's handcuff, signed by him. During the show they stayed handcuffed together during the breaks. They were sitting in the green room kinda walking around handcuffed together. I checked on Dave several times and he said, "By the way, we're letting you go." I said, "And I was so close to the end." [Laughs] It was a long time to be cuffed together.

JERRY FOLEY: There were certain nights where if you said to Dave, "We want to handcuff you to a movie star," he wouldn't think that was a good idea. He is a very unpredictable, complicated guy. He always was reading the room and picking up on the energy of what was happening in a particular style, and he went for it. Those shows were so good because Dave was so invested. Sometimes you see these politicians who complete their term and there is a side to them that is relaxed that you never saw on the campaign trail. This is what you are looking at in these last twenty-eight shows. The campaign was over and Dave was free to be as goofy as he wanted to be. He seized this opportunity to put the pretty boy George Clooney into a kind of compromising situation. He can't leave and go to dinner and do his next appearance. "You are gonna stay here and be handcuffed to me."

BRIAN TETA: Clooney had the idea to handcuff himself to Dave. My idea was to keep it running throughout the entire show. Clooney went for it right away. He was a little nervous about, "Where am I going and what am I doing?" The real convincing had to be done to Dave. To his credit, he went for it. It was a little bit like the old NBC show. We did a bit and committed to it.

The second guest is musician Tom Waits. There is now a stool between Dave and Waits, so Clooney can remain, still handcuffed to Dave. Waits comes up with a great quip as he sits down, "I usually have a key on me that will fit that." Tom Waits first guested with Dave on February 21, 1983. He, like John Mellencamp, truly utilizes his sit-down opportunity. He tells a great bit about how New York has changed. He saw a bunch of people waiting in a line. He asked what they were waiting for and they said they were in line for salad. All of his stories are strange and perfectly told, evocative of a *Late Night* guest. This episode truly is a throwback to Letterman's NBC days.

BILL SCHEFT: George Clooney and Tom Waits conspired for one of the great weird shows we've done. The stuff that Clooney did, mostly in silence, during Tom Waits's interview was funnier than in his two segments, and his two segments were damn funny.

LEE ELLENBERG: I love Tom Waits and the fact that Clooney sat there handcuffed to Dave. That was really a wonderful, odd moment.

SHEILA ROGERS: Tom was cool with George Clooney being out there for his segment. Tom's a nice man and he understands performance on television. As long as he was OK with it, I was OK with it. You want everyone out there to feel comfortable, particularly for those guys who are there for Dave. I mean I booked Clooney as well, so while I didn't produce that segment, it is all part of whole show.

JERRY FOLEY: There was fear of not capturing it, or compromising Tom Waits's performance, or overdoing it. There is fear of not getting out of it gracefully. But it is creative fear. No one is gonna get hurt or die. It's the late innings and there are certain factors that could tilt the outcome to the positive or the negative. I look back at that moment, and you have to take Dave's lead on all this stuff. He had ways of signaling that he wanted out or that we are continuing this. You learned to pick up on those cues.

RANDI GROSSACK: Here he is, a big movie star handcuffing himself to Dave. He kept the joke going in such a great way. Then Tom Waits comes out. Tom is nuts, but so interesting to listen to. You hardly ever get to hear him talk.

SHEILA ROGERS: I have a good relationship with Tom Waits and his wife, Kathleen, who works very closely with him creatively. We wanted Tom on the show. He always puts so much thought into his performance—every detail and every song, He had been on the show a number of times before. He was a great interview back in the eighties. We were very happy with it.

Musical Guest

Tom Waits doubles as the musical act. He has written a brand-new song for Dave's retirement. Tom says, "This is for you, Dave." He sings the most beautiful poetry set to music. The lyrics highlight what it means to say goodbye to a place that has meant something in your life. The words collide with Tom Waits's gravelly, growly voice, and become the very essence of the sadness and nostalgia for the life-long journey that Dave and his viewers have taken to this magical ending.

One particular stanza resonates: "This car looks like it could give us a good run. Our choice to leave was a good one." While no one wants to see Dave end the show, his choice is the correct one. Dave is leaving by his own doing. It is time to move on. With that knowledge, Tom Waits implores Dave and his staff to "take one last look at that place that you are leaving. Take one last look."

JOE GROSSMAN: The Tom Waits song was so memorable: take one last look at what you're leaving. It was very appropriate. It is one of those sad, drunken Tom Waits songs, which I tend to enjoy, the kind of song you are just supposed to listen to and cry. He was a longtime fan of the show at NBC. A lot of us kind of glorified that era, whether it was appropriate or not, so it was nice to have someone from that time.

Photo courtesy of Joe Grossman.

Photo courtesy of Bill Scheft.

BARBARA GAINES: That song was beautiful. It is a one-off, you can't get "Take One Last Look."

SHERYL ZELIKSON: I think he was working on a new album at the time, and he reworked the song for Dave. I remember Tom wanting it to be very special, and putting a lot of thought into what he was going to do. It was a really nice relationship there, and he's so entertaining—the man can tell a joke! A lot of the songs that were performed over those last weeks were very important. They were picked for a reason. I remember just listening to the song and how I was struck by how the situation was displayed in those lyrics.

BILL SCHEFT: The Emmy people can do whatever they want, but so much more thought went into the last month of our shows than the other shows. The word that comes to mind is "thoughtful." We had this finite number of shows, and no one asked for my opinion—and they were smart not to—but Barbara, Jude, Matt, Brian, and Sheila, they understood they had this canvas. They really wanted to get it right, and they gave it a lot of thought. They had to piss off a lot of people too. There were a lot of people who wanted to be on in May, people overestimating their own importance, but that is show business.

WORLDWIDE PANTS TAG:

"Dear sweet pants."

"FROM THE ARCTIC TREE LINE..."
IT IS EPISODE 6,025
MAY 15, 2015

"And now . . . the hairdresser of Seville . . . David Letterman." As Dave runs across the stage, viewers see he is not alone. He is, in fact, still handcuffed to George Clooney. Clooney, disheveled with his tie undone, has to run across the stage and make his way to center stage attached to Dave. They receive a standing ovation. "It was a weird night," Dave deadpans. Paul is called over with giant bolt cutters. He tries to free them. It doesn't work. "Don't hurt the movie star," calls out Dave. Clooney says, "Captain Hook is my next role." Backstage Brian Teta, the mastermind behind this carryover from yesterday, is sweating. They were unable to test this. He has no idea if Paul will be able to free them or not.

BRIAN TETA: It was Barbara or I who said we should carry it over into the next show. The big discussion was how we were gonna cut the handcuffs. The idea was they would walk out after the monologue, but how do you end the bit? So we came up with the idea that we would have bolt cutters and Paul would come and cut the chains. Then George would walk off. We realized we didn't have anything backstage that we were able to cut the chains with. We tried a couple of different ones on test handcuffs and we couldn't cut the chain. Dave refused to accept that we could not figure this out. He said, "Just do it. We will have Paul do it." We had giant burly stagehands backstage with all their strength trying to

Photo courtesy of Brian Teta.

cut these things, and they would not cut. There was no delaying the show because we couldn't cut the chains. They do the run, they walk out. Paul brings out these heavy bolt cutters and the first two times they couldn't do it, and my heart stopped. I think it was like when a mother gets super strength when their child is trapped under a car. Paul shattered the handcuffs on the third try and it worked perfectly. I don't think I breathed for about an hour and half because I didn't think we were gonna be able to do this. "Don't hurt the movie star" was a legitimate concern. I kept thinking, "God help me if I take off George Clooney's fingers."

BARBARA GAINES: I couldn't decide if he should still be handcuffed or not. Brian and I discussed it. We weren't sure if it was too much or not, but we did it anyway. It kind of worked. I liked it, but it could have gone either way.

BILL SCHEFT: Dave didn't come out and do the Q&A with the handcuffs on. They took them off and then put them back on. That would have been way too distracting for the warm-up. I don't think they were told they were gonna come out cuffed together. It kind of doesn't matter, because it is George Clooney.

Freed, Clooney walks off and Dave performs the monologue. He says, "As you grow older you have to keep an open mind. Ten years ago if someone would have said, 'Would you like to spend the night handcuffed to George Clooney?' I would have said, 'No.' Now everything is different." Dave's retirement joke is, "People ask, will I get bored in retirement? Hell, I only have to fill an extra hour."

The Top Ten List is "Thoughts Going Through Dave's Mind While Presenting the Top Ten List." Number one? Johnny never had to do this shit. The best-of montage is a collection of fun things Dave and the crew did outside of the studio: dropping things off the roof, stunts on 53rd Street, Dave riding a motorcycle around the block—the kind of fun moments that could be found only on the *Late Show*.

BRIAN TETA: Having 53rd Street to play with was such an amazing resource. It's incredible to think about it now, but we could close down a block in New York City on pretty much just a whim and launch someone from a cannon or set up a batting cage or a football field. We'd shatter the window of the Hello Deli with a Serena Williams-served tennis ball. Just about anything we could come up with, that team could execute in almost no time at all.

JEREMY WEINER: Dropping stuff off the roof was one of the weirdest assignments we would get as writers. "We need stuff to drop off the roof, but it can't be food." It was interesting to see what the writers would come up with, be it pinball machines or drum sets. One year we had a Dave mannequin laying on the sidewalk and we dropped a safe off the roof and it split the mannequin in half at the base of Dave's tie. It was a perfect shot.

BILL SCHEFT: For me, the funniest moment on that show was Alan Kalter's line in Act 5, the long break where we do the audience pan. Ninety percent of these Alan utterances were written by Steve Young. No one has been through more sensibility changes in the show's comedy than Steve, and nobody could have adjusted and thrived more consistently. He wrote this line for Alan: "Hey, does anybody know how to delete the complete browsing history for a CBS-owned computer?" Deeply perfect.

STEVE YOUNG: I would write all the weird lines that Alan Kalter would say going out of the acts into commercial. That was an area of the show that I particularly liked, because it was one of the last areas where a pure sensibility could exist, because it didn't rise or fall on audience reaction. Dave was willing to be more experimental with it.

The first guest is Oprah Winfrey. Paul plays a song he wrote, "It Ain't Oprah Till It's Oprah," for her walk-on music. Paul used to play this song when Dave was trying to convince Oprah to guest on his show back in the days when she wouldn't. Oprah and Dave have had a rocky television relationship over the years. That was all patched up in 2005.

They discuss selfies and Oprah's college fund for girls. Oprah asks Dave if he has started to clean out his office. He says he is only taking one personal item with him. "When we came over here from NBC, they had refurbished the theater and the office building that comes with the theater. They gave me a lovely, enormous office."

He goes on to explain how he needed a stopper for the sink drain for when he shaved. He says, "They got a rubber stopper on a chain and the chain was too long to fit the sink, so they had tied it into multiple knots to fit into the hole into the sink. So the only thing I am taking is the rubber stopper and the chain." Oprah is baffled by this. She asks, "That's the only thing you are taking?" Dave simply says, "Yep."

BILL SCHEFT: I have a picture of Oprah walking over to hug me like I was a long-lost uncle, because I spent the day with her when she interviewed Dave at Ball State. I was very happy that they came to an understanding about each other. It was a misunderstanding that got righted.

The second guest is Norm Macdonald. His first appearance was on May 9, 1990. Dave introduces him with, "Our next guest made his stand-up debut with us twenty-five years ago this week." Norm Macdonald walks out and performs what just might be the best stand-up routine in *Late Show* history. Don't believe me? Believe everyone who worked there. Without exception every single person I interviewed pointed to this appearance as his or her favorite in the last six weeks. Besides having killer jokes, it hit the perfect emotion. What could be better for the final stand-up set performed on *Late Show With David Letterman?*

He begins with a line that shows he has been writing up to the last moment. He says, "I don't want to brag, but me and Oprah are making the same money tonight." He does one killer bit after another. He talks about photos on our phones, LSD flashbacks, and how the news tries to scare us. The best bit is about Germany and how it took on the world in a war . . . twice.

Each joke builds on the previous one as he nails every setup and punchline. At the height, he turns our attention back to the true moment at hand: "Listen, folks, this will be my last time on the David Letterman show, I understand. We all know that David Letterman was the greatest talk show host who ever lived." The audience explodes with applause. "I remember Dave differently, because the first time I saw him I was thirteen years old . . . " At this point, Norm Macdonald has to stop speaking because emotion is winning the battle within him. He shoots out a fake laugh as he tries not to break down in tears. It takes him a few seconds (a lifetime in the middle of a stand-up set) to compose himself.

He continues, "I was living in Toronto, Canada, and I went to a talk show they had there, and David Letterman was the stand-up comedian on the show. I loved stand-up and David Letterman did this joke." He asks if the audience wants to hear it. Applause. He tries to compose himself again. He proceeds to tell Dave's early joke about a garbage truck and how it says, "Please do not follow the garbage truck too closely." He delivers Dave's punchline, "Another of life's simple pleasures ruined by a meddling bureaucracy. Remember the old days when dad would pile the kids in the station wagon and we'd all go out and follow a garbage truck?"

Norm swings his arms back and forth, clapping his hands, trying to get through his final thought. "I know that Mr. Letterman is not for the mawkish, and he has no truck for the sentimental, but if something is true it is not sentimental, and I say in truth, I love you."

Dave is flabbergasted as he gets up from his desk to join Norm at the epicenter of where comedy lived for the past twenty-two years. Norm can no longer hold his emotions in. Jerry Foley wisely cuts to the back of the theater, bringing into view the studio audience, now standing to applaud Norm's declaration. Dave is unsure how to explain this, "Norm?" he asks in wonder. "Very funny. Thanks for everything," Dave says as he puts his hand on Norm's shoulder. Norm is trying hard to not break down, but that ship has sailed. He just paid the ultimate tribute to his hero. He was funny, truthful, and real. This is the pinnacle of the final six weeks with the right sentiment at the right time. I am not alone in this thought.

BRIAN TETA: Norm is probably my favorite segment of the entire run. It was so real. Dave seemed genuinely moved. He had such respect for Norm. I love that he was one of the last stand-ups. These spots on the show were pretty coveted at the end. The fact that Norm was allotted one of them tells you what Dave thought of him. It was probably the most emotional of all the appearances at the end.

BILL SCHEFT: I have known Norm a long time. He is weird, crazy, and brilliant and he is not emotional. That was quite magical and right up there for me. I can't think of anything ahead of that.

@LETTERMAN

MIKE BUCZKIEWICZ: Norm said, "Can I do stand-up?" We said, "Yeah." When I met up with him in the green room, he turns around and has a notebook of ideas that he was writing in on the way to the theater because he kept trying to make it better. You look at these notes and you could tell he had been working on them for three months. It was incredible to see how much work he put into his craft. He had cocktail napkins, notes, and full notebooks. It comes out as clear as day, what it meant for him to be there. It affected everybody immensely. I would be hard-pressed to find a guest that it meant more to than Norm.

BILL SCHEFT: I saw him backstage at 1:30, five and a half hours before he would go on. You show up that early, it's either going to go incredibly well or horribly wrong. But Norm had something in his pocket, something to go out on: an old bit of Dave's he heard him do years ago. Know this about comics: they love nothing more than another comic doing a piece of their act to them. It was utterly simple, utterly ingenious—just like Norm's act.

LEE ELLENBERG: Like everybody, it is hard not to think of Norm Macdonald. It was such a killer stand-up set, and then to end it on such a truly touching, emotional note. It was really wonderful and a great moment from the show. I will always remember that. "Germany went to war with the world" is one of the funniest lines. Then again they decided to go to war with THE WORLD. I am not a stand-up. To me it's a different skill set, but what is fascinating about that joke is we have all heard the phrase "world war" countless times through our lives. He seized upon it and turned it into one of the funniest stand-up jokes I have ever heard. That was astounding.

JERRY FOLEY: I really hadn't spent a lot of time with Norm over the years. He came to the theater that day way earlier than most guests. It was so sweet, and you just wanted to do everything you could for Norm because he was nervous. He wasn't sure where he was gonna go with his material.

BILL SCHEFT: Dave is a walking contradiction. Stuff means a lot to him, and then you tell him what he means to other people and he is the first person to say that is crazy. I would tell him how much it meant for comics to come on his show and how similar it was for comics coming up to go on Carson. He would not hear it. But then someone like Norm is reduced to tears. That gets his attention. Things meant a lot to him, but he couldn't understand what he meant to other people.

JERRY FOLEY: Norm was stressing himself about the best way to do it and not make Dave uncomfortable and get the point across how important Dave was to Norm's career. Norm just wanted to be around the studio as much as he could, to capture as much in his mind's eye as he could. He was there all day. He wouldn't tell us what he had in mind. I took it upon myself to get a sense of what he was gonna say, because you want a fighting chance to capture it all and do it justice. After talking to Norm quite a bit that day, he slowly shared with me what he was thinking and what he was gonna say. It turned out to be one of the most genuine moments in the whole run of the show.

SHEILA ROGERS: Norm is normally a lead guest. He said, "I will be after Oprah." I talked to Norm's manager, Marc Gurvitz, about him being on the show. Marc came back saying Norm wanted to do stand-up. It was Norm's idea. That was one of the best spots.

JOE GROSSMAN: It has become one of the most memorable moments in the final stretch. Someone who was always seen as cynical and detached becomes emotional because you know he had so much admiration for Dave. He, like many of us working there, felt like Dave played a huge part in our lives even before we worked at the show. That is what made us gravitate toward Dave. So to see someone appear on the show to feel that connection with Dave, that was a highlight.

JEREMY WEINER: The Norm stand-up was such a special thing. It was my favorite. It was such a tight, well-conceived set. He sort of it built in a perfect way. It was fun to see someone so expertly pull that off.

KATHY MAVRIKAKIS: I think Norm Macdonald was the most memorable. His emotional ending was moving to me, and I ran back stage immediately and said, "That was amazing." That is my favorite of the whole last six weeks.

LEE ELLENBERG: Even Norm's phrasing, I remember he said, "I know Mr. Letterman has no truck for sentimentality." You don't hear that phrase often, "no truck." Clearly he gave it some thought as to what he wanted to say, and then you get this completely unguarded moment. It's not like he said, "Thank you." He said, "I love you."

JERRY FOLEY: I've seen performers break down. Then they do it two more times in rehearsal. Not this time. That was as honest as it could get.

BARBARA GAINES: I mean, he cried at the end. Dave looked a little startled, like, "Norm, get a hold of yourself." I think it was very touching. Dave is honestly fond of him in a big way. It was such a great idea for Norm to be our last stand-up comedian.

WORLDWIDE PANTS TAG:

"The pants people."

12

Splendid Isolation

THE ED SULLIVAN THEATER & WORLDWIDE PANTS

LETTERMAN'S MOVE TO CBS IN 1993 precipitated two major changes. The CBS show would be owned by Letterman's company, Worldwide Pants, which meant the staffers were no longer employees of a network. Dave and his team created a company to handle all of the business operations, including a human resources department. The other major difference was the nature of the venue. At NBC, they taped at a typical television studio, inside 30 Rockefeller Plaza. At CBS, they taped at the legendary Ed Sullivan Theater. These two factors allowed the *Late Show* to exist in splendid isolation.

PART 1
THE ED SULLIVAN THEATER

When David Letterman left NBC in 1993, Hal Gurnee, the show's director at that time, led the effort to find a home for the new show on CBS. He had the interesting idea of taping in the Ed Sullivan Theater. CBS purchased and renovated the theater, located on the corner of Broadway and 53rd Street. The theater had been the home of *The Ed Sullivan Show* (originally titled *Toast of the Town*), which ran from 1953 through 1971. When CBS purchased the theater in 1993, the building was in complete disarray. Through the years Dave would create a lot of comedy out of the size of the rats that had resided there before he arrived. Once CBS took Dave from a studio to a theater, it allowed Dave and his staff to enrich the history of the place, which had created so many iconic moments in pop culture, including appearances of Elvis Presley and The Beatles.

"I love the Ed Sullivan Theater. We were looking at different facilities around the city. We went in there and it was a minute or two from being condemned in actuality. By God, in a very short period of time they turned it from whatever it had been into just a first-rate television facility. I am from the school that you do TV in a studio, so I was wondering if it could in fact be done from a theater, but the place is fantastic."

—DAVID LETTERMAN, CNN, MAY 29, 2012

Photo by Scott Ryan

JERRY FOLEY: I absolutely was aware of how special and unique that theater was. That included Ed Sullivan's history with it. It was never lost on me that we were in an iconic spot.

JILL GOODWIN: Being on our own you were kind of isolated and an island away from other shows and productions. You felt like your own thing. You felt proud going to work there every day. The seats were really cool in the old theater in the balcony.

JANICE PENINO (Human Resources, Worldwide Pants): I have two of the chairs from that era in my basement. When we moved there from NBC, they were throwing away all the chairs. I have a piece of the Ed Sullivan Theater in my basement.

LEE ELLENBERG: You do have that sense of history. We would get off the elevator on the seventh floor and there were these very large photos of Jack Paar and Jackie Gleason. It was thrilling. Our show was in a theater. It was like going to see a Broadway show. You came in, the doors closed, you took your seat and watched a show. That really did add a flavor that other shows didn't have.

MIKE BUCZKIEWICZ: I did it for ten years, and it always took my breath away, to be on that floor. It is almost like a living, breathing organism. It is a wonderful venue. You knew you were part of the history there because of the lore of that building. I have worked at several places before and since; those were TV studios. The Ed Sullivan was a magical theater.

BARBARA GAINES: Being able to walk out and be in the city was fantastic. Being in the legacy of the Ed Sullivan Theater was great. But it had a lot of difficulties.

BILL SCHEFT: I remember running into Lorne Michaels [executive producer of *Saturday Night Live*], and he said, "I still never understood why you guys went to the theater. You have total control of the environment in a television studio and you don't in a theater." I think that is why when we first came to CBS, we would do these big stunt-driven pieces, because it was this big barn.

BARBARA GAINES: I thought it was difficult to work in the theater as opposed to a studio. Over at NBC, I would run right outside the door and there was the control room. I would run through the green room and it was all right there. It was convenient and easy to get to the booth. In the theater, it was harder to light and to get the best sound. It is cool, but broadcast is supposed to be in a studio. Thirty Rock is the dream. There is every restaurant right there. Going from 30 Rock to the Ed Sullivan Theater was hard.

JAY JOHNSON: At first, it was very difficult to leave the comforts of 30 Rock and move over to 53rd and Broadway. Thirty Rock is a like a TV-show factory, with all the excitement and energy that one would expect with that. At the Ed Sullivan Theater, we were alone and isolated, and the staff expanded between NBC and CBS to the point where we went from working together on one office floor to being spread over five floors. It changed the dynamic of the workplace. I always missed the intimacy we had at NBC.

BRIAN TETA: The theater always felt majestic to me. No matter how much was going wrong, or how stressful a week was, when I'd get off the subway and look across the street at that marquee, I felt incredibly lucky that this was where I was going to work. It could also be isolated and insular. Television is a small industry in New York—everybody kind of knows everybody—but the *Late Show* was different. I remember that before I worked there the show felt like an impenetrable fortress for people trying to break in from the outside.

BILL SCHEFT: The one bad thing in coming to CBS was not going to work at 30 Rock, because you really felt like you were in television there. The Ed Sullivan Theater was this great venue, but it wasn't television. We had to create that. There was standing water, and it had been in disrepair for so long. I think it took a while to get used to it. We revitalized that neighborhood. Businesses boomed, and they moved other businesses out to get bigger rent. The show really had an effect on that neighborhood.

RUPERT JEE (Hello Deli Owner): The building was in pretty poor condition. It wasn't fully occupied, so Dave moving into this area created the renaissance of this neighborhood. It was a double-edged sword because rent prices skyrocketed, but it became a better neighborhood because of that.

BARBARA GAINES: That neighborhood was dead and had nothing. It is absolutely true we did influence it.

JEREMY WEINER: The staff worked in the office building next door, but when you got called down to the theater to see a rehearsal, you would go through those doors and feel that rush of cold air from the theater. It was such a special thing. I never took it for granted.

EDDIE VALK: You would walk in and feel cool standing on that set. You always felt like you were a part of something special. It was as if the studio had this magical, special feeling. Some people couldn't believe this was where Elvis and The Beatles stood.

JERRY FOLEY: The Beatles probably defined the history of that theater more than any other group or performer. Their personality was in the bones of that stage. That was present in my mind every single day. I can remember repeating to myself, "I am not gonna wait until this thing is over and gone to appreciate this theater."

LEE ELLENBERG: There is something about knowing that The Beatles really performed there, because I am looking at the stage. That is where they stood. They were four guys. They set up their instruments and they played. It exists in our mind as this iconic moment, but when you are there . . . I don't know. It doesn't matter what it is, to touch that thing where it happened is something. I felt that way the first time I touched Dave's desk.

STEVE YOUNG: I think the first time it really hit me that this is where it happened was in February 1994. It was the thirtieth anniversary, and that day on the in-house TV system on the monitors they showed the footage from that *Ed Sullivan Show*. You would see these women screaming, but you would see the same Gothic architectural details of the railings and the walls. You go, "Oh, my God, that really was right there."

JERRY FOLEY: A few years back, we had Paul and Ringo at the theater on the anniversary of their Sullivan appearance. Dave did an interview with them. Imagine the moment of Paul McCartney and Ringo Starr standing on that stage chatting. Even before we turned the cameras on, they were just chatting and taking it all in.

JAY JOHNSON: When Paul McCartney and Ringo Starr came to the Ed Sullivan Theater to tape a Beatles anniversary special with Dave, I was one of the people allowed to photograph the three them together on the stage. That's something I never would have dreamed of doing growing up as a fan of both Dave and The Beatles. That photo is one of my most cherished possessions.

LEE ELLENBERG: I think about when Paul McCartney came on the show, or when the Foo Fighters did their webcast and they made the set look like it did back in 1964. They wore the suits like The Beatles.

Rick Scheckman outside the building and Paul McCartney on top of the Marquee. Photo courtesy of Rick Scheckman.

JOE GROSSMAN: I was always surprised they let me in the building. Why is there an office with my name on it? Why are they not throwing me out on the sidewalk? Here is this building where all kinds of crazy things happened both with Letterman and Sullivan. I think we are all Beatles fans. It is hard to imagine that the same stage where I stood there and pretended to drink urine is the same stage where they played all those songs. It never seemed real to me. I am told that all that did actually happen.

JILL GOODWIN: Your parents who watched *Ed Sullivan* could look around and see where The Beatles and Elvis performed. It wasn't that I worked at a TV show; I worked at the Ed Sullivan Theater. It was a big deal.

LEE ELLENBERG: It was amazing to walk through the little alleyways that Ed Sullivan, Jackie Gleason, and The Beatles walked through to escape the hoards of people outside. There were tons of secret passageways. You could walk from backstage through a bunch of twisted paths and come outside of the door right next to the marquee. I had once heard that Jackie Gleason had put that in because after his show he wanted to avoid all the people gathered outside and wanted to go right to the bar next store. Now it's Angelo's Pizza, but it used to be a bar, and there is a way to get backstage all the way to a back entrance of that bar. It did feel very old New York.

MIKE BUCZKIEWICZ: Because of the way the theater was constructed, the place behind the curtain was not a very large space. You were six to ten feet from Dave conducting an interview, so you had to be super quiet.

LEE ELLENBERG: There was a scene in *Taxi Driver* that was shot in the theater. I always get a kick out of it when I see it—the scene where Robert De Niro is on the payphone. The camera drifts right and you can see our elevator back there.

JERRY FOLEY: Many nights right before we would start the show, I would walk through on my way to the control room and have the thought, "This is a really cool place and a unique situation, and it will not be here forever. Enjoy it and absorb it and take it in as much and as often as you can."

PART 2
WORLDWIDE PANTS

BARBARA GAINES: At *Late Night* we worked for NBC, and all it did was make us closer because we were against the man. We were all together against NBC as the corporate people. At CBS working for Worldwide Pants, we couldn't complain about the company because the company was us.

EDDIE VALK: There was no corporate feel, because everyone respected everyone's role. It was a lot of pressure, but always fun.

JAY JOHNSON: I started with Dave in May 1988. When I was hired on staff, we were all working as "temporary employees" of NBC. As a result, we had no benefits to speak of. Not long after I started, some of the staff passed around a petition asking for health insurance, 401k, etc. To his credit, Dave took action, and soon after we became employees of Worldwide Pants, with full benefits. Dave was a great boss who genuinely cared for the well-being of those who worked for him.

JANICE PENINO: I knew so many people that worked there. It was like they were my kids. They came in as kids. I hired them. They got promoted. Some of them are married to each other and had kids. Some of them left and did other things.

JILL GOODWIN: Everyone who worked there had a really great sense of humor. It attracted people who were fans of Dave and had a quirky sense of humor. Other shows aren't like that. It was a different brand of workplace.

JANICE PENINO: I hired all the interns. Our process was very much a group effort. We would select the kids and they would meet with me and the department that they were applying for. Each department would pick the candidate they wanted, and then I would try to match them with what the kids were studying. Once you had been a good intern, you were valuable to us. You understand the language and we all felt you paid your dues. It was a really great way to have people tested out. Not a hundred percent of the staff was hired that way, but a lot of people were.

JAY JOHNSON: I was an intern straight out of college. On my last day, I got hired on staff. I stayed there till the end. I worked with Barbara Gaines and Barbara Sheehan, who was the production coordinate on the show at the time. We *were* the production department at the time. Then I moved over to the talent department, where I was a talent researcher. Then I worked my way up to head talent researcher. In 1996, Walter Kim and I formed the digital department for Worldwide Pants.

JILL GOODWIN: I started as an intern in the spring of 2001. I interned in the finance department because I was a business major. I still had to go back and finish school. In 2002, I was hired as a receptionist for a year. That is how I got my foot in the door. It was like a family there, so I knew everyone from being an intern. I was able to work on a couple of projects as a production assistant. Then I switched over to the production side when I was hired as Barbara and Jude's assistant. I did that for three years; then I became the writers' assistant for three years and then a writer for five years after that. It was an odd way of going about becoming a writer.

BARBARA GAINES: It was a magical place to work. You started as a production assistant or intern and then you got promoted. Then you are working at a place where you grew up at. This was the best show even if it might not be the best-rated show. I am with the guy, Dave, and I am with my friends that I grew up with, and everyone stayed.

JAY JOHNSON: The culture of the show was to reward and promote people from within. Other shows often box people into specific roles with very limited opportunities to grow beyond strictly defined duties. At Dave's shows, they wanted the staff to be happy and to grow professionally. It was a very supportive, encouraging atmosphere.

SHEILA ROGERS: I started with Dave at NBC in 1990-91. I had been there my whole career. I worked in journalism prior to that, but working with Dave was my only television experience. It was a good one.

BARBARA GAINES: Jude and I, as the elders, were the ones that became friends and stayed first. Dave wasn't going anywhere, because it was his show. If the staff copied anyone they would copy us, but I think it was inert. It just came from a comfortableness of working there even in the uncomfortableness. In television, you go from show to show. That didn't happen at the *Late Show*.

EDDIE VALK: My last semester I did a college internship that I got credit for. I began to work there about three months after that. I worked my way up. I grew into television at the *Late Show*. I started off as an intern and left as a lead stage manager. I was able to grow at a job where people got a position and then stay there for twenty years. To be able to advance at a place like that was really cool. From the minute I was in TV it was at a huge place like that. I met so many great people there.

BRIAN TETA: I read the Bill Carter book *The Late Shift* when I was sixteen years old. I closed the book and said, "This is what I want to do. I want to work in late night for Dave." I got an internship when I was twenty, graduated, and couldn't get a job there. I worked in daytime TV. I got an opportunity in 2004 to be the "Stupid Pet Trick" booker. It was a step down in title and salary, and I couldn't have cared less. "Get me in the door and let me do this." I was the human-interest booker. I became the sports booker. I booked all the Super Bowl winners and went to the Olympics. I started producing the guests, then I became a segment producer and a producer. At the end of the show, I was producing three or four guests a week.

RICK SCHECKMAN: Dave would not hire an intern if they were still in college. They had to graduate. We hired ninety percent of our intern staff over the years. So many of the executives came from there. Rob Burnett, Maria Pope, Mary Barclay, Kathy Mavrikakis, Jay Johnson, Walter Kim, Nancy Agostini, and Brian Teta all were former interns. They all moved up the organization, and all had a great loyalty to Dave.

BARBARA GAINES: We loved to mentor. My intern Nancy Agostini eventually took over the show. That is a beautiful thing. I couldn't be more proud. She is my dear friend, and I am so proud of her. Kathy Mavrikakis, who started as our assistant, became the supervising producer and knew everything about the show. You can't like that more.

KATHY MAVRIKAKIS: At the end of the show, my title was supervising producer. I made sure that we didn't spend more than we had allotted. I tried to keep us on budget. If CBS wasn't giving us what we wanted in the offices, I was the voice to the network. I would go between Worldwide Pants and the network. I asked for the things we needed for the daily show to keep our offices the way we wanted them to be.

JANICE PENINO: Not everyone stayed forever. There were plenty of people who left. The problem in any organization is that at the top there aren't that many jobs. People would get to a certain place and realize there was nowhere to go. If you look at the credits there are like eight executive producers, because people who were talented and wanted to stay were given bigger and better titles.

JILL GOODWIN: Dave's staff was very loyal, and he was loyal to the staff. Most people had been with him for a couple of decades. If someone was going through a rough time, he would know about it and help people out. He really cared about staffers. If someone lost a family member, he gave you time. He was very generous as a boss. I thought everyone was like that; now I know every place is not like that, as far as taking care of your staff like family.

JANICE PENINO: We were all clinging to each other and wanted to see it through to the very end.

JEREMY WEINER: My philosophy was I was such a fan of the show. It was a dream of mine growing up to have been there at the beginning. Well, I couldn't have been there at the beginning, so I am definitely sticking around till the end. I felt a duty to see it through.

BARBARA GAINES: Jude and I didn't look for other jobs. I don't know if the writers looked. Some people thought they would look when it was over. That loyalty must have come from Dave. I don't know why, because he could be cranky, but we all loved him.

LEE ELLENBERG: When I think of the last six weeks, I think of how we related to each other more than I think of the episodes. It wasn't that the show was ending. It was that this work life was ending.

JOE GROSSMAN: The closer we got to the end, it felt different, and not in a good way. It is tough because it is the end of not just a job, but for many it was the only job they had in their adult lives, like Gaines. She was there thirty-five years. For me, it was eleven years. My entire routine is being upended, my income is going away, I don't know if I can get another job, and I won't get to see my friends anymore. It was very stressful and gloomy. It was the end of a big chunk of our lives.

RICK SCHECKMAN: When the show was going off the air, I told the researchers, who were all young, "You have to look for another job." They said, "No, we want to stay." I said, "You can't afford to do that. I can retire after this, you can't. The show is going off in May and the shows for September will be filled." They stayed. They wanted to be there at the end. That is due to Dave.

JILL GOODWIN: Looking back, maybe more of us should have jumped ship, but we didn't want to miss anything. It meant something to us, so much so that we were willing to forgo other job prospects. We probably all considered it. But it is such a good memory to have been there. No one was mad at the people who did leave. It goes to show the loyalty.

STEVE YOUNG: I think a lot of senior people thought if we had been through it this far, we want to be there when we crossed the finish line, that it will be an accomplishment and an experience that we think is gonna be worth it, and I think it was. Everyone came out of it feeling that we were glad that we came into the last station on that train.

JANICE PENINO: I think everyone who worked there thought it was the best in the business, and "Where else am I gonna go?" It was a family. That group of people—Barbara, Jude, Bill, and Kathy—they had been together for so many years. They built something and worked together. They had this person who became a legend that they worked with, and they also had each other and the work. Where else are you gonna go?

EDDIE VALK: You got to a place where you fit in with the family and you kind of grow. There is no place like it and I will never have another job like it again. I can be at a place that is permanent, yearswise, but every other show I work on I will carry with me that I worked at *Late Show With David Letterman.*

JAY JOHNSON: I worked on a reunion party for the Letterman staff at the New York Friars Club. This was the Saturday before the last week of shows.

RICK SCHECKMAN: Jay Johnson put the Friars Club party together. He came up with that idea. It was one of the greatest nights in our thirty-three years.

JAY JOHNSON: It was my own fault, because any time we talked about when the show would end, I would say we have to have a huge reunion party and bring everyone who worked on staff back. People would say, "Who would put that together?" When Dave announced his retirement, everyone looked at me and said, "Are you gonna make this happen?"

BARBARA GAINES: Jay Johnson decided to take on this idea of doing a reunion of all three shows. He invited everyone. People flew in from California. It was packed. All these people got together to see each other. It was crazy.

MIKE BUCZKIEWICZ: I still don't understand how Jay did all the planning. I don't know how many people the Friars Club holds, but the place was packed. I only knew a small fraction of the people that were there.

BRIAN TETA: The Friars Club was an amazing night. I had worked at the show for eleven years and I was a fan before that, so I knew everyone's name and I had heard all of the stories. But being in the room with all of that legendary talent and watching them interact with each other was a real thrill.

JAY JOHNSON: The last several months of the show I worked on pulling together contact information from several hundred people.

RICK SCHECKMAN: The idea was we would all pay a bit to cover the costs like a high school reunion. We didn't want to ask Dave to pay for it. It was something we wanted to do. When he found out about it, Dave wanted to pay for it.

JEREMY WEINER: Some old writers came back. Carter Bays and Craig Thomas from *How I Met Your Mother* came back. They worked at the show when I first started. Tom Ruprecht was at the Friars Club. It was a lot of fun.

JANICE PENINO: There are many floors at the Friars Club and a stairway to take you from one floor to the next. There were people you didn't even get to see because you didn't get to that floor.

JAY JOHNSON: When I did have the opportunity to sit down, I parked myself at a table with a group of people who started at the show back in 1982 and who had long since moved on to other things. I had heard their names so many times, but never had the opportunity to hear their stories. They were so excited to be there and to talk about what working on Dave's show had meant in their lives. The whole party was a love fest. Any burned bridges that existed were repaired that night, and it provided a lovely sense of closure to this incredible shared experience.

RICK SCHECKMAN: Morty [Robert Morton, executive producer 1985-1995] was there. He took me upstairs to this private room and said, "This is where we made the *Late Show* deal." Apparently they had discussion for the CBS deal in the Friars Club. There was just so many people there from all three shows.

JILL GOODWIN: I don't think we knew if Dave would show up. It was such a good idea to have everyone who had ever worked on the show come and be in the same place at the same time. Even if someone worked there for a year or two, they flew across the country. It meant a lot to them to have worked on the show and be there.

BARBARA GAINES: The morning-show people, who worked together for eighteen weeks in 1980, almost all showed up. That is how this show affects people. Tom Gammill, Max Pross, George Meyer, Stephen Winer [writers]—all these guys from 1982, everyone came. It was insane.

MIKE BUCZKIEWICZ: It was neat to see all the people who passed through the *Late Show* family, people that were from different eras. You could share war stories and similar experiences. For many of us, it was the first time to put faces with names you only heard about or you saw their name in old segments notes. You were like, "Oh, so you were that guy."

JAY JOHNSON: Dave came and had a great time. We packed the Friars Club. It was like speed dating. You would be talking to one person you hadn't seen in several years and then you'd turn your head and see someone else you hadn't seen. You didn't really have full conversations. You would say hello and move on.

RICK SCHECKMAN: Dave kind of parked himself by the staircase and greeted people.

BARBARA GAINES: People loved it. For Jay, it was a lot of pressure to decide to do it and put it on. But it was a great success.

JANICE PENINO: I had been through a job ending before, and I thought I was completely prepared for this. Then I went to that party and there were hundreds of people there, people I had hired years before who had gone on to do other things. They were coming up to me and saying, "Thank you for giving me my start." You got to see people you haven't seen in ten years.

MIKE BUCZKIEWICZ: You left that night being blown away by the tremendous amount of talent that was in that house that night and that you were a part of that show. Of all the things we talk about in the last six weeks of the show, I think that event is in people's top five.

BARBARA GAINES: It was overwhelming, because it was so many people. I didn't stay that long. I know people stayed and went to another place after the party. I am not that good in social situations.

RICK SCHECKMAN: A bunch of people went to P.J. Clarke's after and they were all there till like six in the morning. It was pouring down rain and so I went home.

JANICE PENINO: When the party was over, I left with Kathy Mavrikakis and her husband. It was then I realized, "Holy crap, this was a special place to work." When you are in it every day, you are not thinking about it, but when you saw all those people together it really took your breath away. We were really a part of something. That is when it hit me: this really is over. This family is splitting up and it's never gonna be the same again. The turning point for me was that party.

JILL GOODWIN: Some people were sad, but there was so much excitement. The whole country was all eyes on Letterman. It was really special to be a part of the end and to be able to share it with hundreds of other people who had experiences like we had. It felt like a big family party.

JAY JOHNSON: We thought if we had done it after the end of the series, it might not have been as much fun. There was an anticipation knowing that the final show was coming just around the corner. Everybody was soaking in the final days of the show. It was great fun. It was hard to pull together, but it was one of the most fun things I ever did there.

BARBARA GAINES: It was too much for me. I was very singular in my mind of having a show to do. I get nervous and I am worried about the show. I make myself crazy. It doesn't matter if it is Dave's final episode or a fifth-grade production. I get very serious because I don't want to screw up. I would have been much more relaxed if we had done it the Saturday after. I was still in my countdown. I still had three shows to put on.

Dave's wardrobe room at the Ed Sullivan Theater. Photo courtesy of Jill Goodwin.

13

The Final Week

EPISODES 6,026–6,027

"FROM SIMULTANEOUSLY EVERYWHERE AND NOWHERE..."
IT IS EPISODE 6,026
MAY 18, 2015

"And now . . . down the stretch he comes . . . David Letterman." For many years, Dave would have announcer Dave Johnson on the show before the Kentucky Derby to say, "Down the stretch . . ." The audience doesn't hold back as Dave comes to the center of the stage. This is the first audience in the final run to start chanting "Dave" as he receives a standing ovation.

> **BRIAN TETA:** Audiences were instructed throughout to not do standing ovations. It slows the shows down. It isn't something that Dave wanted. There is no applause sign that was lit at the *Late Show.* He didn't want artificial praise, laughs, or anything else. As a producer I always wanted them to happen. When they did happen it was very gratifying. On other shows you see the producers throwing their hands up, saying, "Get up." Dave wouldn't like that and wouldn't want it to be artificial.

Act 2 has the Top Ten "Things I'll Miss About Working at the *Late Show*," presented by longtime staff and crew. This is what *they* will miss, not what Dave will miss. The staffers include Barbara Gaines, Steve Young, Kathy Mavrikakis, Pat Farmer, Sue Hum, Todd Seda, Jude Brennan, Biff Henderson, Alan Kalter, and Paul Shaffer. Looking at the group of people, Dave says, "I remember most of you guys." The staffers begin listing insults about working with Dave. Barbara Gaines says, "Until I met Dave, I didn't know I could put my fist through a wall." Steve Young says, "Because he's not tech savvy, Dave never notices when you steal jokes from Twitter."

STEVE YOUNG: I don't know who wrote that joke. I had been a guest on the show talking about a book I co-wrote, so I was a little used to being on the show, and I had been in comedy bits. Your adrenaline gets up, and it's live in front of hundreds of people. You don't want to screw it up.

BRIAN TETA: There are people who have worked there so long. It was a big part of my life, working at that show, and I am not a drop in the bucket to the people who have been there thirty years, like Nancy, Barbara, Jude. It was probably Matt Roberts who picked the people. It was reserved for the people who are on Mount Rushmore there.

STEVE YOUNG: I felt it was a sweet honor. I had been with the show since 1990. I was in the upper echelon of people in terms of seniority. Whether it is an affirmation of anything else, I don't know.

JOE GROSSMAN: You can do some inside jokes, which may not be satisfying to the audience but are to us. It is also a way to vent at Dave, which is what a lot of those are.

The first guest is Tom Hanks, who is making his thirty-third appearance. Paul plays "Hanky Panky" as Hanks receives a standing ovation. Hanks begins with, "There has been a line of two-time Oscar winners for the last two months hoping to get a seat on this couch." The running joke in this interview is Tom Hanks's impression of director Ron Howard. Tom keeps going back to talking like Ron Howard directing Hanks in a green-screen scene where drones are after his character. "They are back. OK, they are gone. They are back." Dave loves this and keeps saying it throughout the interview.

Hanks has come filled with stories, rattling them off one after another. He talks about *Bosom Buddies*, the closing of F.A.O. Schwarz, and Bob Dylan, and introduces his wife, Rita Wilson, from the green room. He also talks about Dave leaving. He says, "Much like your audience, on Thursday I am pulling the plug. I am cutting the cord. I am going off the grid. There is no reason for that idiot box in the seven rooms in my house any longer. I can get any seven-minute bit on the YouTube. I can get that on my phone." Truer words may not have been spoken during this run. Once Dave closes up shop, it will be internet clips, streams, and likes that late-night television shows will pursue.

Hanks, whose first appearance was on April 4, 1984, ends the interview by bringing out a selfie stick and taking photos with Dave, the audience, and the stage. Dave gets the last word with, "I will never be able to repay this man's kindness, his generosity, and his talent for the world. It's our friend, Tom Hanks."

BRIAN TETA: Tom Hanks carried around a notebook so that he could write down things that he could save for doing Letterman. The people who are the most gifted storytellers spent the most time preparing for the show.

BILL SCHEFT: Hanks was characteristically great. It is a small club of guests who were incredibly generous with their time, who never came just to do a spot. I will tell you what Nancy Agostini, the woman behind the podium who produced the taping from the floor, said about Tom Hanks: "He is the only one who always remembers me and always says hello. No one else."

BRIAN TETA: That was my first time working with Tom. He usually worked with Maria Pope. He is probably the most "money" talk show guest you can find. I never thought in my life I would have to say these words: "Well, Tom Hanks, this has been great, but I really need to go." I couldn't get off the phone with him. He would not stop telling stories. We were on the phone for two hours. That is how much he concentrated and worked on these appearances. He loved and respected Dave. He wanted to do a good job, and worked on it. You would have people who haven't been famous for thirty minutes who wouldn't give a second thought to this. Then you have Tom Hanks, one of the most accomplished actors of his generation, who would come with so much material.

Musical Guest

Eddie Vedder is the musical guest. He first appeared on the show with Pearl Jam on February 27, 1996. He is on the show to perform "Better Man." The song begins with a piano, acoustic feel. Jerry Foley has lighted the stage with a mixture of red and blue lights, bathing the stage in a completely new way. Vedder is backed by Paul and the band. He stands in a similar spot to where John Mayer stood. This way viewers can see the audience, the stage, Paul playing piano, and Vedder up front playing electric guitar.

When the song kicks in during the second chorus, we see that the audience has been standing the entire time. It was something I had not seen on the show before, the audience on their feet, before the song even began. Eddie Vedder and the band truly own this rock and roll performance. By the end of the song Vedder is jumping up and down; he breaks a string on his guitar. They blow the roof off the dump. Vedder shakes Paul's hand when he finishes and then Dave walks over. "This is one we will remember."

JAY JOHNSON: So much of the final weeks were a blur. I went down to see Eddie Vedder. I stood in the studio for that. I was just behind Paul and the band watching it. It was a phenomenal performance. To see Eddie pouring his heart out for Dave was pretty cool.

BILL SCHEFT: I had the same feeling watching Eddie Vedder rip the place up as I did watching Bruce Springsteen when he closed *Late Night* on June 25, 1993. Before the show I had no feeling for or about Springsteen, but thirty seconds after he began to play, I completely understood why he is who he is. Exact same experience with Eddie. The band backed him on "Better Man," and I can't remember when I saw Anton play with more joy. When I saw him the next day and told him, Anton said, "When the guy is that great, you just want to play really well for him."

SHEILA ROGERS: Many years ago, there was a Pearl Jam song that Dave kept referring to in the monologue and kept singing a bit of it. It turned into a thing. We got a call that Eddie wanted to come on and talk to someone about Dave doing that. We parlayed that into a comedy bit. He became a friend of the show, and Pearl Jam was frequently on the show.

WORLDWIDE PANTS TAG:

"Pants for life."

"FROM THE LIGHT SHINING AT THE END OF A LONG, DARK TUNNEL..."
IT IS EPISODE 6,027
MAY 19, 2015

"And now . . . Broadway's most in-demand triple threat . . . David Letterman." Dave receives a standing ovation for his last regular episode of the *Late Show*. His retirement joke is that he is being forced to leave because he gave money to the Clinton Foundation. He plays a video of actual CBS affiliates mistakenly saying Dave is leaving *The Tonight Show*.

Regis Philbin, who holds the record for guest appearances on the show, with over 150, interrupts the monologue. Regis kisses Dave on the cheek and asks if he can be on the last show. Dave says, "Last show is booked solid. We couldn't even squeeze you in for this bit." Regis then slowly leaves the stage through the audience, shaking hands with each person on the aisle. Dave stands there, impatiently waiting for Regis to make his way out of the theater. Dave has a line ready to go, but Paul is playing loud music as Regis leaves. Dave just slightly glances in Paul's direction and Paul stops playing. Dave says, "Go ahead and take your time, Regis. This is not a fundraiser, for God's sake." Regis, still in no hurry, finally exits through the back doors of the theater.

SHEILA ROGERS: We wanted to make sure that Regis was a part of those last six weeks. He did a walk-on. Things were quite full and he had been on fairly recently, which is why he wasn't a sit-down guest.

The Top Ten is "Famous Last Words." Since tomorrow's list will be read by celebrities, this is the actual last Top Ten that Dave ever delivers. His final entry is "And the number-one famous last words . . . 'One scoop of Blue Bell ice cream, please.'" Rupert Jee enters and sits in the guest chair. Paul plays "Hello Dolly" as he takes his seat.

RUPERT JEE: My last appearance was the day before the last show. It caught me by surprise, because the show was so full of things to reminisce about. I didn't think they would have me on, but they did. It was rough going on stage for the last time. It was a sad occasion. The next day he would be gone. All the fun and camaraderie we had enjoyed would be gone forever.

Before Dave plays the best-of montage, "Fun With Rupert," from 1994, he asks, "Why did we have to stop doing this?" Rupert answers, "Someone pulled a knife on us." Dave says, "But it was fun right up till then." Rupert's first appearance on the *Late Show* was the sixteenth program, on September 20, 1993. (For more on Rupert Jee, see Chapter 10.)

> **RUPERT JEE:** Everyone loves when I came out with my finger in the girl's glass. I do believe that bit gave rise to a lot of other people, like Tom Green and Johnny Knoxville from *Jackass*. They took it to the next level.

The first guest is Bill Murray. Dave introduces him, and the cityscape scrim rises to reveal a huge cake decorated with "Goodbye, Dave," flanked by two models. Bill Murray busts through from inside the cake. He doesn't come out of the top; he comes right through the entire cake, like the Kool-Aid Man, falling to the stage floor. He is wearing goggles and is completely covered in cake, from head to toe. He immediately hugs Dave and wipes cake all over his head and face. He walks into the audience and wipes cake on a few people's faces, kisses an audience member, and shares cake with bass player Felicia Collins. When Murray finally makes it to the seat, Dave says, "This guy is a professional. If you kids at home want to try something like this, don't forget the protective cake goggles."

> **SHEILA ROGERS:** There really wasn't an order to booking Bill Murray. He doesn't have a publicist or agent that you deal with. I would text him and never know when I was gonna hear back from him. Sometimes he would text back something that would be funny, but wouldn't really be an answer. He was another one that said, "Of course I'll be here." He was always a handful, but great. He was the first guest on the show and the last guest.

Photo courtesy of Brian Teta.

BRIAN TETA: I was at the desk with Dave and Mike Buczkiewicz right before Bill Murray walked out. Part of my job as a segment producer was that I go through the questions with Dave. You are screaming because the band is playing. I said, "I think this is it, this is the last one." Dave said, "I guess it is. Thank you, boys. Thank you very much." I said, "It's been an honor." It was a nice moment before the last guest. It was my goodbye with Dave.

MIKE BUCZKIEWICZ: There was cake on my leg. There was cake in Brian's office later that night. "Why do I smell like frosting?" We would find cake in our notebooks days later. It was a lot of cake.

BRIAN TETA: That cake was a mess. He was supposed to emerge from the cake not popping out of it as much as it ended up being. It kind of happened. I loved that he hugged Dave with all the cake. I was hoping he would do that. You can't suggest that to Dave, but he did it and it was great.

Bill Murray remembers he left something in the cake and pulls out two more supermodels, who are also covered in cake. They put more cake in Dave's face. Dave and Murray sit down and have a good discussion. Dave says, "You were on our first show here. You were on our first show at NBC. You became such a big part of our program that the doors through which you entered the first time you were on this show were immediately named and still today are referred to as the 'Bill Murray Doors.' Right over there. It's the first exit. Part of the show vernacular."

RANDI GROSSACK: I thought everyone knew we always called them that. On the first show, Bill pulled Dave on the street to 53rd Street. If someone had to walk out, we said, "Have them go out the 'Bill Murray Doors.'"

They discuss Murray's classic film *Caddyshack*. The staff has compiled a montage of all of Bill Murray's entrances throughout the years, from his first appearance, on October 6, 1980, on the morning show, through spray-painting "Dave" on the desk, to entrances dressed as Liberace or flying

in like Peter Pan. After the clips, Murray suddenly remembers he has to do a commercial for a Slovenia vodka. He pulls out a bottle and two shot glasses and starts doing shots with Dave.

MIKE BUCZKIEWICZ: It was always a high production when Bill Murray was on. Brian and I were doing the last one. Bill shows up early. I get this call from a production assistant. They say, "Bill Murray is here." No publicist. Bill Murray. He wanted to

These are the "Bill Murray Doors." Photo taken in 2018 by Scott Ryan.

see the cake. We went to the green room and talked about the interview. He said, "I got one more idea." He explains that he wants to do a commercial for Vodka. It was hysterical. I said, "I can have props get a bottle of vodka." He pulls out this bottle and says, "I have one." Normally what we would do is have Pat Farmer take the bottle, dump out the alcohol, and replace it with water. He said, "Dump it out? Give me that bottle back."

BRIAN TETA: Bill pours us each a very large glass—straight. He said, "Drink that and we'll keep talking." It's like two in the afternoon! We did it.

MIKE BUCZKIEWICZ: So now I am drinking with Bill Murray and one of my best friends. This is gonna go horribly awry because we still have to produce the second-to-last *Late Show*. Then we had to go back to Dave's office to tell him about the fake commercial. That was the time of day when we would normally talk to him about the guest. You kind of felt like you were back in high school and your parents came home early and you may or may not have been drinking. You are always a little on edge when you go talk to Dave. You are emotional because it is second-to-last show, you are drinking, and you have to see Dave. I think we looked for gum.

Murray decides Dave shouldn't ever leave, and he needs to start the movement. Dave wonders if it's the vodka talking. "We just want you to stay and not give up. We just want more." Murray gets the audience to start cheering, "More! More! More!" Dave thanks him for the "friendship you brought to this program." Murray decides it is up to the American people to organize to make Dave stay. He gets up and exits through the "Bill Murray Doors" one last time.

He walks up the street interacting with fans who are waiting outside. He has them get in a circle on the middle of Broadway, stopping traffic. He starts singing to the John Lennon song "Give Peace a Chance." His reworked lyrics are "All we are saying . . . is more Worldwide Pants." A large crowd engulfs the comic legend. They sing and chant along. The screen fades to commercial, and "All Along the Watchtower" is the song Paul decides to play for this break, preparing the audience for the musical guest: Bob Dylan.

KATHY MAVRIKAKIS: Originally he wanted to bring the entire audience out with him. We tried to explain to him that it wasn't possible. We needed them back in the theater for Bob Dylan. You can't unload 500 people and then reload them and keep to our time schedule. We kept saying, "Logistically this is not a good idea." I didn't need to have security other than a couple of NYC police around because it wasn't something where everyone saw us rehearse it. It was gonna be one of those things where it happens before people can get mobilized and realize what is happening. We really didn't plan too much. Then he got out there and got surrounded.

BRIAN TETA: I wanted very much for Bill to walk out the "Bill Murray doors," like he did on the first show. He did that. We had a bigger idea that couldn't work out for safety reasons where at one point Bill was gonna be on top of a double-decker bus doing a New York tour.

MIKE BUCZKIEWICZ: It was very chaotic. I think the street singing went on for another five minutes that didn't air. There was such a mob scene around him so fast. He had security, and it was fine in the end. He ended up being right by the marquee, and he ducked back in that way.

BILL SCHEFT: Bill was a valuable guest. That night, after his appearance, I was waiting for Dave outside the dressing room to run the final monologue for the next day. Bill and Dave had a really nice conversation. It was like two guys who don't get to have this kind of conversation with anyone and they got to have it with each other. They clearly respected each other. There are show business friends and real friends. I think the two of them are real friends.

EDDIE VALK: Coming out with that cake, it's like organized chaos. It's like a dance. It's a hustle once we hit that commercial break. All the people cleared the spots where the cake was. We had to make sure there was wardrobe standing by and makeup artists for Dave. We had to spray down the stage and keep it as neat as we can in that short of a time.

Musical Guest

Bob Dylan's baseball card dates his first appearance as March 22, 1984. Dave now has on a new suit jacket, and his face is cake-free. He introduces Dylan with, "I spend a lot of time, like everybody does, driving around with my son, Harry. You take an opportunity to either teach him or reinforce things for him. I say, 'Harry, what are the two more important things to know in the world?'" Dave imitates Harry, in a high-pitched voice: "One, you have to be nice to other people." And the second one? "The greatest songwriter of modern times is Bob Dylan."

The camera cuts to a straight-on wide shot of Dylan and his band. Dylan appears sepia toned thanks to the filter and lighting. The backing band is lit in shadows, shaded in yellow and tan. Dylan sings the standard "The Night We Called It a Day" from his then-new release, *Shadows in the Night.* The entire song is filmed straight ahead, without cuts. The old-fashioned microphone, the coloration, and the single camera are unconventional for a music performance.

The song appropriately concludes with the line "The night we called it a day." Dave enters and Dylan shakes his hand. Dylan strangely glides slowly away from Dave. "There you go, buddy," Dave says, motioning to the audience.

JERRY FOLEY: This is all Bob Dylan. I can take no credit other than that I helped them get what they wanted. Bob had a very specific idea: single camera. He had a lighting plot that he had already worked out. He brought in a few experts that he had worked with. There my job is more to facilitate than to create. I knew what was possible and what they wanted. In rehearsal, during the instrumental segment your instinct is to go to the musician and take the camera off of Bob, who was doing nothing. I knew Bob wanted a single camera. I said to his manager, "I am thinking of pushing by Bob to go to the guitar and then widen out again when the instrumental is over." They couldn't give me an answer. They said, "I'm not sure if we are supposed to do that." I said, "I don't want Bob to look bad because he has nothing to do during this instrumental." We played the round-and-round. Bob was standing there, but what you learn is that you can't always ask. You are supposed to know. The consensus among the managers was, "Let's run it again; do what you think is best and we will find out." I found out. No. Do not take Bob off camera.

LEE ELLENBERG: The performance that really truly moved me was Bob Dylan. My two favorite musical performers are Bob Dylan and Tom Waits. But to see Bob Dylan on our stage—he had performed for Letterman before, but the fact that he did it not when Bob was available. He made a point of doing it for that show. This was a special occasion, and I like the fact that a man that I respect so much respected the man I worked for. I just remembered how much I loved the song and the lights and just on him. It really did hit home. Bob Dylan belongs on the Mount Rushmore of music, and the fact that he chose to do this was very special. The notion that fifty years from now it will be a nice moment to see Bob Dylan on the same stage as David Letterman—giants in their respective fields.

SHERYL ZELIKSON: That was all Sheila Roberts, and it was not an easy task. She worked very, very hard to get Bob Dylan. And it was down to the wire, that I remember.

RICK SCHECKMAN: Bob Dylan didn't come up till the last moment. I think Foo Fighters might have been scheduled for both days.

BRIAN TETA: It didn't happen, but it was very close that the musical guest was gonna be Billy Joel and not Bob Dylan on that show. I wanted the reciprocity. I wanted the circle to come all the way around because Bill Murray and Billy Joel were on the first show on CBS. In my head and I pushed hard internally for this, I really wanted Billy Joel to sing "Miami 2017 (Seen the Lights Go Out on Broadway)." I wanted him to sing it on the marquee. You can't go wrong with Dylan, but I liked the idea of the first guest and musical performance back on the last show.

SHEILA ROGERS: Getting Bob Dylan was a bit of a coup. He doesn't do a lot of TV. He had done our show at NBC, done an anniversary special, and the show at CBS. That took a lot of time to get that in place.

VINCENT FAVALE: Those musical moments were touching. There was a soundtrack to these final shows. Bob Dylan? It was pretty damn impressive. Now I am sad. Thanks for bringing up these horrible memories. [Laughs]

KATHY MAVRIKAKIS: It was the night of wandering gentlemen. I felt like Regis wandered around in the monologue, then wandered out. Bill Murray wandered out of the theater. Then later, when Dave tried to thank Bob Dylan, Dylan just wandered off. I called that the night of wandering old men.

BRIAN TETA: When I was seventeen years old, I was on vacation with my parents. It was somewhere in upstate New York and I had to rent a TV to watch Bill Murray on the first *Late Show* in 1993. The idea that I got to produce his last appearance on the show is the most amazing thing in the world to me. It was so much pressure, so scary, but such a fulfilling, incredible moment to happen.

THIS EPISODE ENDS WITH AN "IN MEMORIAM"
Kathleen Ankers • Dorothy Chambers • Calvert Deforest
Kevin Dronne • Michael "Doc" Goldsmith • Michele O'Callaghan
Thomas Richards • Bobby Savene • Leonard Tepper • Bill Wendell
Benny Williams

WORLDWIDE PANTS TAG:
"Worldwide Pants."

14

My Ride's Here

THE LAST LATE SHOW 6,028

JERRY FOLEY: I don't know what you can compare it to. Maybe the last day of high school? There was this awareness from the minute I woke up that people that I cared so much about were about to disperse. That is a pretty emotional way to start the day.

BILL SCHEFT: The final show had been lovingly built brick by brick by Barbara Gaines over the last six months. Her title was executive producer. Her everlasting credit will be my best friend. By the time we all turned up for work Wednesday, there was almost nothing to do.

JOE GROSSMAN: That last day we came in, the show was all done. We didn't have to pitch anything. It was in the can for days if not weeks. There wasn't a lot of stress. It was more, "We are walking the plank here."

JERRY FOLEY: I did realize very early in the day that this was maybe the single biggest performance of Dave's life. So much of his legacy would be defined by the last couple of things he does on that stage. There was not gonna be a do-over. There was burden there. You didn't want him going home that night second-guessing himself.

BILL SCHEFT: I wanted to wear the same suit that I wore on the last day of the NBC show. Because we had done the monologue the night before, there was nothing to do for any of us. We were just sitting there, "Let's go."

The cold open: In the famous news footage from 1974, President Gerald Ford says, "Our long national nightmare is over." This is followed up by Presidents George H. W. Bush, Bill Clinton, George W. Bush, and Obama saying the same sentence, plus "Letterman is retiring." President Obama is taped standing beside Dave, who says, "You're just kidding, right?" Obama shrugs. That is how the final episode of David Letterman's late-night career begins. Nothing big, just all the living presidents except Jimmy Carter.

Photo courtesy of Jill Goodwin.

MIKE BUCZKIEWICZ: We started working on that last episode shortly after Dave announced he was retiring. We were trying to come up with cold-open ideas. Barbara and Jude asked me who could I get. I think Matt Roberts said, "It would be great if we did 'Our long national nightmare.'" Barbara and Jude thought it was an awesome idea. I had to figure out how to best approach it. The White House had told me to call them as soon as I knew when the final show would be, and then they would backdate it and figure out how to get President Obama there. I reached out to them and said, "Here is the idea. If we can get everybody, would you do it?" They said, "Yes, we will film it while we are there." Then I sent an identical email to Carter, Clinton, and both Bushes. I had pretty good relationships with all of them. I was pretty sure that Clinton was going to do it. His guy asked, "Who else do you have?" I said, "President Obama will do it if everyone else will do it." He asked, "What about President W. Bush?" I said, "I haven't heard from him yet." The guy said, "I have. We are all gonna do it. You will hear from him soon." I just laughed after I hung up. Of course they talk. It's a pretty exclusive club. Obama and Clinton filmed theirs right before their appearances, and the Bushes filmed theirs on their own and sent it in. President Carter was up to do it, but I think he was ill at the time. They said, "Look, we can't really get this together." We completely understood. We left the door open for him. That didn't come through. I was glad that I could deliver those presidents. It was a high point.

"FROM A MAGICAL PLACE NOT FOUND ON ANY MAP..."
IT IS EPISODE 6,028
MAY 20, 2015

"And now . . . a boy from a small town in Indiana . . . David Letterman." The audience cheers as Dave runs across the stage. They are on their feet even before we see them. They start chanting "Dave." Some in the audience are jumping up and down as the cheering goes on and on. Dave unbuttons his jacket and shows the left and right insides of his suit. He all but shimmies his tie back and forth, not sure what to do, as there is no end in sight for this ovation. Dave says, "Please be seated. I don't know what to do." They continue paying tribute to the last time Dave will stand center stage and give a late-night monologue. "All right, that's it. Stop it right there—sit down. Thank you." After they finally start to settle Dave says, "Now we don't have time for the giving-gifts-to-the-audience segment."

Photo courtesy of @Letterman, CBS publicity photo.

RICK SCHECKMAN: It was a regular audience. The only special people in there were his family—Regina, Harry, and Harry's friend. People who were lucky enough to get tickets were in the audience. It wasn't like you get a ticket because you wrote the most viewer-mail letters. He wanted a regular audience.

Dave begins with a joke written by former Carson writers Michael Barrie and Jim Mulholland: "I'll be honest with you: It's beginning to look like I'm not going to get *The Tonight Show*."

JIM MULHOLLAND: We did write that joke. We did various versions of that joke. I don't think we ever insulted Dave with those jokes. That is one thing about Johnny and Letterman: they liked self-deprecating jokes.

STEVE YOUNG: We started to work ahead a little bit on the last show. Everybody wanted to have a piece of that action. We wrote well ahead of time. I wrote a couple pages. Bill Scheft wrote a couple pages. Old-timers, staffers, and former monologue writers submitted jokes.

BILL SCHEFT: *The Tonight Show* joke was always going to be first out of the chute. In twenty-four years, I remember a handful of times when the opening remarks had been set a few hours before the taping, but never the day before.

Dave rolls a videotaped piece in which he says goodbye to the staff. The group gathers, waiting for Dave to stop in the office; instead a hologram appears and waves goodbye.

JILL GOODWIN: I did the bit where Dave says he gathered the staff together to say goodbye. Like most bits, we taped it with whoever was not busy at the moment. Some of the staffers around the table were Steve Kaufman, Pam Narozny, Jeanine Kelly, Neal Fessler, Eddie Valk, and Sarah Eyde. I think we taped it the second-to-last day. There was a lot of school spirit that week, so everyone was wearing their *Late Show* shirts.

Photo courtesy of Jill Goodwin.

BILL SCHEFT: The writers on the show are really writers/producers. They put together their own pieces. They write, edit, and put them together. These guys, like Lee, Jeremy, Steve, Joe, and Jill, have a lot of skills. They cut together a lot of those packages that we saw on the last shows.

Dave does a bit about having to retire because they can't make the lettering on the cue cards any bigger, runs a taped piece called "Comedy We Could Have Done Tomorrow," talks about having to now go on other shows to apologize, and does a joke about his family. He says, "It has been hard on the family. My son keeps saying, 'Why does Daddy have to go to prison?'"

BILL SCHEFT: We were putting the monologue together and we didn't have a joke about Harry. I said, "Steve had a beauty about your kid. I don't remember the set-up, but that your kid doesn't understand what is going on, he keeps saying, 'Why does Daddy have to go to prison?'" To me, only Dave can do that joke. I was a stand-up for thirteen years and my late wife was a stand-up, and she told me really early on, "The best comics do material that only they can do. Nobody else can steal the joke because it's of them."

STEVE YOUNG: It did feel like it was a special occasion, and we knew the family would be in the audience and there would be this added dimension to it. There were natural points to seasonally mention Dave talking about his son. It felt appropriate.

Dave finishes the monologue by rolling clips created by *The Simpsons* and *Wheel of Fortune*. Alan Kalter is given a moment to say goodbye, and is intentionally cut off by an ad for Ford Motors.

RICK SCHECKMAN: It would have been fun if we could have had Tom Brokaw come out and do that first bit from the first *Late Show* about intellectual property during the monologue. I had not thought of it at the time. We had so many grandiose ideas for the final show. Thank God they all got simplified. You saw what Dave wanted. It was a perfect show. We did a very simple show. We didn't shoot ourselves in the foot.

JIM MULHOLLAND: It was a good companion piece to the final *Tonight Show*s. I don't think anything can ever top those last two episodes of the Carson show. It was pretty close. Dave did a very good monologue. It was one of his best monologues, and it was the last one.

BILL SCHEFT: My last effort looked no different in format than my first, which I typed on an IBM Wheelwriter and turned in Monday, October 21, 1991, except that just under "Opening Remarks Scheft 5/20" I wrote the last line of Catullus poem 101 (*"Atque in perpetuum, frater, ave atque vale"*). In the makeup room, Dave asked me to translate the Latin, and I managed to not choke up when I said, "And into eternity, brother, hail and farewell."

Act 2 begins with a clip from the morning show from August 27, 1980, when there was a fire on the set. Dave begins his desk piece by wishing his successor, Stephen Colbert, the best of luck. Dave runs a classic video piece in which he interacts with children. The next bumper, from the morning show, is Andy Kaufman talking about *Taxi* and having snot coming out of his nose.

The final Top Ten List is "Things I've Always Wanted to Say To Dave," and is presented by ten longtime friends of the show. He calls them to the stage one by one to deliver the star-studded Top Ten.

Photo courtesy of @Letterman, CBS publicity photo.

#10 ALEC BALDWIN: Of all the talk shows, yours is most geographically convenient to my home.

#9 BARBARA WALTERS: Dave, did you know that you wear the same cologne as Muammar Qaddafi?

#8 STEVE MARTIN: Your extensive plastic surgery was a necessity and a mistake.

#7 JERRY SEINFELD: Dave, I have no idea what I'll do when you go off the air. You know, I just thought of something . . . I'll be fine.

#6 JIM CARREY: Honestly, Dave, I've always found you to be a bit of an overactor [messes his hair and makes a crazy face and flaps like a bird].

#5 CHRIS ROCK: I'm just glad your show is being given to another white guy.

#4 JULIA LOUIS-DREYFUS: Thanks for letting me take part in another hugely disappointing series finale [camera cuts to Seinfeld looking shocked].

#3 PEYTON MANNING: Dave, you are to comedy what I am to comedy.

#2 TINA FEY: Thanks for finally proving men can be funny.

#1 BILL MURRAY: Dave, I'll never have the money I owe you.

When the segment ends, Dave walks down the aisle and says something to each person. Dave says, "Thank you, Alec, good to see you. Barbara, God bless you. Steve, thank you very much. That was wonderful. Jerry, nice job. Jim, thanks for everything." Carrey says, "I love you so much." Dave continues, "Chris, how're you doing, buddy? Julia, oh my God, your show is tremendous this year, so funny. Mr. Manning, oh, my God, look who it is. That's unbelievable. Tina, again, thank you for everything. And Bill, I saw you on TV last night, are you all right?" He turns and announces, "It's our friends here at the *Late Show*."

JILL GOODWIN: We had interns, old employees, and the staff writing for that Top Ten.

SHEILA ROGERS: I was backstage for the Top Ten. I was hanging out with their publicists and making sure everyone was happy with their lines. We had a tiny dressing-room situation, so when we had all of those people we had to have trailers. It wasn't A-plus accommodations, but everyone was good about it.

JOE GROSSMAN: I wrote the entry for Alec Baldwin. I wrote a version of Chris Rock's joke, but maybe every writer wrote that, because it was an obvious area.

BILL SCHEFT: Being on the show was really important to Chris Rock, and it certainly didn't have to be.

BRIAN TETA: *The Larry Sanders* finale was all I thought of while we were doing the last shows. That last episode was so great when Jim Carrey comes on and does that number to Garry Shandling. What is that gonna be for us? And then we also got Jim Carrey in our last episode.

LEE ELLENBERG: I think I wrote Jerry Seinfeld's entry. I liked the idea of him doing a little acting in it. He is one of those guys that it is hard for him not to be funny. I wrote that pretty late in the game. It is not really a joke. It is contingent on how the line is delivered, and that isn't a worry with Jerry.

SHEILA ROGERS: That was, "Just get the best names you can get." I think I booked them all but Peyton.

BRIAN TETA: I was involved in the booking part of it and brainstorming names. We had a lot of people that you would expect and a couple were surprises. Peyton Manning was the one I was the most involved with. I spent that whole day with Peyton getting him ready. It was a big deal for him to clear his schedule. Dave knew who was coming, but he didn't give any thought to it. He seemed happy and surprised when Peyton came out. Dave can tell a joke as well as anyone, but he can't win a Super Bowl.

LEE ELLENBERG: We all knew that if we had to go twelve rounds over a normal Top Ten List, we knew that this one was going to be a long process. It was pass after pass. The only thing that worried me was that there is a law of diminishing returns. If it is Seinfeld, it seems like I want to write a joke about these three or four things, but the fifteenth pass I am going way off course here. At one point R.J., Zac, Mike, and I were just writing jokes and drinking beer. We knew the celebrities involved would want a say in what they said. It turned out great, but it took a couple of weeks to make everyone happy.

STEVE YOUNG: That seemed to be something that was going back and forth for quite a long time. You had to not only please Dave, but whoever the celebrity was. There were more layers and filters than usual.

BRIAN TETA: I was wondering if Tina Fey was gonna wear a dress. The premise of her last bit was that she wasn't ever going to wear a dress again. Tina had a hard time deciding. She said, "I wasn't sure, because I was still on Letterman, so it would be OK." She opted out of wearing one. I am gonna hold her to it. I have watched her on other late-night talk shows; she has never worn a dress. She has committed to the bit.

BILL SCHEFT: Tina's line was written by Caroline Schaper, a writer's intern. On the last day of the last show, she scored the final two entries on the final Top Ten. She had Bill Murray's line. We were all genuinely thrilled for her. This twenty-one-year-old has all the resumé she needs going forward.

LEE ELLENBERG: When Julia Louis-Dreyfus saw her joke, which I had written, by the way, she said, "I don't like this joke, I want a different joke." She was right. I think it was a joke I had written while we were drinking. I think she turned to Seinfeld and said, "This is a joke they gave me." He said, "Don't do that joke, it sucks."

JOE GROSSMAN: We all agreed it was terrible. We didn't fault Lee for that because you write so many jokes; they are not all gonna be great. It had something to do with, "You are like the brother I never had, but I never had any siblings," or something like that. So Seinfeld and Julia went to the head writer and said, "Can we get a better joke, because this is going to bomb?" He said,

"No, it will be fine." Jerry said, "I know a few things about jokes; this joke is gonna die."

BILL SCHEFT: Julia settled on a line written by Mike Leech, which the next day was proclaimed the winner of the Top Ten.

LEE ELLENBERG: I was just very happy that Mike's joke got on, because we all loved it so much. It got on through sheer happenstance. I was thrilled, because his joke was better. You can put it in bold: **My joke sucked.**

The next act includes the famous videotaped piece of Dave working at Taco Bell, from 1996. The bumper is a classic clip of Larry "Bud" Melman dressed as Santa struggling to read *Twas the Night Before Christmas*. Next up is "A Day in Dave's Life"—a backstage look at what a typical day of work is like for Dave and his staff. It begins with Dave arriving at the 53rd Street entrance early in the morning and takes him through audience Q&A just before taping.

JAY JOHNSON: In the last few weeks of the show, Walter Kim and I were approached by Barbara Gaines and Dave's executive assistant, Mary Barclay, to create a "day in the life of Dave" piece for the final broadcast. They asked us to come in and shoot footage with Dave and edit the piece ourselves with Dave's input. This was probably the highlight of my time with the show. It was an opportunity to work with Dave and create something unique for his final show, but we had little time to actually prepare for it.

RICK SCHECKMAN: Jay and Walter did the day-in-the-life piece. Jay was my intern back in '86. He was the only intern we ever hired on the spot. He worked all over the place—one of the nicest men you are ever going to meet.

JAY JOHNSON: Very quickly we found ourselves shooting staff meetings with Dave, following him down to the studio, filming his preshow conference with producers in his dressing room, and covering various activities around the offices. We would shoot something with Dave, then run back to our office, quickly throw together a rough cut, then send the footage to Dave for notes. For the beginning of the piece, we got up very early in the morning to shoot Dave's arrival at the theater, which was normally around 6 a.m. We had to be poised and ready with our cameras for the moment he arrived. We actually ended up shooting Dave's arrival twice because he didn't like a hat he was wearing the first time around. The second version was shot just two days before the final show.

BRIAN TETA: I watched the show in the green room with all these titans of comedians from the Top Ten. I made one joke during the show when they were showing the day-in-the-life piece. It's an idealized version of working at the *Late Show*. I said under my breath, "Gee, that looks like a fun place to work." I got a big laugh in that room and I thought, "I can die now."

BILL SCHEFT: It was a long, long last break as they set up for the Foo Fighters. The band must have played Ian Hunter's "Central Park and West," Dave's favorite New York City song, for ten minutes. Around minute ten, Paul looked at Nancy Agostini and pointed to his watch. Nancy is staring at stage manager Eddie Valk, waiting for him to give the thirty-second cue. Todd is holding the last cue card, "THANK YOU AND GOODNIGHT," which Dave will utter at the end of his final remarks. Me? I've already said the last thing I will say to my boss: "You know how to do this."

The final act is Dave's goodbye to his fans, viewers, staff, and family. Dave says, "The last six weeks, it's been crazy. People have been saying lovely things about us and it's really been over the top, and I can't tell you how flattering, embarrassing, and gratifying it has all been. I have two things to say about this. We have done over 6,000 shows, and I was here for most of them. I can tell you a pretty high percentage of those shows just absolutely sucked. And also, in light of all of this praise, merited or not, save a little for my funeral. I'd appreciate it."

BRIAN TETA: Paul had that great joke on the last episode. "Dave, I know you'll hate this." That is what they all said. That was right on the money. Every conversation started that way. I am hoping he hated it less as it went on. It was important to me, as a fan of the show, that Dave got what was due to him, that these guests did say these things. It was important whether Dave wanted to hear it or not. They were things that needed to be said.

Dave says, "The crew, what a tremendous crew we have had here. The people you see on the stage, the people you don't see on the stage. The people you see upstairs, the props department, the audio, the cameras, makeup, wardrobe, scenic—it goes on and on. These people night after night have put up with my nonsense and taken great care of not just me, but everybody on the show."

EDDIE VALK: I was close to a lot of people on that show for a long time. It was nice to kind of have that special moment. It wasn't until after the show was actually over that the "holy shit" thought came into play. At that time, it was still, "Things will be OK."

Dave continues, "The staff, what a tremendous staff. We have researchers, and these poor people work in some kind of a subterranean pit. There is no natural light there, but yet they come in day in and day out and they do the work."

RICK SCHECKMAN: The final show was one of the best shows we ever did. Do a monologue, roll some clips, tell some memories, thank some people, and run Barbara's montage.

JANICE PENINO: That last episode we all had the opportunity to stand in the back and watch the second half of the show, which we never had the ability to do. All of us stood along the back wall.

"The talent coordinators, they bring the guests in. We have segment producers, producers, we have people in the control room. I've never been in the control room. Let me have a shot of the control room? Let's keep it to three drinks today, OK?"

JERRY FOLEY: As far as directing opportunity goes, you are not gonna get another one like that. You will do other things, but you are not gonna be wrapping up an icon's career. It was Dave's show when he started, and it was Dave's show when he ended. He was pretty clear in communicating how he wanted it to go. I think it was just as good as it was supposed to be. Art is never finished; it is abandoned. I thought it was done gracefully.

SHEILA ROGERS: I was standing right by Barbara at the podium. I had no idea what Dave was going to say.

"The writers, throughout the years of this show and the show at NBC I have been blessed and lucky to work with men and women who are smarter than I am and funnier than I am. I have always been interested in doing the show that the writers have given me. Now these people collectively that I have just now mentioned and introduced, believe me this is absolutely the truth, deserve more credit for this show than I ever will. Thank you to all of those people."

JILL GOODWIN: It felt like so much electricity in the room. I think I made the right decision to watch in the back of the theater. I mostly watched Dave and tried to think about what he was feeling. There was so much lead-up to the last show that I think he had gone through so many ranges of emotions. I think he was just trying to soak it in and enjoy the moment. At the end of the day, it's the end of a TV show, but not the end of the world. I think he was trying to be in the moment rather than make it a big, heavy thing.

LEE ELLENBERG: It felt like more than a show was ending—something that was so important in my life—and a man who had been a part of my life since I was a kid was gone. To me

David Letterman was always on the outside. He was still on at 12:30, when he would say the only people watching television were prisoners and shut-ins—a guy that if you liked the show you thought you were in on some inside, secret society. "Oh, you watch Letterman? So do I." To go from that to where we were now, that he had come to be the respected figure in broadcasting and he was now saying goodbye, it was wild.

"Now folks we see every day. Thanks to our announcer, Alan Kalter. I don't know of a better announcer. A guy who has been with me for thirty-five years, and mostly every day he and I have been involved in making television shows, Biff Henderson. Thank you, Biff, God bless you. Here is what I will miss most about this show, and we will start now with Felicia Collins, Sid McGinnis, Will Lee, Anton Fig, Tom Malone, Franke Greene, Aaron Heick, and my good, good friend—as good a friend as you can have on television, as good a friend that you can have in life, absolutely a musical genius, Paul Shaffer. It's the CBS Orchestra." Paul Shaffer says, "Thank you, Dave. You've changed our lives. We've loved every second of it."

Photo courtesy of @Letterman, CBS publicity photo.

[Editor's note. The DVR recording of the finale cuts off here, as the show was extended an extra sixteen minutes. This was not advertised or relayed to any of the cable companies. Only people who watched the show live saw the rest of the finale]

RANDI GROSSACK: I think it was a mistake that we made that night not flooding Twitter and Facebook to say the show is running long—"Set your DVR for the right length"—because a lot of people who taped it missed the end.

Dave goes on to thank his mother, and a picture of Betty White shows up on screen, before it is replaced by a photo of Dorothy Letterman. He thanks his wife, Regina, and son, Harry. The audience, seated around the Letterman family, give them a standing ovation. It's a heartwarming moment to see how happy Dave is and how his young son doesn't quite know what to do with the attention. It is a wonderful, human moment. His wife smiles, beautifully, soaking it all in. Dave says, "Seriously, just thank you for being my family. I love you both, and really nothing else matters, does it?" Regina blows him a kiss. Dave continues, "Before the show Harry wanted me to introduce his buddy Tommy Roboto. Here's Tommy. Go get 'em, Tommy." Dave laughs and the audience applauds as the two young boys are shown on screen.

JERRY FOLEY: When he introduced his family in the audience and his son's friend, what if we didn't have cameras in the area? Or they were pointing the wrong way and you weren't able to get the shot? I remember a couple of days afterward thinking, "That would have been a disaster."

Dave thanks the fans at home and then tells the story about the Foo Fighters and his heart surgery. He tells how the band flew from South America to perform when Dave came back from his surgery. The band is back tonight to play the same song. Dave wraps up his thirty-three years of late-night television with:

Photo courtesy of @Letterman, CBS publicity photo.

"THAT IS PRETTY MUCH ALL I GOT. THE ONLY THING I HAVE LEFT TO DO FOR THE LAST TIME ON A TELEVISION PROGRAM: THANK YOU AND GOODNIGHT."

The Foo Fighters perform "Everlong" set to a montage of Dave's career. With that, *Late Show With David Letterman* ends its run.

Musical Guest

The Foo Fighters' song "Everlong," is the grand finale of the last show, but the work started way before the final show, final week, or even the final month.

Photo courtesy of @Letterman, CBS publicity photo.

BARBARA GAINES: A few years ago I was talking to Dave on the phone. He was driving home, and I remember pacing in my closet on the phone. I remember vividly that he said, "If we ever end the show, we are going to have to end it with some kind of big montage or something." I said, "When that day comes, of course, we will do that." He said, "No, don't just say that. It will be such a big project that we are going to need someone else to do it. We will be too busy doing the show. There is someone who does that kind of thing. Find that person and have them start it now, so if it ever happens, we are ready to go." This was years before. I looked around and found a person who was very famous for doing that. We had him start working on it. I didn't tell him it was for Dave's retirement. I told him it was for an anniversary.

RANDI GROSSACK: I put together several reels of the show for him to get an idea of what the show was like. He was working on it, then the anniversary comes and goes and that piece doesn't air. We never heard anything about it.

BARBARA GAINES: When Dave said he was going to retire, I checked in with the person and said, "Let's see what you got." I saw it and I didn't like it. I showed it to Rob Burnett. When it ended he was very quiet and said, "I hate it." I went to Dave and said, "It's no good." He said, "Do others think that?" I said, "Yes, others think that." I said, "I'd like to give it a try."

RANDI GROSSACK: Barbara asked me to work on it with her, which I was thrilled for. Mark Spada was the editor. I was the associate director on it. Mark has amazing patience and poured his love into it, like we all did.

BARBARA GAINES: The three of us would go into a little room. I could only work on it on Fridays because I was doing the show. I was using regular clips with audio. Hillary Clinton saying, "Was that you?"—the regular clips that people have seen over the years.

RANDI GROSSACK: It was all on actual tape. Once we had our reels done we would transfer them to a digital file for the edit session. We called NBC, and they opened the vault for us. I think most of it we had in-house.

BARBARA GAINES: Dave called the editing room and asked, "How's it going?" I said, "I am trying out this thing with Joaquin Phoenix just staring and then you say, 'Wish you had been here.'" Dave interrupts, "Wait, wait, wait, I thought this was all stills?" I said, "What? Stills? No. This is TV and that is moving pictures. What do you mean, stills?" Dave said, "I thought it was stills, boom, boom, boom, a flash and an explosion of images." I said, "You did? [Laughs] Did we have that talk?" He said, "Gaines!" I said, "Great, sure, yes, that is what we are doing." I hung up and I said to Randi and Mark, "Everything we did, scrap it." They just looked at me. We had been doing this for months.

RANDI GROSSACK: We had to rethink the whole concept.

BARBARA GAINES: I started taking pieces of videotape and freeze frame. Freeze. Freeze. Freeze. It was tedious. That is how we would have to get the stills.

RANDI GROSSACK: During the week, I was in the tape area and we started pulling different clips. Everyone would have ideas of what should be in the video.

Randi Grossack, Mark Spada, Barbara Gaines working on the montage early on in the process.

BARBARA GAINES: I took my senior producers—Jude Brennan, Nancy Agostini, Kathy Mavrikakis, Matt Roberts, Sheila Rogers— and I said, "Tell me stuff you remember that you like," and they gave me lists. The writers also gave me lists. I looked through their stuff to pick things that I thought might work. You would look through something and sometimes you couldn't catch the right still or it was really blurry. Some of the early stuff was very grainy. I think somewhere in there Dave said it should be to the Foo Fighters song "Everlong."

RANDI GROSSACK: It was very collaborative. We would go into the room and work on little sections. "Let's focus on comedians, the stuff we did on 53rd Street, or musical acts." We would work on that and make sure we didn't miss anybody. We went through so many different versions and kept tinkering with it. Barbara would take it home overnight.

BARBARA GAINES: I was cutting it to the Foo Fighters. I am trying to cut it really fast, where the drumbeats are. Mark is editing it perfectly to the song. I finally get a version I think is all right. I show it to the staff in my office. It ends and the room is silent. They look at me and say, "It's nice." Jerry says, "You can't end the show with that." I am like, "Oh, no." So I go back to the edit room, and in the meantime this is costing money. Dave keeps saying, "What are people saying?" I said, "I need just a little more time." I make people work over Christmas. Every year without fail after February sweeps week we all had the first week of March off. I took that away, because I said, "You are gonna have the rest of your lives off." Mostly because I was editing.

RANDI GROSSACK: Once we started to set it to music it started to fall into place. Some of the riffs in the music were very fast and the stills became very quick, which makes it interesting, and you can't blink or look away for a second because you will miss something. We started working with different effects.

BARBARA GAINES: We decided to put the explosions at the end. Somehow it just came together. I am not sure how. So I showed it to the staff again. This must have been around the end of March 2015. They said, "Gaines, you've got it. It worked." So I went to Dave and said, "We have it. It's OK." He said, "Really? Who said it's OK?" I worked with the guy my entire life, I still talk to him, but he would still ask, "Did the elevator guy also like it?" "Yes, the elevator guy also liked it." Then he said, "And you've got the Foo Fighters to play live to it?" I said, "Wait, what? No. I edited it to the song, so perfectly. Live? That is never gonna work. How can you have it live? I have edited it perfect." He said, "No one wants to see that. It has to be live." I said, "OK, great. Of course it's live. That is exactly what we were thinking."

KATHY MAVRIKAKIS: It was not Barbara's first stab at it. Dave kind of knew from the beginning what he wanted, but he wasn't being clear about it. He had a different montage in mind than the one we thought he had in mind. When he finally made clear what he wanted, it was more obvious. I think that was what he intended in the beginning.

BARBARA GAINES: So I say to Sheila Rogers, "Can we get the Foo Fighters to do this live? If we have them live, we will barely see them. I don't want to cut back and forth. I have been working so hard on this video. It is all these quick images." Sheila says, "They are going to have to fly in, cancel a gig, and they won't be on camera?" I said, "Right, that is what I want." She said, "I don't know. That seems like an insult to them. I can't ask them that." I said, "Send the DVD to Dave Grohl and see what he says, because this really is what Dave would like. Just see what happens."

SHEILA ROGERS: We wanted to give Dave exactly what he wanted. Word came to me he wanted the Foo Fighters to do "Everlong." The Foo Fighters are sweethearts. They were great about it. We explained we were gonna show this montage. They didn't say, "What? You aren't gonna show us on TV?" They were so cool about that; they didn't care. I can't say enough great things about the Foo Fighters, the band, Dave Grohl, and their management.

BARBARA GAINES: They said, "It would be an honor. We would love to play behind that." Finally, great. We have stills, we have Foo Fighters live. We had it.

BILL SCHEFT: Barbara worked with Randi and Mark for six months. It was her masterpiece. I am no help. I saw the first version of it, cried, and said, "Don't change anything." They did another fifty versions after that. I am no help.

RANDI GROSSACK: We had twenty-one versions. It was version twenty-one that aired. We started doing stills in November 2014. I think prior to that we were working with moving video. Once we moved to stills, it all changed and we started over. I think we worked on that video from November 2014 and we stopped working on it on May 18, 2015.

Sheryl Zelikson, Mike Buczkiewicz, Brian Teta and Sheila Rogers. Photo courtesy of Brian Teta.

SHEILA ROGERS: I can't even imagine the hours Barbara put in for that montage. We were all given a database and given certain years, to be sure that we didn't miss anyone. She put that whole thing together with Randi and Mark. I always find music is what touches the nerve the most, a melody. The combination was pretty overwhelming emotionally, in a good way. I was really proud to be a part of this.

JEREMY WEINER: The live element of the music was so important. It really helped underscore the moment. Gaines's knowledge of the history of the show was incredible. Randi and Mark's cutting of it was really a special thing.

RANDI GROSSACK: In rehearsal, we rolled the video with a live version we found online for the Foo Fighters. I see Dave Grohl has a giant smile on his face as he hears his music as all those images roll for the first time. They got what we were going for and knew how to do it.

EDDIE VALK: I remember in rehearsal a lot of people taking pictures of people because it was the last show. I have fun, happy memories of that day. That was the first time I saw the montage and to see how close the Foo Fighters were to nailing it. They had to time it perfectly to when Farrah Fawcett says, "Wow." The first pass at that was so cool, to see them come up with how much time they had to shave off to hit that perfectly. You knew Dave's affection for the Foo Fighters.

BARBARA GAINES: They played at rehearsal. It was close. It was nothing like I had it when I edited it within an inch of its life and perfect to the drumming, but it was good and close enough. One of the times they rehearsed they had Farrah perfect and one of the times nowhere near it.

RANDI GROSSACK: They got a count to where Farrah happened, but they knew how to hit it properly. They are that good. They knew when and we opened the pod so they could hear it off the track.

KATHY MAVRIKAKIS: I just remember running up onto the stage while it was happening and watching everyone's faces. Being there was amazing. The Foos were playing. It was just great.

JANICE PENINO: I remember trying to see as many musical rehearsals as I could. I have a son who is in college, and they needed a lot of bodies to pack things up. So we hired all our kids to help move stuff. We went down and watched the Foo Fighters rehearse. I remember Barbara running up to Dave Grohl and giving him a big hug. It was just a moment.

BILL SCHEFT: The first time the Foo Fighters performed it, Barbara threw herself at Dave Grohl. I remember Barbara saying to me, she is my best friend, I remember her saying to me with about two weeks left: "I am just living these last shows. This is all there is." It had to be that way. That montage was her baby.

Photo courtesy of Barbara Gaines.

BARBARA GAINES: When they had it perfect, I ran up on stage and hugged Dave Grohl. I don't know him, but I screamed, "That was so amazing!" He's like, "Who? Why? Get this woman off me." I was beyond excited. Someone took a picture of me hugging him. I don't know how, but people were taking pictures everywhere.

RANDI GROSSACK: It all seemed to work beautifully. It was just magical watching it roll. It was like a love letter. All this work that I loved all these years, it is all there.

BRIAN TETA: Barbara's montage was like an epic undertaking. She spent so much time and energy on it. Everybody on the staff watched a hundred different versions of it. The rehearsal was emotional for everyone. It was a great day. Everybody was on set. That show could not have gone any better. It really was just a perfect show. Very rarely do you get to stick the landing.

JOE GROSSMAN: I had not been there as long as everybody else. Most of the images were things I had seen as a viewer when I had watched the NBC show in high school. To see it all condensed into a video, it made an impression, and it was hard not to get emotional. It was such a huge part of our lives. All these people you work with every day, you see them on the screen. I saw my picture go by a couple times. It was very well done. It was a good way to end the show. I remember finding out they were just gonna do stills and thinking, "That is a terrible idea; why would you do that?" I was entirely wrong about that. It was very well done.

Director Jerry Foley works out the shots for the Foo Fighters in rehearsal. Photo courtesy of Jill Goodwin.

JEREMY WEINER: It was unbelievable. It was this flood of memories rushing back, and the music is so great. It was like watching your life flash in front of your eyes, literally. You would see classic stuff and stuff you just hadn't thought about in years. It was a compelling way to end it.

JAY JOHNSON: I thought it was fantastic. She worked so hard on that, as did Randi and Mark. The fact that they were able to pull that off was amazing. Pouring through three decades of footage is no small feat. To find all those highlights and to create a package that was emotional and exhilarating—watching it brought up so many different emotions and memories in anyone who watched it. I thought it was fantastic.

LEE ELLENBERG: All the writers were in the writers' conference room. There were all these shots of Dave at the desk. I didn't have a wave of nostalgia come over me. I was more struck with—this is it. We are pulling into dock. It is over.

The Letterman Writing Staff. Photo courtesy of Lee Ellenberg.

RICK SCHECKMAN: They finished the show with the clip of Dave and Harry skiing. That was how he wanted to finish the final show. I find it difficult to revisit these things. We did it. It's done.

JANICE PENINO: Everyone took one last look around. I don't remember lingering all that long. We went to the wrap party.

EDDIE VALK: We went to an after-party for the staff at [the Museum of Modern Art]. Everyone was there, mostly just the staff. We had a blowout. It was a big party. It was the grand finale of it all.

BRIAN TETA: We had a wrap party at the MOMA. All the guests were there from the Top Ten. Regis, Keith Olbermann, and people who were friends of the show. Dave was there and being social and warm. A lot of the staff after that went to McGee's, which was kind of the office hangout. It was the *How I Met Your Mother* bar. We watched the show there together. It played even better watching it air.

JILL GOODWIN: It was a fun party. I was scared that all this excitement would end and it would feel like falling off a cliff. There was a letdown after that. It was like the drinking blues. You had this great time and then had to wake up the next morning and continue on. I am happy for Dave that everything wrapped up as nicely as it did. The last couple months were great. I can't imagine he would have wanted anything different.

LEE ELLENBERG: We had a party. We were told our offices had to be cleaned out by Friday. I knew I didn't want to come back. So I had taken care of everything. When we left for the party, I knew that was the last time I was ever going to walk through those doors. I remember leaving very soon after the closing credits came on. I picked up my bag and left. I went out the doors I always went out, the side door by Rupert's. My friend R.J. was taking a picture of the marquee, and he happened to catch me exiting for my final moment, crossing the street.

Photo courtesy of Lee Ellenberg.

RANDI GROSSACK: It was very emotional. It was a big part of my life—people I spent twenty-two years with and loved like family, and it was coming to an end. You hit that last Worldwide Pants, then people headed to a party and I'm heading to an edit room.

BARBARA GAINES: The show ends and everyone goes to the wrap party. I go to the edit room. I have to fix the Farrah thing in "Everlong." When the Foo Fighters did it on the show, they didn't get it. It was close, but it wasn't perfect.

RANDI GROSSACK: We wound up having to do a little tweaking because certain effects didn't render properly. So when it rolled it had to be fixed in post. That was a little more involved than we were hoping it would have to be.

BARBARA GAINES: They said, "We would like to go to the wrap party." I said, "How long can it take? It will be so great for Farrah to say 'wow' where I put it." My one little cutesy thing. Besides that we were seventeen minutes over. SEVENTEEN.

The network says, "We'll see what we can do."

VINCENT FAVALE (CBS Network Executive): I was really pissed at Barbara for that one. I was telling anyone who would listen. This was going to be fucking epic. Let me give you an extra half-hour. They kept saying, "No, we can do this in an hour." What happens? They go long and Barbara wants the extra time. It is a big difference when we are giving it to them a month in advance and when they want it right then.

RANDI GROSSACK: It was not a focused edit room because everyone was keyed up and emotional. Everyone was coming to say goodbye. There was a lot of stuff going on, so we didn't get moving as quickly as we would on a normal night. We had permission from CBS to run long, so we weren't taking anything out. There was a problem with a couple of the render effects. Instead of using the version that ran through the control room, the editor wanted to use the cleanest version. So he was just placing the original version on top of it, but then some of the other effects weren't rendering properly.

BARBARA GAINES: We were done at 5:30. It had to air at 11:30, but it was taking us hours and hours. It took us a little time because we got rolling a little later because I went to a meeting after the show. So I probably didn't get down there till 6:30. I started late. Then they had to push everything to re-edit the montage to make it hit for Farrah, which took a long time.

VINCENT FAVALE: I had James Corden already doing a show. It was really fucked up. Whatever she was going through was just as hard for me because I had to navigate those waters. I had to call the West Coast. They had to move a lot of stuff to make it happen. It was so much that I didn't even bother going to the party. I was annoyed, frustrated, and it was late.

BARBARA GAINES: We are editing. An hour in CBS says they want to add in a commercial. So we had to start from the beginning. It was such a, excuse me, pig fuck. As always happens, the machines crashed, so there are five guys just standing looking at a machine. They are just standing there looking! It is getting later and later. None of us got to the wrap party. We are just standing there as the clock tick, tick, ticks. This will be cute. We are not going to air the last show.

RANDI GROSSACK: He had to keep rerendering, and it kept taking longer and longer. Then it was becoming a little more stressful. CBS called at 9:30 and said, "You can't just put the extra time at the end. There is going to be more commercial time in the show now." I had the whole show laid out except the final act. Then I had to relay the entire show to tape, and that is over an hour. Now it is getting close to 10:30, and people are coming back from the party saying, "What are you still doing here?"

VINCENT FAVALE: I am waiting for confirmation for what I already knew, that they were gonna need the extra time. It was a domino effect, because Corden had to collapse his show. The guest that was going to be in Corden's first spot is now going to be on during Letterman's final show, so we need this much commercial time. Then it gets into the minutiae because we need a certain amount of segments. It all worked out, but it was a totally appropriately fucked up way to end the show. I say it with all peace and love.

BARBARA GAINES: They gave us the OK at 9:30, but they added another commercial, which then we had to fit in. We already felt like we had acts one, two, three down, but then we had to fix that to do the extra commercial. It ended up 16:27 over.

RANDI GROSSACK: We needed to get a car waiting to run the tape over to the network. On the last night of the show, I am running down the hall as if it's the scene in *Broadcast News*, with the tape on my chest, because it is such a big moment. Am I gonna get hit by a car taking it over to the broadcast center? It was all much more exciting than it needed to be.

VINCENT FAVALE: I had nothing but a hundred percent confidence with these guys. They were total pros. There was some nights when they didn't deliver the show till 11:30, where we fed the show to the affiliates from the Ed Sullivan. I knew they would get it done. We lost a lot of time scrambling to make this happen. You can't make that decision at 6:30. The drama ended on my end once we figured out the economics and break structure. I knew they would deliver the final show.

BARBARA GAINES: We finished at 11:20. Randi took the tape, like in *Broadcast News*, and ran down the street to a car and brought it to the broadcast center, and we made it to the air.

RANDI GROSSACK: We were still handing it in to the network in 2015. They may be doing it digitally now. It's not as fast as you might think. If you send it digitally, someone on the other end has to sit and watch it because you don't know if there is going to be a glitch. So it needs a tech check on the other side. I am old school. I like knowing it is something I can put my hand on to know it is actually there.

VINCENT FAVALE: This could have been planned better, had all this happened months before.

BARBARA GAINES: It was complicated. They wanted us to do what they wanted us to do. They wanted us to do a prime-time special. They wanted us to do an hour-and-half-long show. We ended up going seventeen minutes over. We didn't want to plan for an hour-and-a-half-long show, because then in the end you are still seventeen minutes over. I love Vinnie, but CBS was awful. I will stand by that. They were cutting our financing. They were not making things easy. I did not feel like we were getting a respectful send-off. I know Vinnie was upset that I was ruining his party, but I don't care. They should have said, "We are sending out a show of thirty-three years, and we will do whatever we can to help them." Maybe if I had gone to the party it would feel different and I would have felt like I got closure. That wasn't how it went. As I sat in the edit room instead of the wrap party, listening to the Foo Fighters over and over, I wondered if anything could ever be this good again. I rushed home to see that it got on the air. I walked in as Alan said, "David Letterman." I felt very proud that I was the captain and I stayed with my ship. It was all I ever wanted. It took me sort of a long time to realize—I no longer had a ship.

Photo courtesy of @Letterman, CBS publicity photo.

OVER THE NEXT 24 HOURS...

Photos courtesy of Jill Goodwin, Rick Scheckman & Joe Grossman.

15

Keep Me In Your Heart for a While

#THANKSDAVE

BILL SCHEFT: The show ends and they take a fucking wrecking ball to the theater the next day. GET OUT. That was stunning.

BARBARA GAINES: I was obsessed with those twenty-eight shows. The fact that the show was over, I kind of put that out of my mind. I didn't feel the doom of it ending. I wanted to make these the best shows ever, but in doing so I wasn't thinking that meant *I* was going out.

RICK SCHECKMAN: I was going around giving people extra TV sets and desk chairs. Pat Farmer gave me an armrest from one of the guest chairs. We had to decamp so quickly. We taped the final show on Wednesday, we went in on Thursday and Friday, and then we were barred from the theater because they destroyed it. It was a work zone. They were destroying the offices on Monday.

BRIAN TETA: People started grabbing stuff quickly. I was resistant and it felt ghoulish, but now I wish I had taken everything, because of what they did. They took it down so fast. I cracked off a lamppost from the cityscape. I wish I had taken more—a bridge or something. It was sad that it was happening.

JEREMY WEINER: I had everything packed up. I came back the next day to load it into the car. I was back for maybe an hour the day after, just to clear things out. They were already tearing it up. I had a few old late-night bumpers that were really cool from years ago. I didn't take any specific piece of the set.

JOE GROSSMAN: We certainly felt a little bit rushed, and there was the sense that they were kind of happy to see us go, but that is OK.

JILL GOODWIN: I felt like people were in there five minutes after the end of the show ripping things apart. It was pretty crazy and sad. Parts of the bridge were going in the dumpster outside. It was like, "No. If we would have known you were going to just throw it away we would have made a list or something."

BARBARA GAINES: The next day there was spray paint on the walls, for which walls they were taking out and which they were leaving alone. So it said on my wall, "Out." It was like "Get out." It was crazy to walk back in to have this giant black paint saying they wanted us out by Friday. Instead of leaving like I should have, I came back on Monday. It was clearly over. CBS threw our set in the garbage. I know it is showbiz, but it felt so harsh.

Photo courtesy of Barbara Gaines.

RICK SCHECKMAN: I was very unhappy and made my displeasure known to a lot of people. It's like a Broadway show. If *Fiddler on the Roof* closes across the street, the next day you see the set being loaded out and everything on the street because someone new is coming. They had to do it, but really on Thursday morning I got in at 10 AM and the theater was gutted. Overnight it was completely gone. So it wasn't like Thursday morning you had a chance to grab stuff. It was gone. Then the mistake CBS did was throwing stuff into open dumpsters without guards. People could just jump in and take stuff—and they were doing it. I saw it. I am not getting in the dumpster to look for souvenirs.

Photo courtesy of Jill Goodwin.

VINCENT FAVALE: The show bears a lot of blame for it. You have a crew there. I thought everything was going to be preserved. I think Dave got the things he wanted and Paul had the things he wanted. But there were still other iconic things there. The job is to strike the set. People have a job to do. It would have been smarter if we put a canopy over what we were loading out so it wasn't a street spectacle—someone, maybe it's me, maybe I am at fault. I should have been the coordinator. I would have put it in my basement, but that didn't happen.

RICK SCHECKMAN: I know there were some angry phone calls to CBS about "Why are there people in the dumpsters?"

BARBARA GAINES: Every theater person knows, when the show is over, a new one is coming in. Even that didn't quite hit me. It just felt like a dark week. "I'll just go back to my office." Then another week goes by. "Maybe I will go back next week." Then suddenly ten months have gone by. It took a long time for me to realize I wasn't working and it was over.

JANICE PENINO: The production offices were on floors eleven, twelve, and fourteen. I was in human resources on eight. We worked for Worldwide Pants. CBS wanted everyone out that Friday, so for most people it was this crazy whirlwind of trying to get these last shows done and all their stuff packed. The next day, after the wrap party, you had to pack and throw stuff out. All of a sudden it was over. For my department, we were gonna be in the office for eight more weeks or so to wrap up the business side. So those last six weeks, for me it was about explaining everyone's severance package. It was all about closing that part down, but we were continuing because we had work to complete. We could pretend that things were gonna be normal for a little while, even though it wasn't.

STEVE YOUNG: As the last show was ending, I went down to the sidewalk, and there were some Letterman fans hanging out at Rupert's. They said, "You've got to go inside; everyone is pulling stuff out off the set." There was lettering on the wall of the fourteenth-floor reception area that said Worldwide Pants. I pulled off the W, W, and P and brought those home. I saved a few cue cards from the last show's monologue that had to do with my jokes or bits.

JAY JOHNSON: The show ended two years ago, but it feels like it's been ten years. My memory is slightly blurry on all of that. On our social media channels the response from the fans was so great. We were getting so many comments and tweets from fans in those final weeks as people shared their feelings about Dave's retirement. It was really an emotional thing to do. I would work a full day and then come home to rewind, and I would read all these comments on Twitter and Facebook that these fans were writing. I think Dave would have been embarrassed by all the outpouring of love, but it was nice to see that people reacted so well to this.

JILL GOODWIN: I still have thirty-five episodes on my DVR that I have not been able to go back and watch. It's just filled with so many thoughts. I wish Dave was still on the air, not that I had to work there. It is like watching old home videos—memories come back.

BILL SCHEFT: We still have these reunions. I see people that hadn't worked on the show in ten years because they wanted to come back and see each other. We were kind of all in this together. We took care of each other. You miss the people. The last time I talked to Dave we sort of laughed at the stuff we thought was so important. "A guy just pitched a no-hitter. We've got to get him to do a Top Ten." [Laughs]

The writing crew watches the show. Photo courtesy of Lee Ellenberg.

BARBARA GAINES: My mother would say, "Who did you meet today?" I met no one. I only concentrated on Dave. I might see Bette Davis out of the corner of my eye, but I am only talking to Dave. He was who I was taking care of.

JANICE PENINO: I don't think any of us will go through anything like that again. We all lived with the fear of the show ending for so long and now that it has, we have survived. I think Dave would say the same thing. He's fine. We won't have each other again, but we had that moment and were a part of it. I never thought of it that way. We weren't thinking about a legacy. No one had the time to think of it. It was bigger than all of us, but then we realized it at the very end. I am thinking as I am talking to you, "Who is gonna read this book? Who is gonna care what we did in the last six weeks?"

JOE GROSSMAN: That is just Dave's voice slipping into all of our heads, because that is what Dave would say. "Who is gonna want to read this?" The first instinct is always the self-deprecating mode. It is still basically an office job. It is just an office job where weird things happen. You spend most of your day sitting at your desk at your computer. You are just trying to write fat jokes instead of corporate reports. It was fun to have this office job where one day there is a kangaroo in my office. You don't get that at most places. Someone said to me in all earnestness, "I am sorry we couldn't get the monkey permit." Where else would you hear about a monkey permit? We were all very lucky and very spoiled to work at a big show and make a good living being stupid all day. Despite any negativity you might hear, ninety-nine percent of my days were just great.

LEE ELLENBERG: Dave gave viewers a chance to see behind the curtain. I used to love "Viewer Mail" because you got to see Dave's office. I felt like Letterman was like Mister Rogers, when you take that trolley to the other world. I used to love getting to see that other world. We like Shecky, let's put him on the show. We fought as much as anybody, but there were times where we tried to show what it was like behind the curtain.

JANICE PENINO: Brian Teta was a really good intern and went off and started to work on other talk shows. A couple years go by and a new page came in and said, "Do you remember Brian? I am his girlfriend." I said, "I am looking for a new pets coordinator." We ended up hiring Brian. So he owes it all to his now wife. That is how things happened there.

JILL GOODWIN: It felt like the end of the show had this manic energy. It was like everyone has senioritis and is going nuts. The writers had all this energy that we didn't know what to do with. In the last month of the show, we would close the door to the writers' room and then whack balls around the room. We broke lamps, people got hurt. We were like five-year-olds. People would be on the outside listening in and you would hear all the thuds and "Ows." Someone showed up wearing a helmet. It felt so stupid. Dave's office was right below us. I don't know if he heard us. It was some childish way of coping with losing our jobs.

JOE GROSSMAN: During the final years there were probably five of us who did the core writing for the show: Lee, Jeremy, Steve, Tom Ruprecht, and myself. That is the core era of my show. You are cranking out so much stuff every day. R.J. came along in the last two years or so. He was another quiet, awkward guy. He and I sat next to each other at the conference table. It was the one part of the table that you knew you were never going to hear anything from.

LEE ELLENBERG: Joe is a brilliant writer and one of my favorites I ever worked with. I was a fifteen-year writer, and I would put him in the top five that I worked with. I always thought Craig Thomas and Carter Bays were consistently good at what they did. They created a lot of references in the few years they were there. Steve Young is up there because he is the guy who wrote things that no one else could ever come up with. His sense of humor is bat-shit crazy. I was a big fan of Meredith Scardino; she makes me laugh to this day. My friend Jeremy Weiner was one of the best all-around writers. You need ten jokes? He'll give you fifty. He is probably the least lazy human being I ever met. Tom Ruprecht is another one. If you had a joke emergency and you needed one joke you go to Tom. You go to Joe. I could also name twenty more, but those are the ones that I looked up to and aspired to be like.

JILL GOODWIN: All my best friends are still people I met there. I started two days after I graduated college, so it really was growing up for me. Scheft, Gaines, Jude, they were great people to take you under their wing.

BILL SCHEFT: The day after the last show, Dave called a lot of people on the staff. He called me and we had a nice discussion about the show. He said, "All those afternoons, just you and me and the cards. We were always trying to get it right. On the last day, I thought we got it right." That is like a rave from him. He never did anything like that. That was one of the last things that was said on that phone call. In the end, it became important to Steve Young, but Dave and I were a club of two that really cared about the monologue for all those years.

BARBARA GAINES: We really did take care of each other: hearing Randi Grossack on my headset, working with Nancy, Kathy, Jude, and all those guys—funny, smart, good people. You don't get that in civilian life.

JEREMY WEINER: Jerry knew how to take whatever Dave was doing and capture it in the realest way possible. When Dave is making it up on the spot, to be able to follow that and put it together in a cohesive way is something. That was a tough gig and he did a great job. He turned that kind of stuff into something. Being in the control room, watching him work, was very exciting.

RANDI GROSSACK: Jerry was great to work with. We worked so long together that if he just made a noise, I would know what it was involved with. He was unbelievably patient and creative. He would get out on the floor and get involved with the staging or the blocking. Like any TV director they have their moments, but I appreciate all the opportunities he gave me.

EDDIE VALK: Jerry was instrumental in getting me to become a stage manager. He was always great with me. It was such a unique kind of show. I can't explain the vibe. It was more like a family atmosphere. For the amount of stress level that everyone could have had, it always seemed like everything was doable.

JILL GOODWIN: Jerry Foley was great during those last musical performances and trying to do different stuff with them. He did a great job.

Barbara Gaines and Jude Brennan. Photo courtesy of Jill Goodwin.

BARBARA GAINES: I adore Jude Brennan. She is my bestie. She doesn't like to talk. Jude was our steady, our adult. She taught me everything. We started on the morning show together. I was green and she showed me how to do whatever had to be done. One day she said, "I can't get up at five in the morning anymore. I am leaving." She wrote down ten pages in long hand on a legal pad how to do the job and left. When we were coming back to do *Late Night*, she was the first person they asked to come back.

JILL GOODWIN: Jude was really dry and funny. She is the kind of person that could have been a writer. She and Barbara are best friends and are polar opposites. Barbara is like the crazy aunt at Thanksgiving and Jude is the put-together aunt, the buttoned-up voice of reason. She always was the last voice when no one knew what to do or was freaking out. "Does this joke cross the line? What does Jude say?" She came across as someone you didn't want to cross. I worked closely with her for three years. Seeing her opposite Barbara and that dynamic, their whole careers were spent there with each other. They were almost like these really smart sisters. They were both fantastic bosses.

KATHY MAVRIKAKIS: Jude Brennan was a wonderful mentor to me. She taught me how to not get upset about the bullshit, how to stay focused on what we were doing that day. She was supportive, wonderful, and shared her knowledge generously. She gave me parts of her job when I was her assistant so she could do more and then I increased my value over time. I owe her a lot.

BARBARA GAINES: The upper women in the company would be Jude, me, and then Kathy. Those three women were the top women and luckily had no ego. We just wanted the show to go well. I always said, "My show comes first and you guys are all part of the show. So tell me what you got." Dave came first, then the actual production, then the staff, but I cared about all of it. If there was any maternal instinct in me, it came from Jude. Jude took care of me until I grew up a little—you know, until I was fifty.

BRIAN TETA: I will tell you this. At this point in my career, I have been lucky enough that I have met every single hero I had as a kid and adult. Presidents, Super Bowl-winning quarterbacks, actors and actresses in movies that I loved as a child. They tell you to never meet your heroes, and that is true, but Dave never disappointed. He was always so real on television; there was nothing artificial about what he was doing. Is he a little cranky? Sure, but you know that going in. He is smart, sarcastic, and funny. You are not looking for hugs when you go to work with Dave. There is nothing to disappoint you. He is kind of going to be what you expect.

LEE ELLENBERG: The kind of quality that I liked in Dave I see in certain movie stars, where I could watch them do anything. I don't know what it is. There are just some people who can just sit and talk and own the area around them in a way that no one else can. Dave has that. Whether I was there for twenty years or not wouldn't have had any impact on the show. It was all who we worked for. I like to believe I made my contributions, but had I never stepped foot into that office Dave would still be as brilliant as he was.

RANDI GROSSACK: It was the greatest experience of my life. I loved Dave before I worked there, and then to be involved in all of it is such a great gift. To have met and worked with people who are amazingly talented, smart, funny, and now are some of my closest friends, that means the world to me. To be so incredibly involved in the final piece, I was touched to be asked to work on it, and it became so important to me. I can't thank Dave and Barbara enough to have been asked to work on it. I am so proud of what I did.

EDDIE VALK: I kind of learned from Dave that you always want to make it count, just his passion for knowledge. He always knew everything going on. He knew the camera is here, that Paul is there, absorbed what was going on and maintained a level of awareness. That is something I would love to reach.

JANICE PENINO: Dave was a guy that was so talented yet so hard on himself. He spent a long time focusing on the wrong thing. Going forward I try to be very mindful of that, to focus on the right thing, as he is doing now. I am proud to be part of that group of people and to have had that camaraderie there. I got to make a difference in the lives of the people that worked there. I also learned loyalty. He did a lot of things for a lot of people that he never talked about. He always did right.

BILL SCHEFT: I learned a lot of practical things. I learned to always put the very funniest word or phrase at the end of the joke, and put the strongest joke at the end of the run. To not be satisfied. He taught me a real work ethic. I thought I was a pretty hard worker before I went to work there. I really wasn't. I was Mr. Shortcut. You turn in fifty jokes and on a good day he checked ten, put eight on cards, and did five. You realized that whether he took ten jokes or he took none, you were still a writer. There was value in what he did and what you did.

JILL GOODWIN: Maybe Dave wasn't in the writers' room with us, but he still had a hand in all the writing and wanting it to be his vision. When someone worked on your script, you always wonder, "Is this making it better?" When Dave made changes, it always made it better. If it came back from Dave all marked up, you didn't feel that Dave hated it. You thought he cared enough to make it better. He was the employee who was at the office the longest. First in, last out. Somewhat of a private guy, but had a crazy work ethic.

STEVE YOUNG: I learned to try my own sensibility and let it take the time to breath and to emerge. In my case and over many years, I did become the whole version of myself, which was usually something helpful to the show. "How can this be made better? Sharper? Shorter?" Dave was always in search of something good being made better, which I think I have absorbed.

JEREMY WEINER: One of my big takeaways from the show is to always try to push past that first take on things. Don't just settle for the first thing that comes to your mind. Try to explore it and push beyond. Try to find a deeper or funnier way to do things. He came to play. That sort of informed my comedic world view. There was always a plan, but when things go awry, let it go and just see where it takes you. The best stuff was the stuff that wasn't planned, and Dave just rolled with it and turned it into something magical.

SHEILA ROGERS: I learned working for Dave that you always would try to do the best possible job. You wouldn't settle. Of course we did have to settle all the time, because it's all about compromise. We all just tried our best for him. You wanted to make him happy. You wanted to be proud of the work you did for him. You didn't want to disappoint him. I learned how important camaraderie is with your co-workers. We all felt very much part of a team.

SHERYL ZELIKSON: When I was in high school, I wanted to work for David Letterman. That show on NBC meant everything to me, and then to get that job as an intern, starting in the mailroom. David Letterman is curious, and I think that is such an important part of the show. He wanted to introduce you to things he liked that were not necessarily always mainstream. He was a voice that influenced culture, without a doubt. What I learned from the show was how to work at that level, to be curious, to do the extra work, run a tight ship, all the production things I learned from him. Everything that I've accomplished in my career is due to the fact that I worked at *Late Show With David Letterman*.

MIKE BUCZKIEWICZ: Dave has shown me to have a natural curiosity. I think part of that is that I handled so many requests that were of a personal nature for him—that being guest segments about climate change, electric cars, Indy racing, and real-world events. I held oil from an oil spill in my hands. He was always a student to educate himself. He never put on an air of "I don't need to know about that because I am David Letterman." You can't stop asking questions, because you stop growing as a person if you do.

JOE GROSSMAN: That is where I learned how to write for television—not to get too committed to material, expect that all your stuff is going to get thrown out and don't take it personally. He was such an influence on us all comedically and personally. Even though I rarely talked to him, everyone around the offices talked like him. All of us were so immersed in that voice, especially the writers, because we had to write in that voice. We all spoke in that odd language that he does—sometimes overly formal or archaic, and I still do it. It made us all better writers because of the good things we did at the show, and the not-good things. It taught me how to survive at a TV show. It changed my life for the better. I never thought I would get to work there, and I did. Dave actually knows who I am and would say my name sometimes and bring me out on the show. It's still overwhelming to me. It's hard for me to not believe that it was all some hallucination that I had.

RANDI GROSSACK: There was just so much to take away from what he did. When I went through personal things in my life, he reached out to me and it was very touching. I always had heard stories about how he reached out to other people on the staff and quietly gave to charities.

LEE ELLENBERG: Professionally, short and funny is better than long and funny. It used to drive us crazy when we were writers there, but now I realize how important it is to be economical. If

I have a comedic voice, Dave is one of those people that helped me get there. I don't think comedy writing should be the most interesting thing about you, and I got that from watching Dave. You always got the sense that there was something deeper going on with him. He always acted like there was something he wanted to do more when the show was over. I thought that made the show better.

VINCENT FAVALE: I learned that when you are the figurehead, you have to be the hardest-working person. As hard as everyone worked on that show, no one worked harder than Dave. He set an example for me outside of my job. I am the first one in and the last one out because it is my brand. I surround myself with people that share my vision. Be true to yourself and be comfortable saying no. Dave had no problem saying no.

RICK SCHECKMAN: I learned everything. I owe my life, my career to Dave. He was the one who made me a success. He led me to other business ventures because of the show. He always treated us so well. He had funds set aside if a staffer became ill, wanted to get a graduate degree. I would do anything for Dave. Right now if he called me and he had a flat tire and I had to come get him, I'd be in the car, hanging up on you.

BRIAN TETA: Dreams do come true. That is an actual thing. I think I learned that when you are working on a show like that, the next show is always going to come. There is always gonna be another chance at something, so you have to take big swings. You have to try, and it's OK to fail. You have an idea to shoot Ben Stiller out of a cannon on 53rd Street? Maybe it will look silly, but it is worth taking a shot because there will be another idea tomorrow. No idea is too big. It is important to take those big swings.

JERRY FOLEY: Professionally, you're given these opportunities, and at no time do you ever lessen your effort or take that for granted. Collectively, under his inspiration, there were no half-measures. I respected him for that. As long as you are gonna be in the game, then you better be engaged fully all the time. His work ethic, commitment, and professionalism were something I'll carry with me for as long as I am in this business.

LEE ELLENBERG: The guy gave me a career. I'll be forever grateful for that. He has done so much for me, and probably doesn't know it. This business sucks sometimes. It is hard for someone to give you a shot. It is also hard to overstate the privilege of working for someone like that. If Dave's reputation ages as well as I think it will, it will be cool to say I worked for him. I would like future generations to know he was something special.

JAY JOHNSON: Everything from his approach to comedy to the way he took good care of his staff to his thoroughness in preparing every aspect of the show. Mostly, I guess, it would be to be true to yourself. He never, or rarely ever, did anything that didn't stem from his own beliefs or his own sensibility. He never bowed to pressure or took the easy way out. He couldn't be molded to fit someone else's standards. He is uniquely Dave. And that's what makes him such an icon.

KATHY MAVRIKAKIS: I learned that loyalty and friendship are superimportant to making your career satisfying. When you have that you can work in one place for thirty years. Losing that, even though it is good to move on, is the same as losing a marriage. Not to Dave, but to the people who worked for the show, my compatriots, the people who are in the trenches with me. We miss each other terribly. Over time we became pieces of a puzzle that all fit together. Now we are all thrown into the wind in our own new puzzles, which I am happy about, but at the same time it is like experiencing a divorce.

JERRY FOLEY: I saw Dave challenged by expectations and creative frustrations and I saw his reaction to that, and it was to continue to work and push and obsess. I saw him at high moments of great success, and there was no difference. There were plenty of complicated moments throughout those twenty years, but the takeaway was if you were smart, you found a way to embrace the differences; that would get you through the complexity of it. There was a pretty big reward if you could endure all that. It was worth it for sure.

BARBARA GAINES: I personally was such a mess when I started on that show. I was young and unfocused. I had no idea who I was. Dave tough-loved me into being a human being. I would not be me today without him. He kind of saved me, because I was on a very bad path of drinking and drugging. For me personally it wasn't going well and then it was. I think that is due to him. I learned how to be a manager of people. I gained confidence and got my dream job.

BILL SCHEFT: When he called me two days after the show on the Friday I said, "We couldn't have ended better, but with me your finest hour will be what you did for my wife when she found out she was sick." He made a couple of moves when she was first diagnosed, and he made my situation on the show more humane and I didn't have to tell people. She came through that time but unfortunately didn't subsequent to that. She died a year ago. My wife was a comic, and he always treated her like another comic. He was really demanding, but you look at these other guys, they don't have people work for them for twenty years. The type of loyalty he engendered was because of the type of standards he set. The people I met on that show and worked with for twenty-four years are my best friends and some of the best people I ever met. I wouldn't have had those people in my life if it wasn't for him. That is an enormous legacy. How many people can you say that about? And we took care of him, we did, but because it was something that was worth aspiring to. When it ended, you are not gonna—no point in looking for that again. You are not supposed to have a writing job for twenty-four years.

KATHY MAVRIKAKIS: If I learned one thing from David Letterman, it's that the word "trousers" is funny. And I learned if you walk into the door and kick it with your foot, you can pretend you hit your head on it. Where else would I have learned that?

Photo courtesy of @Letterman, CBS publicity photo.

16

Finishing Touches

SPECIAL THANKS

THERE ARE SO MANY PEOPLE TO THANK for a book like this. An oral history doesn't work unless strangers are willing to share their thoughts with another stranger. When they do, an amazing thing happens. It creates a bond that spawns friendships. I like to aspire to the idea that all of life could be that way too. So here are my thanks to the many people who helped this book to happen.

First and foremost, thanks to **DAVID LETTERMAN**, for entertaining me for so many years and teaching me comedy, interviewing, and the art of knowing when it's the right time to be funny (although my wife doesn't think I learned the last one). It was an honor to watch the classy way you left late night. I hope this book is a reminder to people of what you gave all of us for so many years. Also, I really hope you or your corporate goons don't sue me.

If there is a reason this book happened, it is **BARBARA GAINES**. I hope she is happy about that. I pursued her for an interview for over two years on Twitter before she relented. (See, Twitter hasn't caused only bad things to happen to our country.) Barbara so generously vouched for me with other, more reluctant participants. She also fact-checked the book for me, but mostly she loves Sondheim and Buffy—that is cool enough for me. She had an amazing career, and topped it off with an amazing montage.

I somehow got **BILL SCHEFT**, who has made me laugh for twenty-five years, to write the foreword to my book. I will never get over that. When I read it, I thought, "Oh, man, do I have a book that lives up to this foreword?" I am sure the internet will answer that for me. He also gave me permission to use quotes from the blog he wrote during the final six weeks. Bill wins for longest interview. We talked so long his phone battery died and he had to switch phones. He was honest, open, and hilarious. A highlight for me was that I made *him* laugh once. I wish I had a Bill Scheft to stand off to the side of my desk and make me laugh all day. Wonder if he is looking for a new job?

If you want to know something about the *Late Show*, **RANDI GROSSACK** is your go-to person. She was always so giving of her time. We ended up emailing quite a bit (even from Iceland). She sent me the list of everything that was in the final montage, but it would have made the book even longer, so it got cut.

JAY JOHNSON is such a kind person. He was very helpful in connecting me with other *Late Show* staffers. He did so much for me and this book. But not everything that he could have. He knows Amber Ruffin, and hasn't introduced me yet.

Are you in the mood for a great story? Then **JERRY FOLEY** is your man. I have been lucky to interview many people over the years. There is just something different when you talk to someone who is a master at their craft. Jerry has that quality. I had to beg him to accept my compliments over his directing of John Mayer's "American Pie." Watch the clip again and pay attention to the shots. There is much to learn from him.

I would thank **MIKE BUCZKIEWICZ**, but what's the point? I'd probably just delete it anyway.

RICK SCHECKMAN is a super-nice guy. He read the book early and saved my bacon a few times. He gave me great feedback and really was a major key to this book. If only he talked a little bit faster. Wow, was transcribing his interview a final exam.

SHEILA ROGERS was my second interview and gave me the best quote right at the top. "I am regretting this already." I like to think I won her over in the interview. It was hard not to ask her for other email addresses for stars I want to interview. Do you know how many books I could write if Sheila Rogers would be my best friend? So Sheila, if you ever need a ride to the airport or help moving a couch, let me know.

JOE GROSSMAN was someone I was nervous about interviewing. I had seen him so many times on the show. He ended up being just like his "character" and nothing like him at all. He was actually more sentimental than he wanted to let on. He also sent me a ton of great photos for the book.

STEVE YOUNG is as smart as you would expect him to be. We ended up talking about all kinds of other things on the phone. He was the only person who, as far as I know, recorded the call on his end too. Now if only Mike Buczkiewicz would have done that as well.

BRIAN TETA's life story really stuck with me. His journey through the Letterman years reminded me of mine. Of course, I spent it watching it on TV and he spent it actually working with Dave, but is it really that different? I liked the fact that he had to get up and close his office door while we talked on the phone for two hours. Yes, Whoopi and Joy had to wait while I got my time with Brian.

In doing research, I realized I had to get to **SHERYL ZELIKSON** because I didn't have anyone talking about the music. Then I found out she was picked as one of *Billboard's* 100 Most Powerful Women in Music. Well, heck, one of the perks of being that is not having to talk to people like me. She not only talked to me, she was very responsive to email follow-ups. She has introduced me to a lot of great music through the years. I am very thankful for that. She also sent me a wonderful present which I truly love, thanks.

JANICE PENINO took a chance with me on her first-ever interview. She asked, "You want to talk to me? I was just in HR." It was always surprising to me how none of these people understood what they were a part of. I wish I would have been able to interview for her years ago. I wonder if she would have picked me to intern at my dream job?

KATHY MAVRIKAKIS made the elevators run at the building. She kept the money flowing and kept everyone on schedule. She also was very kind in getting back to me with all the little details I needed. Her extra detail on remembering that "Happy" was playing when she heard that Dave was retiring is such a perfect detail for a book. Of course now when I hear the song, I think of the end of the *Late Show* too. Nice job. Although if I'm in a situation where I am hearing that song, something has gone terribly wrong. I also thank her for giving me the last line for the book. When she first said, it, I knew it was my ending.

I am pretty sure that **VINCENT FAVALE** was the only person who outright laughed at my concept. He said, "You don't want to put anything snarky in your book? Who does that?" Well, my "kindness-first" motto must have worked, because he generously tapped me as the host for an upcoming *The Art of Letterman* podcast. artofletterman.com

Whenever I wondered if I was getting too deep into the weeds I thought about hearing **JEREMY WEINER** talk about Calvert DeForest reading *Twas the Night Before Christmas*. I figured if someone who worked there for so long could still be tickled by a small moment like that, I was on the right path.

JILL GOODWIN was such a fun interview. I could feel how much she loved working there. She also mentioned having a lot of extra *Late Show* jackets. I'm just saying. I get cold sometimes too. One day out of nowhere she sent me thirty-three backstage photos. I love emails like that. Her path to becoming a comedy writer is so inspiring. To start out answering phones, move on to being an assistant, and end up being a comedy writer for David Letterman is mind blowing.

RUPERT JEE was nice to me fifteen years ago when I first went into the Hello Deli and asked him for a picture. He was the same kind person when I went in to interview him in 2018. He answered my questions, waited on customers, and treated everyone the same. He also agreed to sell the book there, so I hope you bought it there.

I wish I could have used more of **EDDIE VALK**'s comments about being there for Dave. He was the stage manager who stood off camera for Dave. The way he took care of Dave was impressive and moving. One thing I truly learned is that Dave inspired loyalty in an amazing way. He said, "It didn't matter to me who was on the show. It was, 'How was Dave that day and what can I do to help him?'" I like that.

Somehow I talked to **JIM MULHOLLAND** and **MICHAEL BARRIE**. They freaking wrote for Johnny Carson. I didn't have the heart to tell them, when told me they started working for Johnny in the spring of 1970, "Hey, that is when I was born." They also very generously sent me the retirement jokes that they wrote for Dave over the last six weeks. That was really classy. My favorite one? "I'm ready for retirement. I've got my engineer's cap and electric train set."

Usually when I begin an interview, I try to create a bridge between the person and myself. **LEE ELLENBERG** started by saying he knew about my last book, *thirtysomething at thirty*. Heck, that is all I wanted to talk about. Where? Did he read it? What did he think? But we had to talk about Letterman again. It's always about Dave. Lee wrote some of the best comedy bits over the years. It was truly an honor to talk to him. He was the Toby to Dave's Bartlet.

Did I forget anyone? Oh, I guess **MIKE BUCZKIEWICZ** does deserve two thanks. He did have to do two interviews. After nine years of doing this, I mistakenly deleted his first interview. I felt so bad. I told Mike to just look at it like it was a pre-interview. He is so busy out there getting former presidents to do cold opens. Even so, he made time to talk with me again. Thanks.

Thanks to my editor, David Bushman.

Thanks to Mark Karis, for jumping in at the last moment and saving the design of this book.

Thanks to Mo Smith for transcribing an interview for me.

Thanks to Wayne Barnes for the wonderful drawing of John Mayer.

Thanks to CBS, @Letterman, and Worldwide Pants for all the photos you tweeted and Facebooked out as publicity stills. I tried to credit all the photos to the person who gave them to me. If I made a mistake, no slight was intended. Everyone was so giving in their photos. Thanks to everyone who supplied pictures for the book.

Thanks to Warren Zevon for all the titles and all the music.

Thanks to Don Giller for sharing a few of the episodes with me that I needed. Also a shout-out to the folks at AFL.

Thanks to my friends: Special Treatment Lisa, Holly Brothers, Tiffany Fluharty, Huppie, Jami Huppert, Lisa Mercado Fernandez, Courtenay Stallings, Bob Canode, Brad Dukes, John Thorne, Janet Jarnagin, Melanie Mullen, Mya McBriar, and Amanda Beatty.

Thanks to my family: Thanks Mom for always supporting your artist son. Joyce Ryan, Michael Ryan, Sherry Ryan, Alex Ryan, Rebecca Ryan, Reagan Surber, Gillian Surber, Steve Clark, Mary Caye Clark, Josh Minton, Rachel Minton, and Kaylee Landis.

A special thanks to my loving wife, Jennifer Ryan. She supports me in every project. I never take what she has given me for granted. She goes to work every day so that I can write and create. I am lucky. Wherever is her heart, I call home.

About the Author

Scott Ryan is the author of *thirtysomething at thirty: an oral history* (Bear Manor Media; order at ScottRyanProductions.com). He wrote a comic essay book, *Scott Luck Stories* (eBook), in 2014. He is the managing editor with John Thorne of the *Twin Peaks* magazine *The Blue Rose*. He is a founding partner of Fayetteville Mafia Press. His writing has been published in *The Sondheim Review* and *Fan Phenomena: Twin Peaks* (Intellect Press). He wrote and directed the independent films *Meet Abby* (Streaming) and *A Voyage to Twin Peaks* (Streaming). He is the host of the podcasts *Red Room Podcast, Scott Luck Stories, Big Bad Buffy Interviews, The thirtysomething Podcast*, and *The Art of Letterman*. He is told he is happily married and has children out there in the world.

Check out ScottRyanProductions.com for blogs, podcasts, and products.

Go to ArtofLetterman.com for a new Dave Podcast. Follow on Twitter @artofletterman

Follow Scott Ryan on Twitter @scottluckstory or @bluerosemag1

Send only *complimentary* emails about the book to superted455@gmail.com

All they ever want is repetition.
All they really like is what they know.
—STEPHEN SONDHEIM, PUTTING IT TOGETHER

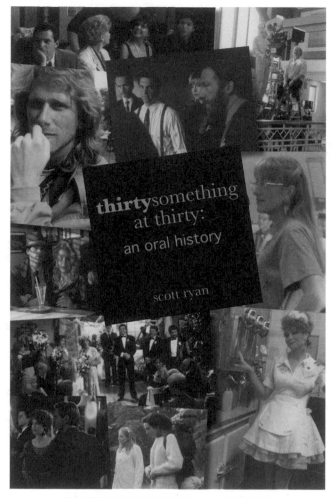

THIRTYSOMETHING AT THIRTY

ScottRyanProductions.com

SCOTT LUCK STORIES

Available online.

THE BLUE ROSE MAGAZINE

bluerosemag.com

Available online

Checkout FayettevilleMafiaPress.com for upcoming books.

Do you have a strong social media presence and an idea for a book?
Pitch it to Fayettevillemafiapress@gmail.com

COMING IN 2019 FROM FAYETTEVILLE MAFIA PRESS
The Women of David Lynch
An anthology of essays about the work of David Lynch written by
female authors.

The Mark Frost Tapes
Written by David Bushman

Last thought: If I have your attention in this moment, can I pitch you my religion? It is called Kindness. This book is a product of people being kind and generous with their time. The goal in life is to be kind in every situation with no regard to whether or not it is returned. Be kind in line at a coffee shop, in the car, and on the internet. Give out as much as you can. It will be returned or it won't.